From Conflict to Modern Slavery

CLARENDON STUDIES IN CRIMINOLOGY

Published under the auspices of the Institute of Criminology, University of Cambridge; the Mannheim Centre, London School of Economics; and the Centre for Criminology, University of Oxford.

Recent Titles in this Series:

A Precarious Life: Community and Conflict in a Deindustrialized Town
Willis

Exporting the UK Policing Brand 1989-2021
Sinclair

Penality in the Underground: The IRA's Pursuit of Informers
Dudai

Assessing the Harms of Crime: A New Framework for Criminal Policy
Greenfield and Paoli

Armed Robbers: Identity and Cultural Mythscapes in the Lucky Country
Taylor

Crime, Justice, and Social Order: Essays in Honour of A. E. Bottoms
Liebling, Shapland, Sparks, and Tankebe

Policing Human Rights
Martin

Normalizing Extreme Imprisonment: The Case of Life Without Parole in California
Vannier

Respect and Criminal Justice
Watson

Neighbourhood Policing: The Rise and Fall of a Policing Model
Innes, Roberts, Lowe, Innes

From Conflict to Modern Slavery

The Drivers and Deterrents

Alicia Heys

OXFORD
UNIVERSITY PRESS

OXFORD
UNIVERSITY PRESS

Great Clarendon Street, Oxford, OX2 6DP,
United Kingdom

Oxford University Press is a department of the University of Oxford.
It furthers the University's objective of excellence in research, scholarship,
and education by publishing worldwide. Oxford is a registered trade mark of
Oxford University Press in the UK and in certain other countries

First Edition published in 2023

Published in the United States of America by Oxford University Press
198 Madison Avenue, New York, NY 10016, United States of America

British Library Cataloguing in Publication Data

Data available

Library of Congress Control Number: 2023935577

ISBN 978–0–19–284654–9

DOI: 10.1093/oso/9780192846549.001.0001

Printed and bound in the UK
by TJ Books Limited

For Mum and Dad, who went to great lengths to avoid having to read this book.

General Editors' Introduction

The *Clarendon Studies in Criminology* series aims to provide a forum for outstanding theoretical and empirical work in all aspects of criminology and criminal justice, broadly understood. The editors welcome submissions from established scholars, as well as excellent PhD work. The Series was inaugurated in 1994, with Roger Hood as its first General Editor, following discussions between Oxford University Press and Oxford's Centre for Criminological Research. It is currently edited under the auspices of three institutions: the Centre for Criminology at the University of Oxford, the Mannheim Centre for Criminology at the London School of Economics, and the Institute of Criminology at the University of Cambridge. Each university supplies members of the Editorial Board and, in turn, the Series Editor or Editors.

Alicia Heys' contribution to this series focuses on modern slavery. Through careful qualitative research with a wide range of participants, Heys uncovers the impact of conflict—which she defines broadly—on rendering people vulnerable to this form of exploitation. While some are victimized as they flee family violence or war, others are exploited after they have arrived in the UK looking for safety.

From Conflict to Modern Slavery is rich in empirical material and attentive to the historical and policy context. In drawing on people's first-hand experiences, Heys offers a vivid and moving account of this crime, the structural factors which underpin it, and its aftermath. In so doing, Heys returns us to foundational questions about structure and agency, which invite us to imagine a world in which both conflict and exploitation were ended.

While the UK is often considered to be, and likes to refer to itself as, an innovator in devising protections for vulnerable people under the Modern Slavery Act, Heys offers a more critical account of people's experiences on arrival. From immigration enforcement, to exclusion from labour protections due to the location and nature of their (domestic) work, the people Heys has interviewed have often found it very hard to access help. Those who had applied for asylum were particularly distressed.

In these examples, Heys paints a depressing, albeit familiar picture of the intersections between immigration and criminal law. Notwithstanding statutory provisions, foreign nationals often find it particularly hard to access legal protections under the rubric of modern slavery. Recent announcements by Prime Minister Rishi Sunak in December 2022 suggest matters are set to worsen.

As issues of modern slavery not only remain high on the political agenda but also indelibly affect people's lives, the need for academic evidence and careful analysis is ever more urgent. In the final portion of this book, Heys offers a range of practical suggestions that could help vulnerable people. We hope that this book finds the audience it deserves and contributes to a more nuanced debate and response. We are pleased to include it in this series.

Mary Bosworth and Carolyn Hoyle
Centre for Criminology
University of Oxford
December 2022

Acknowledgements

There are so many people I must thank for their support in making this monograph possible. First, to all those who shared their stories, thank you for your time and your trust. I have learned so much from each of you.

Second, I'd like to thank my colleagues at the Wilberforce Institute at the University of Hull. Professor Trevor Burnard for his valuable feedback and for never rolling his eyes (as far as I know) when another draft chapter appeared in his inbox. Dr Judith Spicksley and Dr Nick Evans for their patience and encouragement as I lingered at their office doors for chats. Cristina Talens and Beki Bloomfield whose enthusiasm knows no bounds. Professor John Oldfield for making me think it was actually possible that I might be able to write a book. And Andrew Smith whose friendship has been invaluable throughout.

Third, thanks go to Professor Helen Johnston and Professor Simon Green for somehow encouraging me into my academic career—a surprise to many of us! And to reiterate my thanks to Simon who absolutely did not know what he was getting himself into when he agreed to be my mentor, but whose intelligence and wit I have relied on wholeheartedly.

Fourth, my friends: Dr Craig Barlow, Rebecca Craven, Gareth Horton, and Lorna McBride for the texts, coffees, and welfare checks. And my mates on skates for always providing the best distractions.

Finally, Tom and Bishop. The biggest thanks go to you. Sorry there are no pictures.

Contents

List of Tables

Chapter one
Introduction and current context

Modern slavery has become an area of increasing interest among academics, practitioners, and members of the public over the past ten years. Forms of extreme exploitation categorised under this heading of slavery are attention-grabbing and barely a week goes by without a newspaper article announcing another example of how our goods are infiltrated by labour exploitation, of women held in brothels, or children forced to run drugs. While the regularity of these articles reflects the growing interest in these issues, there continues to be little comprehension of the specific root causes that put individuals at risk.

Current approaches to modern slavery often focus on the end result: the slavery experiences. They discuss the different forms of slavery (Craig et al., 2007; Kara, 2009; Anti-Slavery International, 2017), the experiences of suffering (Bales and Trodd, 2008; Murphy, 2014) and life after the exploitation (Human Trafficking Foundation, 2015, 2016). However, in comparison, less attention has been paid to the root causes of modern slavery and without such insight any attempt to tackle modern slavery can only combat that which is currently in progress and cannot endeavour to implement successful prevention programmes.

In this book I go beyond this approach, taking conflict as an example of one root cause for modern slavery. I investigate the existing literature and add to it with first-hand insights from those with lived experience and the professionals who support them, in order to draw conclusions as to the precise vulnerabilities caused by conflict that increase a person's risk of becoming a victim of modern slavery.

While there is significant literature addressing both conflict and modern slavery separately, there is a paucity identifying any link between the two. That which does exist considers conflict only in the sense of war and, in so doing, overlooks the vast remit of the term. In this work I challenge this limited approach by bringing together legal, practical, and dictionary definitions with insights from those who have self-identified

From Conflict to Modern Slavery. Alicia Heys, Oxford University Press. © Alicia Heys 2023.
DOI: 10.1093/oso/9780192846549.003.0001

having experienced conflict to generate a broader definition that incorporates all forms of conflict both including, and beyond, war. I use this definition to investigate what it is about conflict in this broad sense that can increase a person's vulnerability both within the conflict situation and in their movement away from it. I look at life during the conflict, the movement out of the conflict, but also what happens when people search for safety in the UK. In doing this, I discover that there are two key vulnerabilities generated by conflict: a reduction in the options available to people, and a breakdown in their support networks. These vulnerabilities increase the risk of a person going on to experience modern slavery. However, when investigating these issues in terms of people's experiences after arriving in the UK, I discover that it is not just conflict that creates these vulnerabilities, but that there are restrictive policies in the UK which generate the very same vulnerabilities and therefore increase the risk of modern slavery.

With this new understanding about how certain structural conditions can generate specific vulnerabilities that encourage modern slavery to occur, I also consider the interplay between structure and agency. While the general consensus is that a victim of modern slavery must experience some degree of a reduction in their agency, I show that it is uncommon for victims to suffer a complete removal of their agency and they often have some degree of choice in the decisions that lead them towards their exploitation. I encourage a move away from recognising victims only if they reflect the notion of the 'ideal victim' which implies that victims have no agency. Instead, I propose that victimhood and agency should be understood on a scale as opposed to as binary opposites. A true understanding of victims of modern slavery shows that having agency does not negate their experience of having been victimised.

I take these discussions of both structure and agency to demonstrate how situations of modern slavery occur through an interaction between them both. Individuals often still have the ability to take actions and make decisions to some degree, but their options are commonly severely limited by overarching structures. As such, while approaches to tackling modern slavery should not overlook the agentic processes at play, it is important that they consider how structural factors can significantly increase risk where, for many, a modern slavery experience would not have been possible without the impact of restrictive structural conditions.

1.1 Conducting the research

To conduct the research that this work is based on, I gathered data through in-depth interviews with those who had fled conflict, those who had fled conflict and experienced modern slavery, and those who work with either of these groups. By using first-hand accounts provided by these respondents through interviews, my aim was to identify precisely how conflict increases the likelihood that a person would become a victim of modern slavery. In this work, I assess a variety of forms of conflict in a range of different countries and compare the stories of those who fled and experienced modern slavery to those who fled and remained safe. This comparison provides new insight into a little-studied area in order to identify where the vulnerabilities are generated, how they develop, and what could be done to tackle them. I then consider how those who search for safety in the UK could continue to be at risk because of some of the restrictive policies in place in the country.

This research gives voice to those with lived experience and uses their accounts to identify how approaches to tackling modern slavery in the UK could be improved. It goes beyond the tendency of suggesting that people become victims of modern slavery because they were 'vulnerable in some way' prior to their exploitation. Instead, the research identifies some of the specific vulnerabilities that put those fleeing conflict at risk of modern slavery, focusing particularly on the impact that conflict has on generating a lack of choice and a lack of support. Consideration is also given to how these vulnerabilities are mirrored by certain UK policies. The remainder of this chapter outlines the approach to the research, including how the research was undertaken, ethical considerations, and limitations; it then provides an overview of each of the remaining chapters.

1.1.1 Research questions and approach

The primary purpose of the research undertaken for this title was to tackle the overarching question: *what is the relationship between conflict and modern slavery?* This question is deliberately broad in its scope in acknowledgement of the limited targeted research that has been conducted in this area, as outlined in detail in chapter three. In tackling this question, the research incorporated three subsidiary questions:

1. What are examples of conflict that make people vulnerable to modern slavery?
2. What are the specific features of conflict that cause someone to become vulnerable to modern slavery?
3. What are the methods through which someone might become a victim of modern slavery as they flee conflict?

For the research, I identified three distinct groups of respondents that I wished to interview in order to generate understandings to help answer the research questions:

1. Those who had fled conflict
2. Those who had fled conflict and experienced modern slavery
3. Those who work with either of the above groups

These groups were all experts by experience, either because they had experienced conflict and sometimes also modern slavery themselves, or because they were professionals working in relevant fields and therefore experts in both supporting those with lived experience and in the socio-political environment facing those who have experienced conflict or modern slavery.

As discussed in detail in chapter two, there is considerable debate around the definitions of both 'conflict' and 'modern slavery'. In order to place the respondents as experts by experience, I invited people to respond to the call for participants based on them self-identifying having lived through conflict. While I had initially anticipated that those identifying having lived through conflict would be presenting from war-torn areas, respondents presented having experienced much broader forms of conflict which led to a reassessment of my understanding of the concept 'conflict'. This is detailed in chapter two where I generate a new definition of conflict, based not only upon research, legal definitions, and definitions used in practice, but which also incorporates the understandings of those who self-identified having lived through a conflict.

Although there is statistical data available relating to both conflict and modern slavery, quantitative research played a minor role in this research, being used only to provide context regarding the known extent of modern slavery in the UK. Because the interrelation between conflict and modern slavery remains understudied, as outlined in chapter three, this research required an approach that allowed for the development of unconsidered motives and meanings which are difficult to access through quantitative approaches. As Lave and Kvale (1995) discuss, only a human has the capacity to learn about human experience, meaning that while there may be quantitative figures providing statistics about a particular group, it takes human interpretation to decipher the meanings behind those numbers. In short, this research looked to understand the experiences and meanings behind the subjects' pasts, rather than the statistical differences between those experiences.

1.1.2 Sampling

Purposeful sampling was used for this study in order to assist in identifying information-rich cases to get the most material out of limited sources (Patton, 2002). This type of sampling considers not only the people who fit the required criteria, but their knowledge and experience (Cresswell and Plano Clark, 2011) as well as their willingness and availability to take part in the research (Bernard, 2002). In trying to maximise the sample size, this study did not limit the respondents to a specific geographical region. Calls for respondents were sent to recipients across the UK with no limitations on their nationality; the only stipulation was that they self-identified as having lived through a conflict (or were supporting people who had lived through conflict), with further calls for those who had experienced both conflict and modern slavery (and those working to support them).

I employed snowball sampling as a tested method of accessing 'hidden' populations (Faugier and Sargeant, 1997; Atkinson and Flint, 2001; Raymond et al., 2002). When there is the possibility that respondents could be living in precarious situations, perhaps waiting for asylum decisions, and unconfident in confiding in strangers, snowball sampling can be a valuable asset.

In this study I relied on professionals from support organisations to act as gatekeepers in providing access to potential respondents (and in becoming respondents themselves). I reached out to multiple organisations working in the fields of modern slavery, homelessness, migration, and asylum who worked directly with clients who might be able to offer insights into their experiences of conflict and modern slavery. The organisations contacted all directly and proactively offered support to individuals who had experienced conflict and/or modern slavery and included, for example, non-governmental organisations (NGOs) as well as statutory organisations including local authorities.

1.1.3 Accessing respondents

The assistance of gatekeepers proved particularly useful in the recruitment of research participants for this study. Gatekeepers are often trusted individuals who can help talk through any concerns or anxieties that potential participants may have, and those participants may be more willing to engage with the research if they are approached about it from a trusted source rather than an unknown researcher.

In this study, however, there were a number of situations in which gatekeepers would not allow access to their clients and this brought to light concerns around issues of agency regarding the gatekeepers denying their clients the opportunity to decide for themselves whether or not they would like to take part in the research. In some instances, a compromise was reached whereby, instead of asking a client if they would like to be directly involved in the research, the gatekeepers asked the clients if they would be happy for that gatekeeper to share their story. One instance in which this happened was in relation to a client who had already had to retell her story to numerous different organisations: doctors, counsellors, immigration officials, the police, and decision-makers in the National Referral Mechanism (the system in the UK for identifying and supporting potential victims of modern slavery). In this situation, the gatekeeper felt that it would be unfair and potentially counterproductive to her client's recovery to ask that client to repeat her traumatic story once again for the benefit of a researcher. Instead, the gatekeeper agreed, with her client's permission, to study the client's case notes and be interviewed in her place. While this offered access to an experience that I would otherwise not have been able to include in the research, it must be acknowledged that a person's own lived experience and interpretation of it will likely be different to that of a caseworker who knows the story only second hand, and who puts their own biases and interpretations upon it.

In researching hidden populations, some previous knowledge of the community can be very valuable, not only for accessing gatekeepers, but to have an awareness of how best to interact with respondents (Atkinson and Flint, 2001). My own previous front-line experience of working in an anti-slavery charity, interacting directly with both support providers and victims of modern slavery, was hugely beneficial in guiding and influencing this research as well as in accessing potential respondents and advice on the topic. I am confident that my existing working relationships with support organisations meant my approaches to gatekeepers were received more favourably than perhaps other researchers who did not have a pre-existing relationship (see Bosworth et al., 2011, for example).

Gatekeepers can play a significant role in a research project when it comes to allowing—or denying—access to research participants (McFayden and Rankin, 2016). However, it is important to remember that these gatekeepers, by the very role they play in having a relationship with the potential respondents, are also experts in their own right. With this in mind, I included representatives of support organisations as research subjects within this study, alongside individuals who had lived experience of conflict or of conflict and modern slavery. Not only did including gatekeepers as participants allow for access to case studies of individuals who were not accessible directly—where the gatekeeper was interviewed on their behalf as discussed earlier in this section—but it offered the chance to delve into the experiences of the individuals that work closely with people fleeing conflict or who have experienced modern slavery. These individuals have a broad oversight of the experiences of their clients, as well as a working knowledge of the field in which they practise. As such, their insights of the broader picture were valuable in gaining a better understanding of the processes at play for individuals who had fled conflict and were looking for support regarding modern slavery, immigration, or asylum in the UK.

In order to find respondents, I reached out to approximately 260 people, which led to twenty-four interviews being conducted. Eleven of these interviews were with individuals who had fled conflict, thirteen were with agency workers, and the stories of another sixteen clients were elicited through these interviews with agency workers. Not all these interviews are referenced in the content of this work for a number of reasons, including withdrawal of consent by the respondent and lack of applicability for the research (for instance one person's experience of conflict related back to early childhood and they had limited recollection of the circumstances).

Tables 1.1 and 1.2 offer a breakdown of all the interviews that were undertaken with individuals who had fled conflict, and with agency workers respectively. Table 1.3 summarises the sixteen client stories that were obtained from the interviews with agency workers. All names are pseudonyms.

Table 1.1 Respondents who had fled conflict

Pseudonym	Country
Barak	Syria
Fredrika	Uganda
Gamba	Cameroon
Hasim	Uganda
Hattie	Vietnam
Imogen	Bangladesh
Isaac	Democratic Republic of the Congo
James	Iran
Nadim	Syria
Oscar	Palestine (Gaza)
Sakti	Bosnia

Table 1.2 Agency worker respondents

Pseudonym	Organisation works with
Andrew	Children
Carly	Counselling
Daisy	Victims of exploitation
Emma	Counselling
Esther	Medical treatment
Fadi	Refugees
Gain	Asylum seekers
Gloria	Refugees
Harriet	Victims of modern slavery
Isobel	Vulnerable women
Jane	Refugees
Kafu	Asylum seekers
Lusala	Child soldiers

Table 1.3 Narratives provided by agency workers

Pseudonym	Country
Andrea	Uganda
Beth	Uganda
Catherine	Albania
Chiku	Sierra Leone
David	Bosnia
Ifra	Afghanistan
Francine	Gambia
Helen	Poland
Louise	Armenia
Mahal	Democratic Republic of the Congo
Nadia	Eritrea
Ofira	Eritrea
Padma	Ivory Coast
Tara	Nigeria
Verity	Somalia
Zoe	South Sudan

1.1.4 Interviews

Individual interviews are the most widely used data collection strategy in qualitative research (Sandelowski, 2002; Nunkoosing, 2005). They offer the opportunity to cover topics in depth and afford the respondent the chance to really scrutinise the reasons behind their thoughts and opinions (Berent, 1966), and as such, they were my preferred method of data collection in this study.

I employed semi-structured interviews for this research; they allowed for the development of a list of topics to be covered and, within each topic, a list of suggested questions. The intention was to allow the respondent to steer the interview while ensuring that key topics were covered. The interviews used open questions to allow the respondents to offer the answers that they felt most suitable, without implying there should be any limit to their responses. This permitted the respondents to assign their own meaning to their experiences without having to make them fit a multiple-choice option. 'Elite' models of interviewing were also applied. This entails holding the respondent as the expert on the topic, recognising that they have more knowledge than the researcher. This model is advocated by several academics researching hidden populations (Hogeland and Rosen, 1990; Raymond et al., 2002; Bosworth et al., 2011).

Having three distinct groups of respondents as outlined above: those who had fled conflict, those who had fled conflict and experienced modern slavery, and those who worked with either group, meant that the questions varied slightly depending on the respondent, but all followed a similar narrative. Without wishing to go into the minutiae of conducting interviews here, I began each with some time dedicated to building rapport. The interviews covered sensitive topics, for some, this would involve the retelling of traumatic personal stories, so it was important to build a level of trust with the respondents (Labott et al., 2013).

I then gradually moved onto more personal questions. They were kept as open as possible, prompting the respondent to set the direction of the answers. Early questions concentrated on topics based around life before the conflict: family, daily life, work, and school. This then led on to generating a better idea of how respondents managed to flee conflict, and how those who were victims of modern slavery became exploited. From here, the interviews delved deeper into the more sensitive topics, probing at experiences of modern slavery and of the UK asylum and immigration systems. The final section of the interviews considered what life was like now, taking account of any specific issues that the respondents faced, how they were settling in to the community, and what their hopes were for the future.

Locations of the interviews varied, with all respondents providing suggestions for their own preferred locations to ensure that we met in a setting they felt comfortable in. These included rooms in council buildings, drop-in centres, and libraries and all were chosen with easy access for the respondent in mind, so as to limit any inconvenience in terms of them having to travel.

The analysis of data from the interviews centred on grounded theory, one of the world's most prevalent research strategies (Strauss and Corbin, 1997; Birks and Mills, 2011). Rather than beginning with a hypothesis, grounded theory is the process by which the analysis of data leads to the construction of theories by focusing on a question with no expected outcome. As the researcher collects data, they concurrently analyse it and, with the progressive collection of more data, themes become identified until they can be grouped into categories. These categories are then used to construct or develop theories. This stands in contrast to the traditional positivist approach of the social sciences whereby a researcher will gather data to show how the topic under question relates to pre-existing theory. Simply put, grounded theory methods 'consist of systematic, yet flexible guidelines for collecting and analysing qualitative data to construct theories "grounded" in the data themselves' (Glaser and Strauss, 1999; Charmaz, 2006:2).

Grounded theory is promoted for studies relating to culturally sensitive topics as it allows the researcher to discover from their respondents how they understand their own experiences (Sammut-Scerri et al., 2012). It is also particularly useful for fields of study where there is little pre-existing research, as is the case when investigating the relationship between conflict and modern slavery as outlined in chapter three.

With each set of data collected, by identifying and labelling key words, I generated initial codes for topics that regularly occurred. From these, categories, which are groups of related codes (Holloway, 2008), were developed. I continued to generate categories until no new ones arose. From here, I was able to identify patterns, similarities, and anomalies between the findings. This led to the identification of five core categories, which contained those who:

- had experienced modern slavery during conflict
- had experienced modern slavery in the UK after fleeing a conflict
- had experienced modern slavery in an interim country after fleeing conflict but before arriving in the UK
- had fled conflict to the UK in relative safety
- continued to experience risk factors in the UK after fleeing conflict

These five categories were then used to structure the findings.

1.1.5 Ethical considerations

There are a number of issues to contemplate regarding ethics when undertaking research around sensitive topics with hard-to-reach, potentially vulnerable respondents. Some of the key ethical considerations relating to this research are discussed below.

First, the sensitive nature of the topics raised in the interviews was evident from the outset of the project, and a number of respondents were anxious about confidentiality. In acknowledgement of this, all respondents were assigned a pseudonym and any information that could potentially identify them was anonymised.

Second, as the interviews related to difficult topics, it was important to recognise the potential for distress during interviews. While it would be unsuitable for the research process to simply remove upsetting topics, because this research was based on traumatic events it was pertinent to limit potential occurrences of distress (McCosker et al., 2001) and to be prepared to respond appropriately. There were instances in some of the interviews where the respondent became visibly distressed and it was necessary to react according to the individual's wishes, offering them the chance to take a break or end the interview. Some respondents chose to take regular breaks, while others preferred to carry on when they became upset; no respondents wished to end their interview early.

A final point to note in relation to ethics is that five of the respondents required interpreters. Practical reasons led to two of the interviews being undertaken with a face-to- face interpreter and the remaining three with interpreters on the phone (all found via the National Register of Public Service Interpreters). While telephone interpreting held risks, especially in relation to volume and lack of context, these interviews flowed smoothly and the interpreters were better at interpreting direct questions and responses than the face-to-face interpretation where there were occasional brief exchanges between the respondent and interpreter before interpreting their replies. The main difficulty with telephone interpreters occurred when the respondents got upset. While the respondents were trying to compose themselves, they were often quiet. On multiple occasions the telephone interpreters mistook this for poor signal and they needed regular reassurance that the line was still active. Of course, this was not a problem with face-to-face interviewers as the interpreters were part of the situation. It is also key to mention that the involvement of interpreters can cause confusion in transcriptions as there is a tendency to fluctuate between pronouns, switching between I/me and he/she when referring to the respondent. In all the quotes used in this title, unless stated otherwise, the discussions relate to the respondents themselves as opposed to the interpreters.

1.1.6 Limitations and implications

Perhaps the most obvious limitation of this research is the relatively small sample size. The number of accessible people who have fled a conflict and experienced modern slavery is limited, but this number is reduced further when considering those who are willing to be interviewed, and further still in relation to the practicalities of organising convenient dates, times, and locations for the interviews. Having existing working relationships assisted significantly in this regard, and including agency workers as respondents helped to increase the sample size. The sample size was, however, adequate, and towards the last few interviews it became evident that no new themes or categories were emerging.

However, it is important to note that with snowball sampling, as was used for this research, the sample is unlikely to be entirely representative (Kaplan et al., 1987). The sampling method used is not random but is dependent on, and subject to, the first respondents. This makes it difficult to draw true generalisations from the study; it means it is not possible to compile a complete, accurate sampling frame, and it must be acknowledged that there are limitations in applying generalisations from the sample to the general population (Bloch, 1999).

One further limitation of this research relates to a lack of data regarding individuals who had fled to the UK but who had been denied asylum and were facing repatriation. Although some of the interview respondents had received negative asylum decisions, they had all appealed the decisions and continued to wait for the next outcome. It is possible that those who have been denied asylum and who are facing repatriation will have different experiences to those who opened a fresh claim after a negative asylum decision. Their stories could provide insight into the vulnerabilities that such individuals face both in the UK after receiving word that they are to be repatriated, and upon return to their home countries.

While this work focuses on research regarding the links between conflict and modern slavery, it must be acknowledged that conflict is not the only root cause of vulnerabilities. Although examining the impact of conflict here provides new understandings regarding some of the issues that put individuals at risk of modern slavery, it is only one of many root causes and there is scope and necessity for much wider research that explores the impact of other potential sources of risk. That being said, this title highlights that conflict increases the risk of modern slavery by generating vulnerabilities in the form of reducing a person's available options and their support networks. These are vulnerabilities that, as this work shows, are mirrored by restrictive immigration policies in the UK, and therefore likely present when tracing modern slavery back to other root causes.

In this work, I discuss the aspects of conflict that leave people vulnerable to modern slavery both as they leave the conflict situation and after they have arrived in the UK looking for safety. In uncovering these areas of risk, this work reaches beyond academic curiosity to offer insight and suggest practical applications as to where changes could be made to effectively implement prevention strategies to reduce the likelihood of individuals fleeing conflict situations becoming victims of modern slavery.

1.2 Chapter outline

In this title, by investigating the experiences of individuals who have experienced conflict, I demonstrate that conflict increases the likelihood that a person will become a victim of modern slavery by generating two key vulnerabilities. First, conflict reduces the options available to someone, often leaving them to choose between limited options that all hold inherent risk. Second, conflict commonly reduces a person's support network, leaving them to have to either cope on their own, or turn to strangers if they need help or assistance. The chapters are laid out as follows:

Chapter two: defining slavery and conflict. With widespread disagreement on the definitions of both 'slavery' and 'conflict', this chapter works through the terminological debates. It looks at definitions of slavery over time and how the term has been used as legislation has developed since the abolition of the transatlantic slave trade. Consideration is also given to whether it is necessary—or even possible—to distinguish between modern slavery and exploitation. Understandings of conflict are considered in terms of both legal and non-legal definitions as well as whether the motivations for a conflict can alter its definition. A new definition for conflict is developed in this chapter which brings together these concepts along with insights from those with lived experience who identified having lived through examples of conflict that extended beyond armed violence. These definitions of slavery and conflict are then used throughout the title to discuss current understandings and highlight new findings on the relationship that exists between conflict and modern slavery.

Chapter three: current understandings of conflict and modern slavery. In this chapter, I consider the extant literature relating to the relationship between conflict and modern slavery. While both conflict and modern slavery receive a great deal of interest in isolation, there is little academic literature that considers the relationship between the two, and less still when ideas of conflict are expanded beyond the notion of war. This chapter highlights the three most common topics of discussion in existing literature: victims of modern slavery during conflict, perpetrators of modern slavery during conflict, and immediate post-conflict zones. Scrutinising this literature emphasises how discussions of conflict generally fail to move beyond war and underlines a gap in the literature that calls for a broader understanding of conflict. This chapter also highlights a need to understand that vulnerabilities to modern slavery triggered by conflict continue beyond the immediate post-conflict period.

Chapter four: fleeing conflict to modern slavery. In this chapter I assess the stories of those who fled conflict and experienced modern slavery, be it in the same country as the conflict, in the UK, or in an interim country. While all those who suffered modern slavery had vastly different experiences, there were two key vulnerabilities that conflict had generated for all the respondents, regardless of the form of exploitation or the country in which it occurred. The first vulnerability was a limiting of choices, meaning individuals were left only with options that were all imbued with risk, leaving them to choose the option which appeared to be the lesser evil. The second vulnerability was a breakdown in support networks, which meant individuals no longer had a strong network of people they trusted to be able to turn to when they needed support, assistance, or advice.

Chapter five: fleeing conflict to safety. This chapter assesses the stories of those who fled conflict but did not experience modern slavery. Here, I consider whether those fleeing conflict to safety remained safe as a result of UK government policies or in spite of them. Two methods are highlighted through which individuals may be kept safe from slavery: the support of the government and statutory agencies, and the support of strangers and NGOs. While the former exemplifies ways in which government structures can be successful in identifying and protecting potentially vulnerable people, the latter relates to situations in which those systems can fail and individuals remain safe only through interventions by strangers or NGOs.

Chapter six: generating the conditions for risk. This chapter focuses on two key areas: intersectionality and structural dynamics, and the impact of some of the UK's restrictive policies. It pays particular attention to the UK's current approach towards modern slavery including the way modern slavery is conflated with immigration crime. It also considers the impact of the asylum system and the hostile environment in which it sits, as well as the impact of tied visas. In considering these aspects, this chapter demonstrates how some of these restrictive policies can serve to generate the very same vulnerabilities as conflict and therefore create environments which actually encourage modern slavery to occur.

Chapter seven: from victim blaming to victim agency. This chapter considers the role of agency in generating situations of modern slavery. It addresses a number of issues including victim terminology, the flaws of understanding modern slavery through a victim/agent binary, and the role of agency in leading people into situations of modern slavery. This chapter determines that victim terminology can have a detrimental impact on those who experience modern slavery but who do not fit the expectations of an 'ideal victim'. It encourages an understanding whereby victimhood and agency sit on a spectrum as opposed to a binary in order to reflect lived reality that having agency does not negate a person's experience of having been a victim. Finally, it considers how agency and structure interact in generating situations of modern slavery.

Chapter eight: conclusion. This chapter evidences how the findings of this research extend past academic interest to offer a new understanding of how conflict can increase vulnerabilities to modern slavery. It goes beyond the current tendency of suggesting that people become victims of modern slavery because of 'some pre-existing vulnerability' and evidences how these same vulnerabilities are also developed by restrictive policies in the UK. By identifying what these vulnerabilities are—the reduction of available options, and a breakdown in support networks—this research provides new information to enable the development of effective interventions to specifically target those most at risk. In the conclusion, I draw together the key findings and topics covered within the title. I then conclude by highlighting the practical applications and further research that could be developed as a result of the findings.

Chapter two
Defining slavery and conflict

Both 'conflict' and 'slavery' are complex terms with debated definitions. In this title, I use the Bellagio-Harvard Guidelines' definition of slavery, and provide a new definition of conflict. In this chapter I demonstrate how I came to settle on these definitions which are then used throughout this work to discuss current understandings of the issues and highlight new findings on the relationship that exists between conflict and modern slavery.

2.1 Definition of slavery

The definition of slavery is contentious and much debated. Its meanings vary across law, history, social sciences, and lived experience. Starting with the first references to slavery in international law, the following section works through the key legislation and definitions used through time, alongside their limitations, in order to articulate the rationale behind the definition chosen for this work.

2.1.1 The abolition of the transatlantic slave trade

In 1803, Denmark became the first sovereign state to permanently, legally abolish their slave trade. Four years later in 1807, both Britain and the United States enacted legislation following suit with the Act for the Abolition of the Slave Trade and the Act Prohibiting Importation of Slaves respectively. This obviated the trade and forced labour of millions of Africans; however, the terminology was limited in scope as these Acts abolished the slave *trade* but not slavery itself. Further, in the United States, abolition related only to the *international* trading of the enslaved. In Britain it was not until 1833 that slavery was legally abolished throughout

From Conflict to Modern Slavery. Alicia Heys, Oxford University Press. © Alicia Heys 2023.
DOI: 10.1093/oso/9780192846549.003.0002

the British Empire under the Slavery Abolition Act of 1833. In the United States, slavery itself remained legal until 1865 when the Thirteenth Amendment to the United States Constitution was enacted; however, neither of these national laws actually provided a definition for the term 'slavery'. Prior to this time, the terminological parameters of slavery were less contentious due to the clear legal guidelines that allowed human beings to be understood as the property of others. However, once slavery began to exist outside of these legal boundaries, the concept of slavery became more ambiguous.

Following abolition, the next widely cited historical discussion of slavery came in the early 1900s surrounding the term 'white slavery'. The 1904 International Agreement for the Suppression of the White Slave Traffic was renegotiated into the 1910 International Convention for the Suppression of the White Slave Traffic. The resulting convention was ratified by forty-one states after coming into force in 1920 as a response to widespread concern over white women and girls being trafficked into prostitution (Bales and Robbins, 2001). The use of the word 'white' in this convention highlights the reluctance at the time to directly link this form of slavery with the transatlantic slave trade, where it was generally understood that only Black people could be enslaved. The 1910 convention was ratified in 1921 by the League of Nations, after incorporating the word 'children' in the title, and became the International Convention for the Suppression of the Traffic in Women and Children. It is here that the notion of 'trafficking' first entered international legal understandings of slavery.

Five years later, the 1926 League of Nations' slavery convention was introduced. The Convention to Suppress the Slave Trade and Slavery (the 1926 Convention) provided the first definition of slavery in an international agreement, describing it as 'the status of a person over whom any or all of the rights attaching to ownership are exercised' (United Nations General Assembly, 1926). It prohibited all aspects of the slave trade, which it defined as:

> includ[ing] all acts involved in the capture, acquisition or disposal of a person with intent to reduce him to slavery; all acts involved in the acquisition of a slave with a view to selling or exchanging him; all acts of disposal by sale or exchange of a slave acquired with a view to being sold or exchanged, and, in general, every act of trade or transport in slaves. (ibid.)

Article 2 of the convention required that states were to 'bring about, progressively and as soon as possible, the complete abolition of slavery in all its forms' (ibid.). The convention was controversial as it was introduced at a time when forced labour was common practice under the colonial administrations of the 1920s (Bales and Robbins, 2001). To overcome this issue, the convention stipulated that 'forced labor may only be exacted for public purposes' and it required states 'to prevent compulsory or forced labor from developing into conditions analogous to slavery' (United Nations General Assembly, 1926). The convention was therefore significant in opening the way for understandings of slavery to go beyond the previously restricted interpretation of slavery as only the enslavement of Black people via chattel slavery.

In response to this convention, the International Labour Organization acknowledged the reading of forced labour as slavery, leading to the development in 1930 of the Forced Labour Convention. The aim of this convention was to prohibit forced labour regardless of the type of work it involved, thereby retracting the stipulations of the 1926 Convention which permitted forced labour for public purposes.

Subsequent focus on slavery came with the Universal Declaration of Human Rights in 1948 which stated that 'no one shall be held in slavery or servitude; slavery and the slave trade shall be prohibited in all their forms' (United Nations General Assembly, 1948). The adoption of this declaration by the United Nations General Assembly was a reaffirmation of the international stance on slavery. The European Convention on Human Rights (also known as the Human Rights Convention) used similar wording when it came into force in 1953, stating that 'no one shall be held in slavery or servitude' and that 'no one shall be required to perform forced or compulsory labour' (Council of Europe, 2010:7).

2.1.2 Widening parameters in international understandings of slavery

The 1926 Convention was updated in 1956 with the Supplementary Convention on the Abolition of Slavery, the Slave Trade and Institutions and Practices Similar to Slavery of 1956 (the 1956 Convention), alternatively known as the Supplementary Convention. This was a response to a UN decision that the 1926 Convention omitted some practices which were tantamount to slavery. The 1956 Convention obligated states to abolish any institutions and practices which were homologous to slavery, known as servile statuses, regardless of whether they were covered by the 1926 Convention. These servile statuses included debt bondage; serfdom; servile marriage; and the transfer of a person under eighteen years old by his guardian(s) to another person, regardless of reward, with the intention of exploiting them or their labour. The 1956 Convention then expanded on the 1926 Convention's recognition of different forms of slavery. It confirmed that there were multiple manifestations of slavery, each of equal importance, and emphasised that chattel slavery was no longer the only, or even the predominant, form of slavery. The definition provided by the 1956 Convention adds to, rather than replaces, the definition of the 1926 Convention. From an international standpoint, it is the amalgamation of these two conventions that provides the basis for any current legal definition of slavery.

The 1998 Rome Final Act established the International Criminal Court and employs a definition of slavery that is based on the 1926 and 1956 Conventions. It defines slavery as 'the exercise of any or all of the powers attaching to the right of ownership over a person and includes the exercise of such power in the course of trafficking in persons, in particular women and children' (United Nations General Assembly, 1998). The Rome Final Act extends the legal definition to include trafficking but, like the International Convention for the Suppression of the Traffic in Women and Children, it specifically highlights the plight of women and children. Whether this is based on ideas that women and children are more vulnerable to slavery, or perhaps considered more deserving of assistance, is a point not widely discussed.

In 2000, the Protocol to Prevent, Suppress and Punish Trafficking in Persons, especially Women and Children (better known as one of the Palermo Protocols) was introduced as part of the Convention against Transnational Organized Crime. The terminology in the titling of the protocol again indicates a bias towards women and children, but also emphasises its purpose of focusing on human trafficking, with no mention of slavery in the title. It is notably different in its definition to the conventions that preceded it, as it extends beyond just the exertion of notions of possession over a person. It states that:

(a) 'Trafficking in persons' shall mean the recruitment, transportation, transfer, harbouring or receipt of persons, by means of the threat or use of force or other forms of coercion, of abduction, of fraud, of deception, of the abuse of power or of a position of vulnerability or of the giving or receiving of payments or benefits to achieve the consent of a person having control over another person, for the purpose of exploitation. Exploitation shall include, at a minimum, the exploitation of prostitution of others or other forms of sexual exploitation, forced labour or services, slavery, servitude, or the removal of organs;

(b) The consent of a victim of trafficking in persons to the intended exploitation set forth in subparagraph (a) of this article shall be irrelevant where any of the means set forth in subparagraph (a) have been used;

(c) The recruitment, transportation, transfer, harbouring or receipt of a child for the purpose of exploitation shall be considered 'trafficking in persons' even if this does not involve any of the means set forth in subparagraph (a) of this article;

(d) 'Child' shall mean any person under eighteen years of age. (United Nations General Assembly, 2000a:2)

To simplify this definition, human trafficking according to this Palermo Protocol must contain three elements: the Act, the Means, and the Purpose. The Act refers to what is done, the Means refers to how it is done, and the Purpose refers to the form of exploitation. While this Palermo Protocol offers more detail of the elements of human trafficking, it continues the previous conventions' failures of defining slavery, simply listing it as one of numerous forms of human trafficking.

There is often confusion around the term 'human trafficking', with a propensity for it to be confused with people smuggling. While people smuggling does have the potential to become human trafficking, the terms are not interchangeable and there are distinct differences between the two which are important to elucidate. As summarised, human trafficking involves three elements: the Act (recruitment, transportation, transfer, harbouring, or receipt of persons); the Means (threat or use of force, or other forms of coercion, of abduction, of fraud, of deception, of the abuse of power or of a position of vulnerability, or of the giving or receiving of payments or benefits to achieve the consent of a person having control over another person); and the Purpose (the type of exploitation).

In the same year as the adoption of the Palermo Protocol, the UN Protocol against the Smuggling of Migrants by Land, Sea and Air was also established (United Nations General Assembly, 2000b). This defined the parameters of people smuggling as: 'the procurement, in order to obtain, directly or indirectly, a financial or other material benefit, of the illegal entry of a person into a State Party of which the person is not a national or a permanent resident'. Although people who are trafficked may well experience an illegal border crossing (or illegal entry), they may equally be taken to a destination in which they are legally entitled to reside.

Overall, the clearest way to differentiate between people smuggling and human trafficking is by identifying the point at which the relationship between those travelling and those organising the travelling ends. The relationship with those being smuggled will end upon arrival at the destination, while the relationship with those being trafficked will not. Although the confusion between people smuggling and human trafficking is understandable—especially when, for many, the conditions in which they are smuggled is poor—by defining trafficking using the Act, the Means, and the Purpose, the Palermo Protocol provides clear parameters which differentiate human trafficking from people smuggling.

2.1.3 Diversification of terminology: successes and limitations

Within the definition of human trafficking provided by the Palermo Protocol, it is perhaps surprising, considering the force and severe historical connotations surrounding the word 'slavery', that it is placed as a subheading of human trafficking as opposed to an issue in its own right. This framing of human trafficking and slavery is reversed in the UK's Modern Slavery Act.

As the UK Home Office was developing plans for the Modern Slavery Act, the term 'human trafficking' was used less by media and practitioners and was commonly replaced with the term 'modern slavery'. Yet little attention was paid to the meanings of the terms and they were often used interchangeably. Considerable and lengthy debate ensued among the working group preparing the first draft of the Modern Slavery Bill about 'slavery', 'trafficking', and how either might be defined. Only with the introduction of the Modern Slavery Act in March 2015 was a definition of the differences properly elucidated.

Unlike the Palermo Protocol, the Modern Slavery Act sets 'modern slavery' as an umbrella term where human trafficking is one of two subcategories, alongside 'slavery, servitude, forced or compulsory labour' (Home Office, 2014:9). This helps to overcome the problem whereby situations of slavery which do not incorporate movement are overlooked. Using the Act, the Means, and the Purpose criteria again, the Modern Slavery Act states that human trafficking requires the presence of all three criteria, while 'slavery, servitude, forced or compulsory labour' only require the Means and the Purpose (though the Means is not required for a child under eighteen years old to fit the criteria of being a victim of either human trafficking or slavery, servitude, forced, or compulsory labour).

However, the Act lacks clarity by identifying slavery as a subset of modern slavery without providing any definitions for its use. The legislation states that:

> (1) A person commits an offence if—
> (a) the person holds another person in slavery or servitude and the circumstances are such that the person knows or ought to know that the other person is held in slavery or servitude, or
> (b) the person requires another person to perform forced or compulsory labour and the circumstances are such that the person knows or ought to know that the other person is being required to perform forced or compulsory labour. (Modern Slavery Act UK, 2015)

The only mention of defining slavery is the statement that 'the references to holding a person in slavery or servitude or requiring a person to perform forced or compulsory labour are to be construed in accordance with Article 4 of the Human Rights Convention' (Modern Slavery Act UK, 2015). However, as discussed in section 2.1.1, the Human Rights Convention simply states that:

> 1. No one shall be held in slavery or servitude.
> 2. No one shall be required to perform forced or compulsory labour. (Council of Europe, 2010:7)

In effect, the Modern Slavery Act is a simple repeat of Article 4 of the Human Rights Convention with the addition of human trafficking but, like the Human Rights Convention, it fails to provide a definition of slavery. This exemplifies how legal understandings of slavery continue to date back to the 1926 Convention. Each time legislation is passed without clarifying a definition, previous legislation must be consulted for clarification. The point has now been reached where the basis of the legal definition of slavery is almost 100 years old, yet understandings of the crime continue to morph and expand.

Academic disagreement on the definition of slavery continues. Some claim that slavery is a form of exploitation manifested as a system through political violence, captivity, and theft (Meillassoux, 1991). Others understand it as 'institutionalized marginality' (Miers and Kopytoff, 1977:3–77). Some argue that the defining factor of slavery is that the victims are outcasts (Testart, 2002), while others suggest it is a form of social death whereby the victim suffers powerlessness, degradation, and removal from their familial claims and obligations (Patterson, 1982). Some of these definitions look for a common factor or defining theme that can be used to identify a situation of slavery whereas the conventions discussed above tend to rely on exemplifying *types of slavery*, which allows for a more open-ended depiction of slavery. While a broader definition of slavery increases the likelihood that victims of wider forms of exploitation will receive support, it risks expanding the definition to a point where it becomes so general as to be redundant. As Quirk (2011) suggests, wider definitions of slavery risk becoming overgeneralised to a point where they could incorporate potentially any type of exploitation that involves some extent of dominance. Such generalised definitions risk slavery becoming an evocative concept relating to extreme forms of human maltreatment, rather than a specific analytical category.

Other academics criticise the use of the term modern slavery in reference to forms of extreme exploitation occurring since abolition. These claims are based on the notion that there is no clear segregation between modern slavery and other forms of exploitation, including labour, marriage, and debt (O'Connell Davidson, 2015; Quirk, 2015a). Others suggest that current interest in the term 'modern slavery' is simply reflective of a 'white man's burden', whereby cultural relativism is imposed on other societies (Kempadoo, 2015; Dottridge, 2017). Similar arguments criticise the terminology of modern slavery, claiming that is not reflective of historic practices of slavery and the preoccupation with the topic serves to diminish and trivialise the historical experiences of the enslaved (Beutin, 2017).

It is evident then that there is a lack of a unified definition of modern slavery, and it was in response to such blurred and varied understandings of slavery that the Bellagio-Harvard Guidelines on the Legal Parameters of Slavery (Bellagio-Harvard Guidelines) were written (Allain et al., 2012).

The Bellagio-Harvard Guidelines were developed by the Members of the Research Network on the Legal Parameters of Slavery, a group of leading property scholars and slavery experts, with the intention of overcoming the lack of clarity regarding the definition of slavery in international law. By bringing together the slavery understood by law and the slavery experienced in reality, the Network believes these guidelines to be a reasonable description of slavery.

The overarching theme from the Bellagio-Harvard Guidelines is:

> In cases of slavery, the exercise of 'the powers attaching to the right of ownership' should be understood as constituting control over a person in such a way as to significantly deprive that person of his or her individual liberty, with the intent of exploitation through the use, management, profit, transfer or disposal of that person. Usually this exercise will be supported by and obtained through means such as violent force, deception and/or coercion. (Allain et al., 2012)

This definition progresses the 1926 Convention where 'slavery is the status or condition of a person over whom any or all of the powers attaching to the right of ownership are exercised.' The Bellagio-Harvard Guidelines unpack such powers to equate to the control of a person to an extent that is tantamount to possession, where possession is the most fundamental of the powers relating to ownership. A person cannot sell an item or profit individually from it unless they own it, and this extends to human beings; a person cannot exploit someone else's labour or body entirely for their profit unless they possess them. As it is no longer legal to recognise people as the possessions of others, these guidelines use control to delineate possession, to reflect lived experience.

The Bellagio-Harvard Guidelines expand the 1926 Convention's definition beyond just notions of possession by stipulating that the intent of exploitation must also be in place for a situation to constitute slavery (guideline 2). This addition helps to combat critiques which suggest that defining slavery simply as the possession of others fails because it forms no specific category of persons. As Patterson states, 'proprietary claims and powers are made with respect to many persons who are clearly not slaves' (1982:21). To understand slavery based only on possession would be to include people such as military personnel whose actions are controlled and who are instructed on where they must live and the battles in which they must partake. It would consider prisoners to be enslaved, with their experiences of being controlled and constantly monitored. It could include children, as they may be considered their parents' possessions, or couples who could reasonably be argued to have an extent of possession and control over one another. It would cover victims of kidnapping who are controlled in a way tantamount to possession. Couples in arranged marriages could be deemed to be victims of slavery by this understanding, as their parents are able to exert enough control over them to promise them to another person. By including the clause requiring the intent to exploit, the Bellagio-Harvard Guidelines comfortably overcome this issue and exclude the above examples from definitions of slavery (although, should the intention of exploitation be, or become, present, any of these could decline into situations of slavery).

2.1.4 Distinguishing between exploitation and modern slavery

This discussion leads us to the academic debate about whether—and how—exploitation and modern slavery differ, with some supporting the idea that there is a distinct difference, and others claiming that modern slavery is simply a form of extreme exploitation that cannot be segregated into a category of its own. Proponents of the latter suggest that there are plenty of examples of non-slavery situations where powers attaching to the right of ownership exist (Patterson, 1982; O'Connell Davidson, 2010).

> The distinguishing feature of slavery is widely held to be that it treats human beings as property. Yet, the League of Nations' definition of slavery as 'the status or conditions of a person over whom any or all of the powers attaching to the right of ownership are exercised' does not completely differentiate the master–slave relation from every other social relationship. This is because some of the powers attaching to the right of ownership are also often exercised over spouses, employees and children. (O'Connell Davidson, 2010:246)

However, as the Bellagio-Harvard Guidelines clarify, slavery relates not only to the powers attaching to the right of ownership, but to situations in which there is also an intention of exploitation (Allain et al., 2012). For children, perhaps the powers attaching to the right of ownership are present in that their parents or guardians may have full control over their decisions, but the child could not be deemed as enslaved unless their parents were exploiting or intending to exploit them. Similarly for spouses and employees, although some of the powers attaching to the right of ownership may be present regarding the fact that there is a contract in place between two parties, the spouse or employee still *can* leave the situation. Equally, unless the employer or spouse was exploiting or intending to exploit the employee or husband/wife, then the situation would not meet the grounds to be defined as slavery.

Forced marriage

One topic which is often defined as slavery, but where such a label is commonly questioned, is forced marriage. Some adamantly support the notion that forced marriage constitutes modern slavery (Kelly, 2017; Anti-Slavery International, 2017) and its recent inclusion in the Global Slavery Index (GSI) has both affected the GSI figures and influenced international audiences to this thinking. However, for many, the recognition of forced marriage as slavery is not so evident (Gong-Gershowitz, 2009; Jain, 2009).

It is important to identify that there is a distinction between an arranged and a forced marriage. An arranged marriage is one that is organised on behalf of the couple but where both parties are over eighteen and have the option not to participate. A forced marriage is where one or both parties are coerced into participating (KarmaNirvana, 2022). 'It is this very violation of autonomy and the right to self-determination that makes forced marriage an egregious violation of the victim's personhood' (Jain, 2009:1032).

For those in a forced marriage where there is a third party organising and enforcing the arrangement, there are powers attaching to the right of ownership but these are not held by the individual whom the person is to marry. Either or both parties of the marriage may not consent to the marriage itself, but they are unable to resist due to abuse or pressures placed on them by those enforcing it. For such a situation then, there is a clear demonstration of the powers attaching to the right of ownership whereby the people forced into the marriage are unable to decline; however, the exploitation aspect is much less clear. In such a situation, where the perpetrator is not a member of the marriage, it is unclear as to how the perpetrator could benefit from the exploitation of this person; this implies that forced marriage does not fit the definition of slavery. The actual process of being pressured and forced into a marriage against the person's consent may be defined as exploitative, but that does not necessarily mean that the marriage itself will be exploitative.

However, where the line begins to blur as to whether forced marriage could constitute slavery is when the perpetrator is one of the parties to be married. If this person has organised and enforces the marriage with the intention of benefitting from the exploitation of the other person, then this could be recognised as slavery: the powers attaching to the right of ownership are held by the person the victim is to marry and they intend to use the marriage to benefit from the exploitation of their new spouse. Yet, as Jain (2009:1019) states, 'while forced marriage may involve components of rape, sexual violence and enslavement, these [a]re not determinative of its existence'. As such, it is not possible to make generalisations claiming that all forced marriages represent situations of modern slavery. Instead, each case must be assessed individually to determine whether both the powers attaching to the right of ownership and 'the intent of exploitation through the use, management, profit, transfer or disposal of that person' (Allain et al., 2012) are present. Only then can the situation be determined as one of modern slavery.

Armed forces and prisoners

Other examples that comprise powers attaching to the right of ownership but do not indicate slavery include members of the armed forces and prisoners. Like the employee scenario, members of the armed forces have signed a contract to work and the conditions have been made clear to them. Although some of these conditions might, to some, appear exploitative, the employees have agreed to the conditions and the intention of the armed forces is not to benefit from the exploitation of its employees. Further, although there are some restrictions in place, members of the armed forces do have the option to leave without fear of physical violence as a repercussion. This example, however, clearly does not cover situations of child soldiers who, as discussed in chapter three, may be recruited against their will, purposefully exploited, and forbidden from leaving through threats of violent punishment or death; their experience would then be defined as modern slavery.

Being a citizen of a state means agreeing to its laws and consenting that, upon breaking them, the legal repercussions will be accepted, which may involve time in prison. The prisoner is not free to leave the situation as people are in the other examples mentioned, yet the exploitation of prisoners is not the intention of the criminal justice system. However, again, like the forced marriage scenario, if prisoners were to experience exploitation at the hands of those controlling them, then they could meet the definition of being victims of modern slavery. If this were the case, then prisoners would essentially be victims of state-sanctioned exploitation, as discussed by Chase (2015), LeBaron (2015), and Bales and Mayblin (2018); however, this is not generalisable to all prisoners and should be assessed on a case-by-case basis.

An aspect of note regarding prisoners and the people controlling them is that the relationship is not between two individuals, but between the prisoner and the state. This brings to light a question regarding who the perpetrator of the slavery would be if prisoners were to be exploited in a state-sanctioned way: the prison officer who is enforcing the exploitation, or the prison system that expects them to do it. If the prison officer was acting alone or with a group of other like-minded prison officers then the question is easier to answer, but if the exploitation is systematic then understandings of slavery become much more clouded.

Situations of modern slavery have been referred to as 'a relationship between (at least) two people' (Bales, 2006:1). While this implies that the relationship could be between more than one victim and more than one perpetrator, it does not account for situations where there is no identifiable perpetrator; situations, for example, in which the perpetrator is not a person, but a system. Prisons offer just one example to highlight the difficulties in identifying situations of modern slavery where slavery could be a result of a system rather than an individual or group of individuals. Another example might be seen in the UK's tied visa system.

Slavery perpetuated by a system

The tied visa system which restricts overseas domestic workers from changing their employers leaves these workers with limited legal options should their employment become exploitative: they can stay in the exploitative labour, or they can be repatriated (though an amendment in 2016 allows a change of employer if the six-month visa is still valid, but in reality this leaves little space to report and deal with abuse). This means that such employers have the privilege of knowing that their employees will be unlikely to ever raise a complaint against them. Essentially, through the tied visa system, the UK government grants the powers attaching to the right of ownership of the domestic workers to these employers by giving them control over the workers in the sense that they can set the working conditions and pay and the employee has little power to question them. If the workers decide not to accept the prescribed conditions, then they are returned to the government which will repatriate them, likely against their will. As such, the tied visa system creates the perfect environment for unmonitored domestic exploitation to thrive by offering the powers attaching to the right of ownership over that person to their employer. Should such ownership be rejected by the worker, then the legal outcome would be forced movement through the repatriation of that person back to their home country. This is discussed further in chapter six.

Another example of a government system offering the powers attaching to the right of ownership over people can be seen in the UK's asylum system. Here, the majority of asylum seekers are forbidden from undertaking employment or education until a decision is made on their case, and they receive £40.85 per week on which to live while they wait. However, as discussed further in chapters five and six, this is not enough for many to meet their basic needs. As a result, forms of extremely exploitative and forced labour are commonly unavoidable (Lewis et al., 2013).

These individuals have three options. The first option is to avoid the asylum system entirely and find illegal work in order to survive. The second option is to accept the £40.85 per week and find illegal work to supplement this. In these two options, they would not be able to raise a complaint if the labour became exploitative because they would be working when prohibited from doing so. The third (the legal option) is to enter the asylum system and accept the £40.85 per week, resigning themselves to the fact that they may wait a year or more for a decision on their asylum claim, while knowing they could be detained at any time and accepting that repatriation will continue to be a constant threat. To choose this third option is to accept that the state holds the powers attaching to the right of ownership over people in such a situation.

For some asylum seekers, this fear of repatriation encourages them to remain hidden from the authorities in the hope of making a life for themselves in the UK, where not being found means not being returned to the country they fled. The International Labour Organization (2005) reports numerous examples whereby employers have threatened repatriation to their undocumented migrant worker employees as a way of guaranteeing their labour and their silence on exploitative employment. For others, the fear of repatriation means compliance to the system and a reluctance to complain. As O'Connell Davidson asserts:

> the range and number of jobs available to them are more limited than those available to other groups of workers, and the lack of employment opportunities, especially for those who have indebted themselves to migrate, is a powerful motive to consent to poor conditions and wages. (2010:253)

Threats of repatriation used by employers for compliance is simply an easy method to prevent these people from trying to leave the exploitative conditions.

The state also has the power to arrest and detain asylum seekers without providing any information as to the reasons for the detention or how long they will be detained; the detentions also often involve violence (Symonds, 2021). Immigrants in detention may not suffer labour exploitation, but their bodies, by being in detention centres, are generating huge profits for the private companies that run the centres (O'Connell Davidson, 2013a), with figures indicating that some firms make up to 30 per cent profit on Home Office contracts (McIntyre, 2018). This is supported by research exposing the huge profits that are generated by detention facilities which receive on average $124 per day per detainee in the USA. With expanding immigration detention systems and the USA detaining an average of 34,000 people per day (Martin, 2015), this means these companies are set to make millions each year from the detention of immigrants (Conlon and Hiemstra, 2016). In quarter two of 2021, the estimated average cost of holding someone in immigration detention in the UK was £98.78 per day, and the overall financial cost of the UK's detention system for the year ending March 2021 was around £95 million (Silverman et al., 2021). This significantly reflects those situations in which people are defined as victims of modern slavery when they have suffered no physical exploitation but have benefits registered and paid in their name while their exploiter takes all their welfare money and generates a profit from the victim. Further, the state has the power to repatriate people, moving them across borders against their will, in a system that is often backed with coercion and violence (Binberg Peirce and Partners et al., 2008). Interestingly, these situations of detention and repatriation are not identified as situations of modern slavery despite the distinct similarities they have to situations which *are* defined as such. As O'Connell Davidson succinctly concludes:

> States use razor wire and guns to prevent people from moving where they wish to move. They detain them against their will. They use the

> threat of separation from their loved ones to make them comply with demands to move and they forcibly transport them from one territory to another. When states do these things their actions are not described as 'trafficking' or 'modern slavery', but are generally either applauded or accepted as integral to the legitimacy of the modern nation-state that claims a monopoly over the control of mobility, as well as a monopoly on violence. (2010:255)

Such an arbitrary line of differentiating between slavery and exploitation based only on whether threats come from a person rather than a system highlights how, if the asylum system or tied visas were a person, they could be identified as perpetrators of slavery and O'Connell Davidson is right to ask why states are not held to account as perpetrators of slavery when individuals acting the same way would instantly be recognised as such. The Bellagio-Harvard Guidelines could be used here to argue that while these systems essentially hold the powers attaching to the right of ownership, to fit the criteria for them to be accountable for slavery would mean also proving that the systems *intend* for the victims to be exploited. While exploitation is often the outcome of these systems, it is not a stated intention. However, the fact that the asylum system and tied visa system function in the way they do highlights that a government that promotes repatriation, uses violence to detain immigrants, and leaves them little choice but to accept exploitative labour simply cannot also laud itself as a champion in the fight against modern slavery.

The importance of a distinction

These examples highlight the extremely blurred line between what is considered slavery and what is considered exploitation. Not all asylum seekers or overseas domestic workers are victims of slavery and not all are exploited, but at what point does migration become exploitative, and at what point does such exploitation become slavery? Some, like Craig et al. (2007), argue that it is important to distinguish between situations of exploitation and situations of modern slavery. However, such a stance suggests that there should be a line between what is considered acceptable exploitation and what is considered unacceptable exploitation or slavery. Such a suggestion appears illogical; to deem a situation as 'exploitation' is to indicate its unacceptability. This therefore suggests that less focus should be placed on trying to differentiate between exploitation and slavery, and that more focus should be placed on ending exploitative practices as a whole as opposed to one specific subgroup of exploitative practices. This emphasises the tendency of too much attention being placed on terminology over the more pressing issue of human suffering. For those experiencing either modern slavery or exploitation, the definition of their suffering is likely to be far less important to them than an offer of support in ending the situation.

However, it must be acknowledged that without such defining lines, legal responses cannot be consistent, though if sentencing rates remain at their currently insignificant level, then the impact of a lack of clear legal definition will likely be negligible. To illustrate these rates, in 2017, 2018, and 2019 collectively, sixty-four adult offenders were sentenced for section 1 (slavery, servitude, forced, or compulsory labour) and section 2 (human trafficking) offences under the Modern Slavery Act (Sentencing Council, 2021). To put this in context, in the same time frame 22,765 potential victims of modern slavery were referred into the National Referral Mechanism (National Crime Agency, 2018, 2019; Home Office, 2020).

The blurred line between slavery and exploitation is often one of the criticisms against using the terminology of slavery today (O'Connell Davidson, 2010), because the lack of a legal status of slavery makes differentiating between the two extremely difficult. However, even during the transatlantic slave trade and immediately after its abolition, despite the legal status of slavery, the segregation between exploitative labour and slavery was not clear cut. Industrial wage workers of the same era as transatlantic slavery had masters to whom they were bound, but were not considered enslaved (O'Connell Davidson, 2017). Further, 'coolies' worked in exploitative conditions, often comparable to those of enslaved Africans, but were not defined as enslaved. Equally, after abolition, labour exploitation persisted and domestic workers continued to labour under conditions often reminiscent of slavery (Quirk and LeBaron, 2015). If exploitative conditions such as these—that were essentially equal to but not defined as slavery—existed when slavery was legal, then there is little justification to reason that slavery today cannot be defined as such on the basis that there is no clear distinction between exploitation and slavery.

During the eighteenth and nineteenth centuries, abolitionists were focused on ending racialised, African, slavery in the Americas, while overlooking exploitative situations elsewhere that essentially constituted slavery. Decades later, legislation began to identify this discrepancy between slavery and exploitation, and the 1956 Convention called for states to abolish 'slavery-like practices'. The terminology in this convention highlighted how it was not possible to list all forms of slavery, and that there were likely to be situations considered exploitative that had not yet, but should have been, defined as slavery. It is the plight of this supplementary convention that should be recognised today, but instead of trying to widen the definition of slavery to incorporate more situations of exploitation, a move away from ideas of slavery towards the broader framework of exploitation should be encouraged. Moving attention away from the specific and limited experiences of slavery to the more general and widely experienced situations of exploitation or 'slavery-like' practices would help to ensure that government and practitioner responses stop defining one person's experience of exploitation as worthier of attention than another's.

2.1.5 Implications of definitions on accountability

The inclusion of 'intent' is a fundamental aspect of the Bellagio-Harvard Guidelines, which would help protect the systems noted in section 2.1.4 from being identified as perpetrators of modern slavery where, although the resulting exploitation may be the same as that perpetuated by an individual, it is not the *intent* of the asylum system or tied visa system to exploit people. However, the notion of intent is approached differently by the Modern Slavery Act. To refresh, the Modern Slavery Act states that:

> (1) A person commits an offence if—
> (a) the person holds another person in slavery or servitude and the circumstances are such that the person knows or *ought to know* that the other person is held in slavery or servitude, or
> (b) the person requires another person to perform forced or compulsory labour and the circumstances are such that the person knows or *ought to know* that the other person is being required to perform forced or compulsory labour. (Modern Slavery Act UK, 2015, emphasis added)

The added emphasis highlights how the Act implies the possibility of holding a person in slavery without the intention of exploiting them. If a person 'knows or *ought to know*', then there must be cases in which a person *does not* know that they are enslaving a person. Such a situation could be exemplified by agency work, where an employer hires a worker through an agency. The employer believes that payment for wages is being paid to the employee, but the employee's bank account is being controlled by someone at the agency. The employer then ought to know, but could reasonably claim not to know, that the employee is being required to perform forced or compulsory labour. This underlines the lack of clarity afforded by the Modern Slavery Act in stipulating how broadly accountability can be assigned.

This situation is exemplified by 'Operation Fort', the UK's largest anti-slavery operation to date (Crates, 2020). In this operation, the police identified ninety-two potential victims, but believe that up to 400 Polish nationals were exploited.

> The traffickers targeted vulnerable victims in Poland, luring them to the UK with the promise of well-paid jobs and accommodation in the Birmingham area. On arrival, they were forced to live in squalor and work long hours in farms, factories, waste recycling plants and parcel sorting warehouses. In addition, some victims were forced to work extra hours carrying out building and maintenance work on a number of properties owned by the criminal network. (2020:9)

Operation Fort led to the convictions of eight members of a Polish criminal gang for slavery, trafficking, and money laundering offences. The legitimacy of these convictions is unquestionable as the perpetrators were both aware of, and had intended to benefit from, the exploitation of these victims. Yet the lines begin to blur in tracing the products of the crime to the point of distribution. In this case, some of the trafficking occurred in the agri-food sector which is a highly regulated industry and this brings up the question of how far along the supply chain the Modern Slavery Act's stipulation around offences being committed by those who 'ought to know' should be applied. These companies have corporate social responsibility teams and auditing trails into their supply chains. It is therefore not unreasonable to claim that those companies *ought to have known* that people were being required to perform forced or compulsory labour. Despite the lack of direct involvement in the exploitation of the victims, the Modern Slavery Act's definition implies that these companies committed a modern slavery offence. Some large-name retailers who received goods from suppliers where some of the victims worked received communications from the UK's Independent Anti-Slavery Commissioner at the time, expressing her concerns and asking them to outline how they were ensuring their suppliers were not using slave labour. Despite the phrasing of the Modern Slavery Act which indicates these organisations committed an offence because they *ought to have known*, in practice the companies were not charged.

It could similarly be argued that the financial institutions linked to the case *ought to have known* because the perpetrators were operating bank accounts in ways that are consistent with modern slavery and money laundering practices. Or that the labour agencies *ought to have known* because victims were being paid into the same bank account. However, like the retailers, these organisations were not deemed culpable for their involvement in the exploitation of these hundreds of victims.

Using this definition of the Modern Slavery Act links the concept of modern slavery perpetrators being those who *ought to have known* to the discussion in section 2.1.4, and suggests that those making decisions regarding the asylum system and tied visa system *ought to know* that their systems are leading individuals into situations of modern slavery. As such, under the definition of the Modern Slavery Act, they are guilty of an offence because there is plenty of evidence to demonstrate how these systems are perpetuating experiences of modern slavery. However, like the discussion of Operation Fort, it is unlikely that those who have not actively intended for modern slavery to occur will be held accountable.

It is clear then that the Modern Slavery Act fails to provide conclusive parameters as to who is culpable in a situation of modern slavery. In the example of Operation Fort, the Act can demonstrate that an offence has been committed, but it leaves an open-ended possibility as to where the responsibility for the offence lies. Under the Bellagio-Harvard Guidelines, the example would again be defined as slavery, but the assignation of culpability would be much less ambiguous. Here, the blame would rest only with the traffickers—those actively involved in organising and benefitting from the exploitation—as it was their intention from the outset that the victims would be exploited in order that they could personally gain from that exploitation. An equivalent intention on the part of the retailers, the financial institutions, and the labour agencies cannot be proven, meaning the Bellagio-Harvard Guidelines would not identify them as perpetrators in this case.

While it is important to provide parameters to words that represent vast topics and varying experiences to make it possible to identify and compare situations, we must be open to the fact that lived experience should be a key determinant of a definition. The Bellagio-Harvard Guidelines fuse legal understandings of slavery with the lived experience of victims and provide a more practical approach to defining perpetrators of the crime. By basing the definition on control coupled with intent to exploit, the Bellagio-Harvard Guidelines offer the clearest definition of slavery; as such, it is this definition that is used in this work. To repeat this definition for clarification:

> In cases of slavery, the exercise of 'the powers attaching to the right of ownership' should be understood as constituting control over a person in such a way as to significantly deprive that person of his or her individual liberty, with the intent of exploitation through the use, management, profit, transfer or disposal of that person. Usually this exercise will be supported by and obtained through means such as violent force, deception and/or coercion. (Allain et al., 2012)

2.1.6 The terminology of perpetrators and victims

While I have clarified the definition of slavery that I will be using in this work, there are other terminological issues requiring attention. The discussion of Operation Fort in section 2.1.5 uses the term 'trafficker' in reference to those who committed the modern slavery offences. This terminological choice could cause some confusion if the situation is one relating to slavery more generally as opposed to trafficking specifically. To overcome these issues, I use 'perpetrators' to refer to those who commit slavery offences and use 'traffickers' (and trafficking) only rarely and in reference specifically to situations of human trafficking.

Clarifying the terminology of the offenders is important, but it is also necessary to highlight the use of the term 'victim'. There is significant academic discussion which considers whether using the word 'victim' serves to remove agency from the individual, though focus rests predominantly on sexual assault (e.g. Dunn, 2005; Rape, Abuse and Incest National Network, 2009; Jean-Charles, 2014; Williamson and Serna, 2017). Some propose terms such as 'survivor', considering them more empowering and recognising the subject's agency. Advocates of this term claim that such terminology seeks to view the individual more positively, as strong and active, rather than as weak and passive as implied by 'victim' (Alachkar, 2016; Papendick and Bohner, 2017; Schwark and Bohner, 2019). Hunter (2010) highlights the impact of terminology with the argument that those labelled 'victims' commonly find it more difficult to develop a sense of self that goes beyond their victimhood. Other literature concurs that the term 'victim' reinforces a sense of passivity, an almost accusatory word indicating that those in question are not working towards recovery (Dunn, 2005) and one that could cause feelings of shame and guilt.

However, the term 'survivor' also faces criticism with claims that it can put pressure on an individual who may not feel like a survivor (Peternelj-Taylor, 2015). The same can be said for the term 'victim' in some situations of modern slavery; individuals may not identify as victims, especially if they had significant agency in the decisions that led to their exploitation (discussed in more detail in chapter seven) or if the situation of slavery was preferable to their previous circumstances.

Hunter (2010) suggests that 'victim' and 'survivor' sit on a continuum where individuals may initially identify as victims, but after talking about their experiences and confronting or reporting the perpetrators, go on to identify as survivors. As this implies, it is important to understand any preferences that the person being referenced has about the terminology used in relation to their own situation. It is not always possible to identify the terminological preferences of those who have experienced modern slavery, meaning a generalisable term is required here. Because the term 'survivor' is applicable only to situations after the exploitation has ended, its relevance is limited in this work which refers both to those who have escaped situations of slavery *and* to those who continue to be exploited. For these reasons, I choose to use the term victim throughout this title while acknowledging the flaws surrounding it, and emphasising that I do not apply the connotations discussed above to this term.

2.2 Definition of conflict

In order to reach participants for this research, I contacted organisations across the UK who support refugees, asylum seekers, or victims of modern slavery, whether that is the remit of their organisation as a whole or just a part of their work. I provided an information sheet with an outline of what the research was about, and explained that I was looking to interview people who had experienced conflict, and those who had experienced conflict *and* modern slavery. In the process of reaching out to these organisations, I did not provide a definition of the terms 'modern slavery' or 'conflict' that I would be using in the study, instead allowing potential respondents to self-identify their own experiences. I had anticipated those that came forward with experiences of conflict to have lived through armed conflict, war, and violence, but as I began to conduct the interviews, it became clear that the definition of conflict I had in mind was much narrower than the definitions that the respondents identified with. Recognising the fact that respondents were self-identifying as having lived experience of conflict that went beyond war or violence and included issues such as familial conflict, political conflict, and marital conflict encouraged me to really reconsider how I defined conflict and, like the Bellagio-Harvard Guidelines, to ensure I included lived experience within my understanding of the concept. The rest of this chapter summarises how I negotiated the term 'conflict', considering the difficulty in characterising it.

2.2.1 Conflict or competition: the impact of regulation

There is a common tendency to amalgamate conflict and competition (Schmidt and Kochan, 1972). Some, such as Weber, argue that conflict and competition are simply separated by violence: 'A peaceful conflict is "competition" in so far as it consists in a formally peaceful attempt to attain control over opportunities and advantages which are also desired by others' (Weber, 1964:132–3). Others suggest that competition and conflict are different issues separated by regulation (Schmidt and Kochan, 1972), where competition is regulated and conflict is not (Mack, 1965). The opposing parties may well be competing for the same thing: land, wealth, power, etc., yet there is no unilaterally definitive point at which a competition becomes a conflict, and this argument is defeated with the realisation that, with international humanitarian law, conflict can also be regulated.

2.2.2 International humanitarian law

International humanitarian law refers to two distinct forms of conflict: international armed conflict and non-international armed conflict. International armed conflict is defined in the Geneva Conventions of 1949, common article 2 as:

> all cases of declared war or of any armed conflict that may arise between two or more high contracting parties, even if the state of war is not recognized by one of them. The Convention shall also apply to all

> cases of partial or total occupation of the territory of a high contracting party, even if the said occupation meets with no armed resistance. (International Committee of the Red Cross (ICRC), 1949:common article 2)

This is expanded with an additional protocol to include 'armed conflicts in which peoples are fighting against colonial domination and alien occupation and against racist regimes in the exercise of their right of self determination' (ICRC, 1949:additional protocol I, art. 1, para. 4).

Non-international armed conflict is covered by common article 3 of the Geneva Convention, describing 'armed conflicts not of an international character occurring in the territory of one of the high contracting parties' (ICRC, 1949:common article 3). This means that non-international armed conflict can include armed forces that are not linked to a government. The conflict could even be constituted entirely by non-governmental groups. According to international humanitarian law then, international armed conflict is one between the armed forces of two states or for national liberation, while non-international armed conflict is an internal conflict which does not necessarily involve governmental armed groups.

The International Criminal Tribunal for the former Yugoslavia (ICTY) declared that 'an armed conflict exists whenever there is a resort to armed force between States' (ICRC, 2008). However, because this could relate to a dispute between just a few dissidents, to warrant the attention of international humanitarian law, there are two widely accepted criteria that must be met: a minimum level of intensity and a certain degree of organisation within the opposing parties.

The level of intensity is reached when the hostilities are collective or when a police force cannot contain the fighting force, requiring the government to engage its armed forces (ICRC, 2008). The ICTY provides examples of cases where such levels of intensity could be reached, including intense devastation of a small number of buildings, the preparation of combat units, or the use of anti-aircraft equipment without resources for air power (ICTY, 2005). However, this is simply a list of examples; there is no agreed base level, which makes it impossible to create a generalisable definition.

The degree of organisation refers to conflict involving non-state actors. Again, examples are provided in the ICTY document, including situations in which land is divided into zones each with a commander required to provide updates to the general staff. This threshold is much easier to define in that the non-governmental parties involved in the conflict must have organised armed groups with a recognisable structure and the capacity to undertake military operations. Unlike the level of intensity, this is a basic definition that has the potential to be generalised to other conflicts. While the requirement of state involvement is understandable to necessitate the involvement of international humanitarian law, the definitions provided fail to offer a generalisable definition of conflict that goes beyond large-scale armed violence, and further, it is unclear as to why different rules are applied depending on whether the conflict is international or internal.

These definitions provided by international humanitarian law offer legal classifications for those who are signatories to the Geneva Convention. However, they exclude situations that exist beyond the realms of international or non-international armed conflict, for example a conflict between a state and a foreign non-state actor (Belandra, 2007; Duxbury 2007). Further, they refer only to armed conflict, and within that, only to situations which occur on a scale large enough to require the acknowledgement of international law. Finally, they do not provide fixed parameters through which a set definition of conflict can be garnered:

> Although international humanitarian law has at its aim the limitation of the effects of armed conflict, it does not include a full definition of those situations which fall within its material field of application. (Vité, 2009:69)

Of course, the actions of those who exploit people in the form of modern slavery are not stayed by law. Slavery is illegal in all states yet continues to exist in times of conflict, both in terms of war and in wider understandings of the concept. This means that, like the definition of slavery, it is necessary to look further than legal definitions to identify the broader reality of conflict and to establish the common themes that can provide a generalisable definition. However, similar to Quirk's assertions about the risks of broadening definitions of slavery as discussed earlier in section 2.1.3 (2011), Dahrendorf (1958) suggests that reducing all conflicts to a single common principle risks leading to either huge generalisations or unreasonable over-simplifications. In this work I seek to identify a definition of conflict which is both robust and which expands beyond the limited parameters of war in order to recognise the lived experience of those who participated in this research, and who self-identified as having lived through conflict in a sense broader than just war. The discussion in section 2.2.3 moves away from legal definitions of conflict to assess how it is understood in broader contexts.

2.2.3 Non-legal definitions of conflict

Dictionary definitions of conflict provide a variety of suggestions as to how the term might be applied:

1. A serious disagreement or argument, typically a protracted one
   1.1 A prolonged armed struggle
   1.2 A state of mind in which a person experiences a clash of opposing feelings or needs
   1.3 A serious incompatibility between two or more opinions, principles or interests
2. Be incompatible or at variance

(Oxford English Dictionary, 2021)

As this work is concerned with understandings of conflict between people, point 1.2 is disregarded. The remaining points purport that conflict relates to incompatibility, but a pertinent matter to highlight is that the dictionary definitions move beyond conflict being just understood in terms of armed or violent conflict. This is significant, and re-emphasises the respondents' own understandings whereby they self-identified having lived through a conflict, with only a small number of respondents having experienced armed conflict specifically. As such, it is necessary that we move beyond a limited understanding which always connects conflict with violence. It is important to recognise that 'conflict' as a concept has broad and contested boundaries and, indeed, lived experience of conflict extends far beyond just armed conflict. However, the concept of conflict has been debated for decades.

2.2.4 Conflict resolution in defining conflict

The field of conflict resolution was established in the 1950s and 1960s when academics of varying disciplines agreed on the usefulness of studying conflict as a generalised issue where there were commonalities between all forms, regardless of scale. However, before conflict resolution could prove insightful, it was essential that contributors provided some form of definition of 'conflict' to set the parameters of study. There were debates over the variations in conflicts and how they should be categorised. Some scholars generated lists, like LeVine (1961) who limited conflicts to four types: intrafamily, intracommunity, intercommunity, and intercultural. Others created much vaster lists, such as Chase (1951) who characterised eighteen different types of conflict ranging in degrees from personal quarrels to East versus West. In fact, many writers developed lists of types of conflict alongside a caveat stating that the lists were not exhaustive. However, providing examples of situations that can be defined as conflicts—mirroring the 'minimum level of intensity' described earlier in section 2.2.2 in relation to international humanitarian law—does not provide a generalisable definition so much as an incomplete list of illustrative cases.

There is also academic debate over whether conflict always denotes a negative, or whether it could be understood as positive: as a method through which solutions can be created (Tjosvold, 2006); these are, respectively, notions of destructive and constructive conflict. Destructive conflict is deemed negative and to be averted. It generates situations in which no party is content with the circumstances or outcomes. On the other hand, constructive conflict is valuable and sometimes necessary to overcome situations of tension and reach a productive outcome (Deutsch, 1949). It occurs when the interests of both parties are balanced and the parties adapt to the situation, leading to a satisfying, mutually beneficial outcome. Singer (1949) raises an insightful thought on this issue in that, logically speaking, the struggle (e.g. war) could be understood as a method of solving the conflict rather than an example of conflict itself. With this understanding, the conflict is the initial disagreement and war is a response to this, where its purpose is to find a resolution to the initial problem. Throughout this work, I consider conflict to encompass both these notions: a conflict arises when there is a clash between two people or groups of people, and continues as that disagreement endures through whatever means.

2.2.5 The motivations of conflict in generating its definition

Another key concept relating to the definition of conflict is that it has two possible motivations: fighting over the same resource or fighting over differing values. These are the notions of consensual and dissensual conflicts as discussed by Ramsbotham et al. (2011). The former refers to opposing parties fighting for the same thing (such as land, control, autonomy, etc.) and the latter refers to opposing values (such as religion, ethnic bias, etc.); however, there are clearly times when the two overlap.

Defining conflict then becomes even more complex if its reasons for existence form the basis of whether a disagreement can be defined as a conflict. The character of a conflict may change over time and the reasons for its commencement are not necessarily the same as the reasons that promote its continuation.

2.2.6 Widening the remit of conflict

There has been significant disagreement on how narrowly the parameters of conflict should be set. Those who advocate for a narrow definition claim that generalising the term could result in it becoming oversimplified and used to refer to anything 'from war to choices between ice cream sodas or sundaes' (Mack and Snyder (1957) quoted in Fink, 1968:431). However, others such as Dahrendorf (1958) and Ramsbotham et al. (2011) promote a more inclusive understanding of the term to reflect that it really does cover a huge cohort of issues. It is this more generalised approach, reflecting the lived experiences identified by the respondents of this research, that I adopt here to denote conflict through a set of conditions whereby parties identify and act on mutually incompatible goals. Unlike the definitions offered by international humanitarian law and the ICTY, such understandings include non-violent conflicts as well as those that incorporate violence. As Wieviorka asserts (2009), while conflict and violence may merge, they are not codependent:

> conflict is not only not to be confused with violence: it tends basically to be its opposite. Violence closes down discussions rather than opening them up. It makes debates and exchanges—even unequal exchanges—difficult and encourages ruptures or even pure power relations. (Wieviorka, 2009:10)

It is important then that any understanding of conflict is not automatically conflated with violence. However, searching 'non-armed conflict' in academic literature is a futile exercise returning only results of 'armed conflict' or 'non-international armed conflict'. This emphasises the tendency of academia to focus on conflict only in terms of war or armed violence. Extending such a search to 'non-violent conflict' does little to narrow down academic definitions. Although this heading incorporates much more literature that is accepting of the existence of conflict without violence, it continues to fail to provide parameters. As an example, Ackerman and DuVall's book *A Force More Powerful: A Century of Non-Violent Conflict* (2000) provides valuable insight into the ways in which non-violence has been used in conflicts over the past century; however, no concrete definition of 'non-violent conflict' is offered. Another interesting finding in literature on non-violent conflict is the use of the term 'non-violent resistance'. Stephan and Chenoweth define this as 'a civilian-based method used to wage conflict through social, psychological, economic, and political means without the threat or use of violence' (2008:9) and they offer examples including 'boycotts, strikes, protests and organized non co-operation' (2008:8). They discuss how little the literature on non-violent conflict comprehensively analyses all forms of non-violence, instead providing lists of examples, thereby repeating the previously mentioned problem that examples do not constitute a definition. While Stephan and Chenoweth (2008) focus on resistance and offer a rare academic insight into violence-free conflict, they continue to reference conflict without defining its meaning, and they depict non-violent resistance as separate to conflict while offering no clear distinction between the two. Their work suggests that resistance (violent or otherwise) is a *response* to conflict rather than a form of conflict itself, thereby echoing Singer's suggestion that a struggle could be understood as a method of solving the conflict rather than an example of conflict itself (Singer, 1949).

This tendency to overlook a definition of conflict is reflected widely in the literature (see for example Steiner, 1969; Helvey, 2004; Mnookin and Verbeke, 2009). To identify a generalisable definition of conflict, situations must be identified that are not framed purely around armed violence, yet that go beyond listed examples of non-violent resistance. Incorporating non-violent forms of conflict is important to recognise that conflict can exist without violence, and this would then be to acknowledge issues such as familial conflict, marital conflict, political conflict, ethnic conflict, and employment conflict, experiences highlighted by the participants involved in this research. To offer clarity on these issues, familial conflict refers to any dispute within the family. This could be the desires of one family member not being acknowledged by another, for example, a female wanting to take on traditionally male employment. It could be a forced marriage that goes against one of the participant's wishes. It could be a relationship that other family members do not approve of, etc. Marital conflict relates more specifically to a breakdown in the relationship of a married couple, particularly if this were to lead to divorce.

Some instances of political conflict will be covered by international humanitarian law should they reach the required thresholds. Smaller-scale political conflict could include disagreements between parties (as, of course, is commonly the case) or disputes between party members.

Ethnic conflict can be illustrated with examples whereby ethnic discrimination has led to widespread violent conflict, such as with the Rohingya Muslims of Myanmar, the Hutus and Tutsis in Rwanda, and the Nagorno-Karabakh conflict between Azerbaijan and Armenia. Horowitz argues that ethnic conflict may have any number of causes, including religion or politics, and any conflict based on ascriptive qualities could be deemed ethnic (1985). However, as Varshney (2002) counters, while there may be multiple religious and political views within a single ethnic group, to be defined as ethnic conflict the dispute must be explicitly for the societal position of that ethnic group. An ethnic conflict need not lead to widespread displacement, murder, or even violence in order to be defined as conflict; the conflict may simply be between two ethnic groups or members of those groups.

Employment conflict relates to a conflict of interests between two parties: two or more employers, two or more employees, or a dispute between employers and employees. While many employers have policies to ensure that no employment conflict escalates beyond a manageable threshold, this is not always the case. Employers may have human resources teams and employees may be represented by unions, each of which could either heighten or lessen the conflict. Should these prevention methods fail to counter a conflict, there is the possibility that the dispute could progress to an uncontrollable level.

The connection between religion and violent conflict gained significant academic recognition in the early 1990s in response to the fall of communism in the Soviet Union and eastern Europe, where examples of religious conflict ensued, such as in Kosovo and Bosnia and Herzegovina (Little, 2006). As with ethnic conflict, there may be numerous root causes for a religious conflict and multiple political and ethnic representations may exist within that one religion. However, for a situation to be understood as a religious conflict, those in conflict must be in dispute explicitly over the position of their religious group within society. Again, violence or arms are not required for such a situation to meet the definition of being a conflict.

The above examples of non-violent conflict form a non-exhaustive list. However, as raised above, lists of examples do not constitute a definition and the parameters of the term 'conflict' must be identified if it is to be used in a meaningful and generalisable way. I use the ideas generated from the discussions on conflict outlined in this section, coupled with the forms of conflict identified by the respondents who took part in this research, to shape my own, newly developed definition of the term, as detailed in section 2.3.

2.3 Conclusion

In this chapter I have introduced the themes of both slavery and conflict, working through historical and contemporary understandings and providing the definitions (and justification for these definitions) that I will be using throughout this title. While there is no universally accepted definition of either modern slavery or conflict, the following definitions are the ones that I rely on.

The Bellagio-Harvard Guidelines bring together the slavery understood by law with lived experience to determine slavery as follows:

> In cases of slavery, the exercise of 'the powers attaching to the right of ownership' should be understood as constituting control over a person in such a way as to significantly deprive that person of his or her individual liberty, with the intent of exploitation through the use, management, profit, transfer or disposal of that person. Usually this exercise will be supported by and obtained through means such as violent force, deception and/or coercion. (Allain et al., 2012)

Equally, 'conflict' continues to be contested, sometimes framed as a necessary step to meet a goal, other times conflated with competition. In law, the definition is relatively narrow and rests heavily on concepts of violence. I take a broader approach to the remit of conflict to incorporate both legal and non-legal definitions and to ensure that the definition I use also reflects lived experience. To this end, I define conflict as a set of conditions whereby parties identify and act on mutually incompatible goals. While this act may be violent, the presence of violence is not necessary in order for the situation to be defined as conflict. It is possible to be affected by a conflict without being an active participant.

Chapter three uses these definitions as a basis from which to review the existing literature for intersections between conflict and modern slavery in order to assess how the relationship between the two is currently understood.

Chapter three
Current understandings of conflict and modern slavery

As discussed in chapter two, conflict includes, but is not limited to, war and should be understood in much broader terms. However, one pertinent flaw of the extant literature is its failure to do this, with the representations of conflict being almost exclusively in relation to armed violence. Further, despite the fact that in Resolution 2331, the UN Security Council recognises that human trafficking is prevalent in conflict situations, since the passing of UN Resolution 55/25, anti-trafficking policies and documents at the regional level have mainly failed to focus on human trafficking in conflict (Muraszkiewicz et al., 2020a). The lack of concentration on this nexus is also reflected in the extant literature, whereby there are few publications that overtly consider the interplay between conflict and modern slavery or human trafficking. This chapter reviews the available literature, focusing on the limited topics that highlight the explicit links between conflict and modern slavery, namely: understandings of victims and perpetrators of modern slavery during war, and the impact of the post-war period in generating situations of modern slavery.

By reviewing the literature, this chapter highlights the gaps and limitations of current writings that link modern slavery to conflict. It draws attention to the current limited understandings of victims of conflict-related slavery predominantly as child soldiers, and perpetrators as peacekeepers. It also emphasises that there is currently a restricted understanding of slavery-related conflict where focus rests entirely on understanding conflict as war. Having identified this gap in the literature, section 3.4 summarises the findings of a literature search which sought to go beyond these limited understandings of conflict by using search terms of forms of non-violent conflict which authors may not have explicitly defined as such, but which fit the definition of conflict outlined in chapter two.

From Conflict to Modern Slavery. Alicia Heys, Oxford University Press.
DOI: 10.1093/oso/9780192846549.003.0003

3.1 Victims of modern slavery in conflict

Ineffective research methods coupled with a lack of data mean that there is no accurate estimate of the number of victims of modern slavery in conflict situations (Weitzer, 2014). There is also limited acknowledgement of who is affected by modern slavery resulting from conflict; however, Muraszkiewicz et al. (2002b) undertook empirical research with key stakeholders to generate a typology of human trafficking in conflict, and identified seven key ways in which it presents. Trafficking for sexual exploitation is identified twice, once in reference to peacekeepers and humanitarian agencies (where an imbalance of power coupled with immunity from prosecutions creates the perfect conditions to perpetuate sexual exploitation) and again in reference to armed groups (in terms of both a demand for sex and a tactic of war). Other forms in which it presents are the trafficking of children into armed groups and for forced labour, trafficking for the purpose of slavery or practices similar to slavery, trafficking for the purpose of extorting ransom, trafficking for the purpose of forced combat (of those aged 18 or over), and trafficking for the purpose of the removal of organs. Milano (2020) offers another suggestion that trafficking for labour is another category of human trafficking in conflict, where the military may recruit labour forces through trafficking networks, or by buying the services of trafficking victims.

While Milano (2020) and Muraszkiewicz et al. (2020b) consider how trafficking might play out in conflict, both contributions hail from the same title, an edited collection: *Trafficking in Conflict: Context, Causes and the Military* (Muraszkiewicz et al., 2020c). This is one of the most comprehensive titles which addresses linkages between conflict and examples of modern slavery. The book highlights the lack of attention paid to issues of human trafficking in conflict, despite recognition that it is prevalent. Beyond this title, very few studies regarding conflict and modern slavery consider the interplay between the two concepts with the main exceptions being discussions of child soldiers and women. Of these two topics, child soldiers receive significantly more attention; whether this is because children are considered the most vulnerable members of a society in conflict, are most willing to contribute information to researchers, or whether funding and international interest encourages researchers to focus their efforts on children is unclear. However, it is important to note how the terminology of 'child soldiers' could be confusing, leading to understandings of children as active, willing participants in violent conflict when they should be understood as victims of modern slavery.

> A child soldier has been defined as any person under 18 years of age who forms part of an armed force in any capacity, and those accompanying such groups, other than purely as family members, as well as girls recruited for sexual purposes and forced marriage. (Secretary General of the United Nations, Report to the Security Council, S/2000/101, 11 February 2000 quoted in Verhey, 2001:27)

A child soldier then, is simply a child who is attached to the armed forces. They are not necessarily a combatant but could be used to carry out a range of tasks including being a guard, a courier, a domestic labourer, a manual labourer, or a 'wife'. With this definition widely accepted, it is important to emphasise how the experience of child soldiers is a direct result of conflict; without the conflict, their use would not be required. Reiterating the definition of the Bellagio-Harvard Guidelines, child soldiers fit the definition of being victims of modern slavery:

> In cases of slavery, the exercise of 'the powers attaching to the right of ownership' should be understood as constituting control over a person in such a way as to significantly deprive that person of his or her individual liberty, with the intent of exploitation through the use, management, profit, transfer or disposal of that person. Usually this exercise will be supported by and obtained through means such as violent force, deception and/or coercion (Allain et al., 2012).

For child soldiers, the powers attaching to the right of ownership are used to minimise the child's liberty with the intention of exploiting them within their role as a soldier, whatever form this takes. They do not have the freedom to leave, should they wish, and their actions and movements are controlled by those in charge.

3.1.1 Methods of recruitment

A large proportion of the literature on child soldiers focuses on methods of recruitment, be this pre- or mid-conflict. Children are particularly desirable to armed forces because they are so easy to manipulate, they obey instructions, and they eat and earn less than adults (Human Rights Watch and Brett, 2003). There are numerous countries with armed groups that actively recruit children for both armed combat and auxiliary roles (Haer et al., 2019), and there are several methods through which children are recruited into armed forces. Some children claim that they volunteer, which raises issues around children's agency and questions the possibility of whether such 'volunteering' is, in reality, due to a lack of alternatives. For example, if a child comes from a particularly impoverished area where food, employment, and safe shelter are scarce, their situation may be particularly desperate if they are also living in a conflict zone. Human Rights Watch (2003) discusses examples of thousands of children in Ugandan villages and towns, fearing abduction, leaving their homes every night to seek refuge in churches, factories, and bus depots where they hope to be safe. They will then travel back home every morning. Some children see that joining an armed force would at least provide them with food, accommodation, a sense of belonging, and some degree of protection (Verhey, 2001; Human Rights Watch and Brett, 2003; United Nations Department of Economic and Social Affairs, 2005). This will be the case particularly for children who have been separated from their families and who are living in abject poverty with a lack of social services (Watchlist, 2003).

Wars alter both the social and economic roles of children. Their vulnerability to slavery or exploitation becomes heightened if they have also suffered poverty, the death of parents, if they are runaways or live close to places with high demand for child labour or where armed forces recruit new soldiers (Smucker and Murray, 2004). Again, this emphasises how pre-existing vulnerabilities alone are often not enough to push children into slavery, but how conflict can intensify their vulnerabilities to lead them towards such situations.

When people flee from conflict, their community and family support systems often break down. Children may be separated from their families, increasing their vulnerability to recruitment into the armed forces or other forms of exploitation (UNHCR, 2003). Research has shown that some parents even ask commanders to take their children when they can no longer afford to feed them (Human Rights Watch and Brett, 2003), believing that the children will live better lives or at least have a better chance of survival as child soldiers than if they stayed with their families. Other children 'volunteer' into the forces to seek revenge for atrocities suffered by their families (David, 1998), though, again, without the impact of war, those children would likely have no need for revenge, nor an inclination to volunteer. The literature provides plentiful examples of children threatened with murder for refusing to join, and the most common courses of recruitment are through threats, force, and outright kidnapping (David, 1998; UNICEF, 2002; Human Rights Watch and Brett, 2003; United Nations Department of Economic and Social Affairs 2005).

3.1.2 Experiences of exploitation

McKay and Mazurana (2004) discuss child soldiers in depth. One of their focuses is recruitment in Uganda. Here, children tend to be abducted into armed groups where their initiation involves committing atrocities against those from their communities: rape, torture, maiming, and even murder. This serves a double purpose: it initiates the child into the armed force and simultaneously destroys links between them and their family and community. These aspects make it difficult for the child to reintegrate back into their society should they escape or be permitted to leave. Therefore, for these children, the impact of war does not end in their recruitment to the armed forces but continues for the rest of their lives as they lose their pre-war societal connections. This means that should they ever leave the armed force they must make a life for themselves with little or no outside support.

Human Rights Watch (2003) discusses this in further detail, also in relation to children in northern Uganda. Children are abducted from homes, schools, and the streets and forced into sexual exploitation, to burn houses, carry out raids, beat and kill civilians, and abduct other children. Some are forced to fight while others become 'wives' or servants or are given auxiliary roles as guards, spies, miners, domestic servants, porters, or forced labourers (Sommers, 2002). Although being a front-line fighter may appear the least desirable role when other auxiliary roles are less dangerous, often children choose these combat roles, knowing there is a greater chance of escape when they have a weapon (Newman, 2014).

Although girls are recruited by armed forces, many are not given fighting roles, but are taken as 'wives' to commanders (David, 1998; Mazurana et al., 2002; Watchlist, 2003; McKay and Mazurana, 2004). The commanders choose the girls they consider prettiest as their 'wives', and the other girls are given ancillary roles (Human Rights Watch, 2003). The 'wives' may well bear children from the commanders.

3.1.3 Demobilisation and reintegration of child soldiers

Once the conflict ends, children may be reluctant to leave the armed forces for various reasons, chief among them having no family to return to, not knowing the location of their family, or fearing stigma for some of the acts they committed as a soldier (Verhey, 2001; United Nations Department of Economic and Social Affairs, 2005).

Education can help prevent child exploitation and recruitment into armed forces as well as assisting in the prevention of the enslavement of children once the conflict has ended. However, education during an armed conflict is often limited (UNICEF, 2002). Governmental priorities commonly change during times of war and governments may choose to remove funding from education to assist in tackling the conflict. Teachers' salaries may be cut, forcing some of them to leave (and as a result, potentially making them vulnerable to offers of employment that transpire to be exploitative). In post-conflict societies, parents commonly choose not to send their children to school, believing that the schools are unsafe (de Watteville, 2002). Land mines, military gangs, and fear of rape encourage many children to stay at home rather than risk walking to school (Sommers, 2002). Further, many returning child soldiers are unable to attend school because even though the school is free, their books and uniforms have been stolen or destroyed with no family money to replace them. Alternatively, schools may have been closed because of rebels, or families may have been displaced to an area without schools. Other children choose not to return to school because they are ashamed to have to be in classes with younger children due to the schooling they missed because of their time in the armed forces (McKay and Mazurana, 2004). This lack of schooling is a direct result of conflict which leaves children uneducated and naïve to migration rules and to offers of people who may exploit them.

Women and girls face real difficulty if they manage to escape the fighting forces. Their experiences as soldiers are often overlooked and they are disregarded from demobilisation efforts (de Watteville, 2002), yet those girls who were taken on as 'wives' to commanders may be rejected by their communities on their return. Some families do not believe that the child was forced into a relationship with the commander and consider her a traitor (Newman, 2014). This is especially the case if the girl has given birth to children fathered by the commanders; children that the family may refuse to accept as related. These mothers may still be children themselves, but many say that once they have returned, they have no one to look after them and are considered a burden to relatives. They are abused by these relatives, unable to provide for their children, have no permanent home, and no access to education (Newman, 2014). If these mothers have no one to support them and their children, they become pressured into finding work to support themselves. If their community has rejected them, they are likely to move elsewhere in search of work. With a lack of education and assistance, they become vulnerable to exploitative offers or, with an absence of alternative options, tempted to return to the commanders who were exploiting them as the only viable source of support. Again, these are all situations that exist as a direct impact of the conflict.

Post-conflict situations require strategies that encourage youth employment in order to discourage children from being recruited (or re-recruited) into armed forces. However, of course, the job market and trade networks are often negatively affected by conflict (United Nations Department of Economic and Social Affairs, 2005). Ex-combatants can be a burden on their families when they return: physical and emotional trauma means that they are often unable to undertake manual labour, the labour most commonly available in post-conflict areas (Newman, 2014). A lack of support, a dearth of job opportunities, or the inability to undertake the work available in post-conflict situations, means that demobilised child soldiers become vulnerable to being re-enslaved when they are forced to travel to look for employment. Alternatively, the child soldiers' return means that their families have extra people to care for. Those who lack suitable income may be the ones who search elsewhere for better paid jobs, making them perfect targets for people looking to profit from their exploitation.

Verhey (2001) discusses the example of the Angolan Quick Impact Project which has provided funds for a number of families with demobilised child soldiers to establish small businesses, giving the children work to be able to earn an income for the family and bringing economic activity to the local area. Projects such as this are one method through which the risk of enslavement of demobilised child soldiers could be reduced. If children are not required to seek work outside their communities, then they are less likely to be enticed by the offers of those looking to exploit them, or be willing to accept poor conditions in order to meet their basic human needs. This risk of slavery after leaving the armed forces is discussed further in section 3.3 with reference to slavery in post-conflict zones.

3.1.4 Summary

Using the definition provided by the Bellagio-Harvard Guidelines, child soldiers should be understood as victims of modern slavery. Their individual liberty is significantly deprived as they suffer control to an extent that is tantamount to possession. This is done for the purpose of their exploitation and is usually achieved through violence, deception, or coercion. However, the main point to emphasise is that their experiences as child soldiers would not have occurred if not for the impact of conflict. Although many of the children may have been living with various vulnerabilities, it is the war that exacerbates these vulnerabilities to an extent that makes them susceptible to being recruited as soldiers. If not for conflict, or the preparation for it, there would be no call for soldiers. Further, the reasons for becoming child soldiers, the methods used to recruit them (including any indication of consent), and any benefit they may personally achieve from their role does not diminish their status as victims of modern slavery if they continue to be exploited for the benefit of the armed force.

This section has demonstrated that children are vulnerable to slavery at all points of a conflict. Pre- and mid-conflict, they are vulnerable to recruitment, both forced and 'voluntary', into the armed forces whether that be as combatants, 'wives', or in ancillary roles like guards, cleaners, porters, or cooks. Between 2015 and 2020, over 93,000 children were confirmed as having been recruited and used by parties to conflict (UNICEF (United Nations Children's Fund), 2021). The true figures are expected to be much higher than this and Reuters reports that 7,740 children were recruited and used by armed groups in 2019 alone (Wuilbercq, 2021).

Post-conflict, children are vulnerable as they return from the armed forces and are faced with rejection from their families and communities because of the acts they committed (David, 1998). Some are unable to locate their families, are unable to go to school, or are unfit to work because of the physical and psychological trauma they are suffering. This lack of support, education, and employment coupled with the precariousness of living in post-conflict zones where law and order, social services, and healthcare are limited if not non-existent, puts children in significantly unstable situations where searching for employment makes them highly vulnerable to the offers of those looking to profit from their exploitation (post-conflict zones are discussed in more detail in section 3.3). Significantly, if not for the conflict then these vulnerabilities (pre-, during, and post-conflict) would not be exacerbated to the extent that these children are pushed into situations of modern slavery.

3.2 Perpetrators of modern slavery in conflict

Section 3.1 above provided an overview of the literature relating to child soldiers as victims of modern slavery whose exploitation occurs as a result of conflict. Of course it would be inaccurate to suggest that child soldiers are the only victims of modern slavery during conflict and, as Muraszkiewicz et al. (2002b) discuss in their typology, there are multiple different ways that modern slavery can present in a conflict situation. However, there is a dearth of literature that studies the nexus between conflict and modern slavery, less still which focuses on the victims, and that which does exist concentrates almost exclusively on child soldiers.

This section moves on from victims to look at the literature relating to those who commit acts of modern slavery during conflict situations. While there is a little attention paid to those who enlist and exploit child soldiers, discussions in the literature of perpetrators of slavery linked to conflict focus heavily on the role that peacekeepers play in both conflict and post-conflict zones. Perhaps this interest is due to the disjunction between ideas of the values that a peacekeeper should uphold compared to the lived experiences.

Acknowledging the impact of a lack of law and order in post-conflict zones highlights the effect that peacekeeping missions have on modern slavery. The role of peacekeepers is to help maintain law and order and protect citizens living in conflict-afflicted states; however, there is a range of literature that focuses on the methods through which peacekeeping missions can encourage modern slavery (Human Rights Watch, 2002; Amnesty International, 2004; Smith and Miller-de la Cuesta, 2010; Women's International League for Peace and Freedom, 2012; Pehlic, 2020). This literature focuses predominantly on UN peacekeeping missions which send international troops into an area to establish and maintain peace once a conflict has ended. As with any topic of a clandestine nature, obtaining accurate statistics on slavery related to peacekeeping missions can be difficult; this is especially the case with governments who host peacekeeping forces as they are likely to be concerned with downplaying human rights issues to retain a positive international image and to ensure the continuation of funding. However, there are multiple examples citing that some troops have been complicit in trafficking itself, and that foreign troops have served to increase demand for trafficked women and girls in countries all over the world (Muraszkiewicz et al. 2020b).

3.2.1 Generating demand for victims of modern slavery

Studies have shown that the introduction of foreign peacekeepers into conflict zones generates a previously non-existent demand for human trafficking (Smith and Miller-de la Cuesta, 2010; Smith and Smith, 2010). Smith and Miller-de la Cuesta's studies in Kosovo, Haiti and Sierra Leone suggest that the influx of relatively wealthy foreigners encourages the establishment of criminal networks. Although there may already be some degree of demand for sex workers, these criminal networks identify that the foreign troops are likely to bring with them a much higher demand. The criminal networks then begin to traffic women and girls to the area, knowing that they can earn considerable profit by selling their victims' sexual services to the peacekeepers. However, the trafficking may begin before the peacekeepers are even in situ. The International Organization for Migration (2001) discusses how, as soon as there was intelligence to suggest that there would be an international presence in Kosovo, mafia groups began to move in, putting their focus on trafficking women into brothels in anticipation of the arrival of the troops. Similarly, Picarelli (2002) notes how in south eastern Europe, brothels began to open in anticipation of the peacekeepers' arrival, with the expectation that they would pay for sex. These studies also discovered that the increase in human trafficking is directly proportionate to the size of the foreign force, making the link between peacekeeping missions and human trafficking difficult to deny. As peacekeeping troops are introduced to an area only in response to a conflict, this increase in trafficking is therefore a direct result of conflict.

Smith and Smith (2010) also undertook studies in Kosovo, Haiti, and Sierra Leone which all hosted UN peacekeeping forces, and Nepal which did not. Those with peacekeeping forces saw a surge of women and girls trafficked into the region alongside the introduction of the troops, whereas Nepal saw no change in human trafficking, thus providing further support to the hypothesis that peacekeeping troops directly encourage modern slavery.

The Kosovan peacekeeping mission, starting in 1999, perfectly illustrates this point. The UN mission to Kosovo was the largest peacekeeping operation by the UN, where 20,000 peacekeeping troops were deployed to protect civilians from a war between the Kosovo Liberation Army and the Federal Republic of Yugoslavia. The introduction of the foreign force as a result of the conflict brought with it a demand for sex workers that significantly exceeded the local supply. It was soon noticed that there was a substantial increase in human trafficking to the region to meet this demand. The initial deployment of troops was in July 1999. In January 2001, seventy-five premises had been identified for using trafficked women. By the end of 2003, this number had increased to over 200 (Amnesty International,

2004), although, of course, it is difficult to provide these numbers with any certainty. Unfortunately, the lack of knowledge on premises using trafficked women prior to 1999 is unknown, meaning no true comparison can be made, but there remains a clear link between the number of troops and the number of establishments using victims of trafficking.

In Kosovo, the sex-work market was taken over by organised criminal networks and the peacekeeping troops were identified as the sex workers' main client group, comprising 80 per cent of their clients (Picarelli, 2002; Amnesty International, 2004; Smith and Miller-de la Cuesta, 2010; Women's International League for Peace and Freedom, 2012). The post-conflict conditions of Kosovo, alongside the relative wealth that the international troops brought in, turned Kosovo into a profitable and easy destination for traffickers to bring their victims, all as a result of the war.

The International Organization for Migration (2001) further discusses how the increase in international troops directly led to an increase in the demand for sex workers in the post-conflict Balkans, yet this increased demand was not only from international troops but also from local men. The amplified cash flow resulting from the influx of foreigners had increased the spending power of local men, meaning trips to brothels became an affordable possibility. This indicates how the impact on slavery due to peacekeeping troops can last much longer than the duration of the missions. If local men are provided with both an increased income and the opportunity to visit brothels because of the international presence responding to conflict, then this new lifestyle habit could continue once the international troops have left, therefore perpetuating the demand for the trafficking of women and girls.

Without the presence of the international troops, the demand will be lower, but without their custom the victims may become vulnerable in other ways. It may be that the criminal gangs that trafficked them initially force them into other forms of exploitation, such as for labour or for trafficking drugs or arms. Alternatively, they may be abandoned and left without employment, housing, or support in an unfamiliar area; an area they were brought to only because of the international response to a conflict. In this scenario they may become vulnerable to offers of assistance that may be genuine, but which may alternatively lead to further situations of exploitation.

However, the influx of international troops is not the sole factor causing the increase in trafficking for sexual exploitation. Other conditions assist by making trafficking easier for the criminal networks. Kosovo's geographical location makes it a perfect trafficking hot spot. It is close to poverty-stricken source countries in eastern Europe where women face gender discrimination, huge levels of poverty and unemployment, and over ten years of economic imbalance. It is also close to established trafficking routes to the EU and has cooperative links with organised criminal networks in Serbia, Albania, and Macedonia (Amnesty International, 2004). The infrastructure was therefore already in place for trafficking to occur prior to the peacekeeping missions; however, without the troops' demand, these were just plans in waiting. The conflict led to the introduction of the foreign troops, and therefore served as the catalyst to encourage the criminal networks to begin trafficking women and girls to be sold for sex.

3.2.2 Enforcement and convictions of perpetrators

While it will never be clear whether peacekeepers are aware of the conditions under which the sex workers they use are being forced to work, the United Mission to Bosnia in 2002 (discussed in Olsson et al., 2004) claimed that 25 per cent of women and girls working in nightclubs and bars in Bosnia during the peacekeeping mission were trafficked.

The buying of sex is forbidden to all UN peacekeeping troops, yet little is done to enforce this rule or to hold rule breakers to account (Olsson et al., 2004; Pehlic, 2020). Picarelli (2002) discusses how peacekeepers are provided with no-go lists of specific bars and restaurants that also function as brothels in an attempt to prevent the troops from paying for sex. However, this simply meant either that the bars would change their names, new brothels would open, or women from the brothels would be brought to the base (Amnesty International, 2004). This reflects charity scandals where, for example, the ICRC admitted that twenty-one members of staff had either resigned or been fired after allegations of sexual misconduct when they were accused of paying for sex, despite contractually being banned from doing so (Greenfield, 2018). Similarly, Haiti suspended Oxfam GB operations after claims of sexual misconduct regarding paying for sex while working in the country (BBC, 2018). Charities, like peacekeepers, are expected to uphold the highest moral values, which is perhaps what makes their misconduct so startling.

Although it only concerns a few corrupt individuals, the literature does refer to peacekeeping troops who are involved, not only in buying sex from trafficked women and girls, but in trafficking them in the first instance (Picarelli, 2002; Amnesty International, 2004; Pehlic, 2020). Picarelli discusses this in relation to some peacekeeping officers who, after arriving in a country to assist citizens living in a conflict or post-conflict zone, have been implicated in trafficking. Examples include officers transporting victims who are then purchased directly by the peacekeepers' contractors. Equally, corruption allowed perpetrators to move women across borders by paying bribes to the border officials. In contemporary peacekeeping operations, the international troops are often the main, or only, law enforcement, making them responsible for dealing with crimes of human trafficking. However, holding this responsibility makes it easier for those corrupt few to circumnavigate the system and traffic people without consequence. There is evidence that corrupt local police visit brothels and receive sexual services or bribes. They stamp documents to officially register the girls working there and are clearly friends with the brothel owners (Human Rights Watch, 2002; Pehlic, 2020). While the UN can investigate allegations against peacekeepers, it is the home nations that are responsible for punishing them, and 'Some troops have escaped sanction in the past because of the attitudes of their home commanders' (China Daily, 2005).

Amnesty International (2004) discuss this further in relation to Kosovo where prosecutions were unheard of despite a dedicated police force and a regulation which criminalised traffickers and those who knowingly used the services of trafficked women. By 2004 (when their research went to press) there had been no prosecutions whatsoever. This is mirrored in Pehlic's discussion of UN peacekeeping forces in Bosnia and Herzegovina (2020) where women and girls were trafficked from eastern European countries on the promise of well-paid jobs in western Europe, but found themselves in Bosnia and Herzegovina, trapped in sexual exploitation and debt bondage. It was evident that peacekeeping troops were paying for sexual services from these women, but prosecutions never happened. The perpetrators were simply removed from the mission or sent to another mission, and once an officer went home or was transferred, their disciplinary cases were usually closed (although Pehlic does mention that there were some successes in establishing accountability for local police officers). Yet there are some stories of perpetrators being held accountable for acts of sexual abuse, though not directly related to trafficking, and the numbers are insignificant in terms of how rife the problem seems to be.

In 2005, the Moroccan mission to the UN arrested six UN peacekeeping soldiers in the Democratic Republic of the Congo. They were arrested for sexually abusing local girls, and their commander was fired. Following these arrests, there was a call to increase the number of military police accompanying the peacekeeping mission to help prevent abuse by UN forces. This is in addition to measures including increased surveillance of UN military camps, curfews, and shuttering stores that facilitated interactions between soldiers and locals; such measures indicate that there was a recognised problem. Before these arrests, despite widespread allegations, there had been few known prosecutions of troops. One was by South Africa against two of its soldiers, and France also jailed a UN staffer for rape and for making pornographic videos of children (China Daily, 2005). The Associated Press undertook an investigation of peacekeeping missions between 2005 and 2017 and found almost 2,000 allegations of sexual exploitation by peacekeepers and others across the world, yet the punishments were rare and light. For example, in Haiti, 134 Sri Lankan peacekeepers were found to have abused nine children in a sex ring between 2004 and 2007. While 114 were sent home, none of these peacekeepers were imprisoned (Dodds, 2017).

Despite peacekeeping troops having been found to have directly trafficked women, to have used victims of human trafficking for sex, or to have sexually abused local women and children, the perpetrators rarely suffered any consequence more serious than repatriation (Human Rights Watch, 2002; Picarelli, 2002; Women's International League for Peace and Freedom, 2012; Pehlic, 2020); they are simply not held accountable for their actions, which only serves to strengthen the idea that impunity is the norm (Mendelson, 2005).

3.2.3 Summary

The preponderance of discussions relating to perpetrators of modern slavery linked to conflict is focused on peacekeeping missions and, within that, the literature focuses on the trafficking of girls and women for sexual exploitation. This section highlights that there is a demand for sex work that is driven by the increase of international troops, and this encourages the trafficking of girls and women to provide a supply to meet that demand, despite the fact that peacekeepers are forbidden from paying for sex.

There are numerous studies which link an increase in human trafficking directly to the introduction of international peacekeeping forces, with the increase in trafficking proportionate to the number of troops. Pre-existing criminal links and transport networks are used to deceive women and girls into brothels which surround the troops' bases. Although these criminal links, networks, and vulnerabilities were pre-existing, it is the impact of the conflict that drives the slavery, through the introduction of foreign troops sent to intervene in conflict and post-conflict situations. The foreign forces, as anticipated by the criminal gangs, begin to pay for sex, despite being forbidden from doing so. It is this disregard from the troops, alongside established corruption and a lack of will to enforce punishment, that allows the trafficking to flourish. Despite peacekeeping troops being forbidden from paying for sex, there are rarely punitive measures for those who break the rules, which does little to discourage other international troops from paying for sex and assists in perpetuating the demand for trafficking. The increased cash flow resulting from the relative wealth of the foreign troops increases local men's disposable income which, in turn, makes visiting brothels a new possibility. This generates a level of local demand for sex work which did not exist prior to the peacekeeping mission. Those women who were trafficked initially for the use of the peacekeepers may then remain vulnerable once the mission is over, where they may continue to be held in sexual exploitation for local men. Alternatively, if the supply begins to outweigh the demand, the criminal networks who trafficked the victims may either find another lucrative situation in which to exploit them or abandon them without support.

A key issue raised in this section is that while the processes and potential for slavery to occur existed prior to the international troops' presence, it is their introduction that causes the demand for trafficked women and girls. The troops' demand for sex workers exacerbates the pre-existing vulnerabilities, routes, methods, and processes in order to drive modern slavery and cause it to flourish, and their presence is purely a result of conflict.

3.3 Modern slavery in a post-conflict situation

While the impact that peacekeeping missions have on encouraging trafficking is well referenced in the literature, peacekeeping missions are not the sole cause of slavery in post-conflict zones and the literature makes regular reference to the vulnerabilities caused by political and economic transition, corruption, and the particularly precarious situation facing internally displaced persons (IDPs) and refugees. The following section outlines in more detail some of the ways in which post-conflict zones can be conducive to encouraging modern slavery.

3.3.1 The impact of political and economic transition

Cucumanova (2010) reviews Soviet states to identify how restructuring in post-conflict areas could actually serve to generate new conflicts. The Soviet National Migration Policy generated social-political competition between former Soviet states over control of the local power structures. This led to civil wars and ethnic conflicts in a number of the new republics. For example, Tajikistan was hit by violent conflict in 1992, leading to the emigration of 300,000 Tajiks and 692,000 becoming internally displaced; this was in addition to the pre-existing poor security and economic conditions. The Tajiks commonly paid people to help them escape, thinking them to be smugglers but discovering them to be traffickers. This is one example of the frequent story of how conflict can limit the choices of the affected populations; they must either escape in the hope of finding peace and security, or wait in the conflict zone. Either choice makes them vulnerable as the mortality rate of displaced persons is second only to those who remain where the violence occurs (Bellamy, 2017). In such a situation, neither choice can offer guaranteed safety and, in trying to find paid work, there is an inherent risk of accepting offers from people whose intention is to profit from the exploitation of others.

Balkan countries are often used as transit destinations for victims of human trafficking because conflict in the region has led to the disintegration of social, political, and legal structures and controls (International Organization for Migration, 2001). Due to the prioritisation of the conflicts, border controls became a low priority for Balkan states, providing a cautionary example for the development of policy recommendations, which must take into consideration how governmental priorities will change in times of conflict. This made for high rates of unmonitored migration, allowing trafficking to occur unchecked. This breakdown of law and order as a result of conflict can decrease the power of states and the ability of authorities to be able to assist victims and criminalise perpetrators.

3.3.2 The role of corruption

Conflict provides the conditions for corruption to thrive when there are fast-moving changes in priorities, low levels of democracy, widespread instability, and a lack of robust safeguarding or protection measures. An absence of repercussions for crimes, coupled with the poverty of a post-conflict society, can result in an increase in crime that can go unchecked due to the complicity of corrupt officials.

This corruption caused by conflict not only allows trafficking to go unpunished but can actually be the cause of trafficking. For example, the social breakdown caused by conflict marginalises individuals from political, economic, and national domains (Acharya, 2004). This then makes it easier for perpetrators of slavery to operate because the underlying factors that cause slavery are exacerbated and corruption allows it to be tolerated. Human Rights Watch (2002) stress that the Bosnian government has failed, with few exceptions, to prosecute police officers directly involved in human trafficking, reflecting the discussion of peacekeepers in section 3.2 above. They also claim that police and government corruption in post-conflict Bosnia and Herzegovina allowed trafficking to thrive.

Picarelli (2002) discusses how government corruption is driven by organised crime. The criminals are able to infiltrate political and legal systems, finding people who will accept a cut of their profits in return for turning a blind eye to their crimes. In post-conflict areas, this can be relatively effortless because the difficult living situations and extreme poverty causes a point where a need for money overcomes the desire for justice. Similarly, conflict not only increases the number of victims of modern slavery, but also the number of perpetrators. This is particularly true in post-conflict areas where employment opportunities are scarce and poverty is rife, leading some to envisage their survival in the exploitation of others (Martens et al., 2003). Understanding conflict in this way also highlights the impact of strain theory (Agnew and Kaufman, 2010), where this competition for limited resources will leave some unable to attain everything they need, including employment, through legitimate routes. In this sense, the economic implications of modern slavery are a consideration for both the perpetrators who will profit, and the victims who believe that the perpetrators will help them to find work.

The methods through which conflict can cause corruption and economic and political transition can also be emphasised through Durkheim's concept of anomie (1897) which describes instability as a result of the breakdown of individual or societal standards. A conflict, especially in the sense of war where lives may be at risk, causes a rapid change in the values of individuals and societies, meaning issues that were once a priority may no longer be so. Societies in conflict become places of transition where new ways of life may not be compatible with previous ideals. The breakdown of political systems during conflict may lead to corruption where people learn to put profit over justice simply to survive in a society where there is significant competition for limited resources.

3.3.3 Refugees and internally displaced persons at risk

Poverty is one of the most commonly cited push factors for trapping people in perpetrators' false promises (Kaye and McQuade, 2007; Kuhl, 2011; Barner et al., 2014). Following a conflict, various methods can heighten this poverty, including increased living costs, decreased wages, privatisation of public services, increased unemployment resulting from economic restructuring, public spending cuts, decreased social benefits, and the removal of consumer subsidies. Amnesty International (2004) illustrate this with the example of Kosovo where economic conditions failed to recover after the war and unemployment rates reached 60 per cent in 2004. These issues disproportionately affect women who are often excluded from the labour market and who are usually disadvantaged because of the way that economic reconstruction tends to favour men. Further, declining social services put more pressure on women to support their families and to look for work in a society that emphasises male employment. As such, women may begin to look further afield for work and, in doing so, run the risk of becoming vulnerable to modern slavery.

Political and economic changes following conflict can emphasise this poverty and provide the perfect conditions for slavery to flourish. Civil wars and political and economic transition lead to the breakdown of political and legal systems and border controls. This makes for an increase in migration which becomes difficult to monitor in times of instability, making it easier for perpetrators to operate. Klopcic (2004) illustrates this with the example of the fall of the Berlin wall which allowed the movement of people from ex-socialist countries to western Europe. The transition after the fall of the wall meant increased unemployment, increased foreign debt, and economic recession. This resulted in both weakened nation states and an increase in refugees and economic migrants whose experiences of unemployment and poverty put them at risk of being enticed by the offers of perpetrators who intended to benefit from their exploitation.

Refugees are commonly from rural or poor urban regions with little education, where a lack of job opportunities causes people to leave in search for work. These vulnerabilities are rarely recognised by governing bodies, as discussed by Pearson (2003) in reference to the trafficking of women in east Africa. The Ugandan armed conflicts in the north and the west of the country resulted in high numbers of IDPs as well as high refugee numbers from neighbouring countries. Although the conflicts became a governmental priority because of the impact they had on the economics and the politics of the country as well as the citizens, the link between conflict and modern slavery is commonly overlooked and often remains unrecognised (Muraszkiewicz et al., 2020a).

Refugees and internally displaced persons are particularly vulnerable in post-conflict situations. Any pre-existing vulnerabilities are exacerbated by the conflict, which commonly leads to poor living conditions, gender inequality, a lack of basic healthcare or education, poverty, xenophobia, a lack of security, and no certainty of the future. These issues, combined with an inability to earn a living and a lack of access to food and medicine increase susceptibility to trafficking (Kotecha, 2020). Living in such conditions may encourage people to move in the hope that they will find a better life elsewhere, and may lead them into taking risks that they otherwise would not. However, particularly when there are large numbers of people in the same situation, they will likely find themselves competing for the same available living spaces or employment opportunities. In attempting to escape the problems caused by conflict, some families may choose to migrate away, but language barriers and a lack of awareness of immigration rules can make them vulnerable to exploitation, especially if they are from particularly rural areas and are naïve to urban environments or other cultures. This creates an opportunity for perpetrators to make offers of jobs in safe countries; offers that are too good not to accept. Even though some of those who accept these jobs may have had concerns or a degree of scepticism around the reality of the offers, they are really left with little choice but to take the risk.

Nelson et al. (2004) emphasise this effect on refugees. The absence of law and order in a post-conflict situation, coupled with the vast numbers of destitute citizens (homeless, widowed, separated children, refugees, and IDPs) provide the ideal setting for slavery. The struggle in this post-conflict stage is heightened for women and girls whose vulnerability to slavery is increased because of their disproportionate lack of access to education and resources. Their search for employment opportunities and a better quality of life, twinned with a lack of knowledge of migration processes, make these women and girls easy targets for perpetrators (Limanowska, 2005).

3.3.4 The disproportionate effect on women

The effects of war can disproportionately affect women in multiple ways. Wölte (1997) notes how in conflict zones typical gender relations become unstable. The rape of females is sometimes employed as a weapon of war, to reinforce male dominance, or to punish women for taking on traditionally male roles during the conflict (Brown, 2012; Kirby, 2012; Muraszkiewicz et al., 2020b). Domestic violence by men against women increases in war torn countries (de Watteville, 2002), and men may be socialised to violence during the war (Byrne et al., 1995). These issues pose a threat to the women and children to whom these men return. Add to these problems the fact that female recruits are commonly excluded from demobilisation campaigns, making it difficult for them to return or reintegrate and often leaving them no choice but to remain with their exploiters (Dunhill and Kidd, 2020), and it is clear that post-conflict societies specifically affect women in numerous ways.

In many war-torn countries, women are already at a disadvantage to men due to unequal access to benefits, education, healthcare, social services, and jobs. Conflicts can force them out of their homes, increasing their disadvantages and leaving them unable to find any way to make a living. Acharya (2004) discusses how, in Mexico, some parents sell their daughters because they cannot afford to care for them and hope that this will provide them with better opportunities. This reflects an earlier discussion in section 3.1.1 of parents asking commanders to take their children into an armed force because they can no longer afford to care for them. Here they risk selling their children into exploitation and many are aware that this is a potential outcome.

Men returning from war often leads to many women losing their jobs (de Watteville, 2002). This is especially true where the jobs are traditionally 'male' roles and they are offered to the men upon their return, leaving the women redundant. This can have a significant impact, especially for those women who are heads of households due to their husbands still being at war but who find themselves unemployed when their jobs are offered to other men. De Watteville (2002) exemplifies Nicaragua where around 16,000 women lost their jobs when men returned from war. Many other women were forced to accept lower salaries if they wanted to remain employed.

Alternatively, some women were forced to leave their jobs because their husbands believed working and earning an income were men's responsibilities. In losing their employment by either means, women are left without the financial independence or the security required to support themselves or their families (especially if the husband is still at war or is unable to find work). This leaves these women vulnerable to exploitation as they begin to seek out other options for employment, sometimes travelling to areas they are unfamiliar with in search of work.

3.3.5 Demobilisation of armed forces

While demobilisation efforts might be assumed to assist their participants to reintegrate into society, demobilised soldiers are another group that suffer disproportionately in post-conflict zones. Firstly, demobilisation efforts at the end of a war usually focus only on combatants (Dunhill and Kidd, 2020; Verhey, 2001), which overlooks huge numbers of those involved in the conflict but in non-combat roles. Most of these people are women and girls who tend to be given auxiliary roles, such as 'wives', cooks, porters, and guards.

De Watteville (2002) notes how women may be purposefully misinformed about demobilisation efforts and exemplifies Mozambique where many women missed out on encampment due to misinformation. Because they missed this stage, they were denied funding for transport home, and the costs for this transport were more than the women could afford. This left them with limited choices: they were either left desolate or forced to return to the commanders who abused them as their 'wives'. As discussed in relation to child soldiers in section 3.1.3, many women who were taken as 'wives' and raped during war times will be rejected by their families and communities on their return home. They are considered to have disrespected their family, to be a burden, or to be unfit for marriage. Similarly, women who have become pregnant or given birth to children of soldiers will often be left unsupported post-conflict. This leaves these women with the sole responsibility of caring for themselves and their children.

This rejection of girls and women during disarmament, demobilisation, and reintegration programmes is further documented in the 2005 UN Department of Economic and Social Affairs World Youth Report which emphasises how this rejection leads to a lack of physical, economic, and emotional support once the conflict has ended. The lack of support from these programmes, coupled with missed education from time spent in the armed forces, means that many female ex-combatants become locked in a system of long-term poverty. A lack of access to these programmes can lead to homelessness, isolation, and being unable to find safe, paid labour. They are left with limited options, pushing many to remain with their captors, encouraged into early marriage or sex work, or vulnerable to the offers of the perpetrators of slavery. This re-emphasises the impact of conflict on modern slavery; if not for the conflict, then demobilisation would not be required and these girls and women would not be pushed to the margins of society.

Resolution 1325 on women, peace, and security adopted by the UN Security Council (Office of the Special Adviser on Gender Issues and Advancement of Women, 2000) calls for increased representation of women at every level of decision-making on the prevention, management, and resolution of conflict as well as including more women in operations. It calls to provide training to field staff on women's rights, the adoption of a gender perspective in peace agreements, and special measures to protect women and girls from gender-based violence. Farr (2012) notes that women are rarely included in the planning and establishment of disarmament, demobilisation, and reintegration programmes, despite being part of the fighting forces and constituting half of the population.

3.3.6 Summary

The extant literature on modern slavery and conflict highlights a range of issues regarding slavery in post-conflict zones. While structural transformations have brought about required economic and political changes, oversights have been made regarding the impact they would have on the citizens of those states. Some transitions have resulted in the development of new conflicts which have created new vulnerabilities in previously stable communities. Further, corruption and the breakdown in the monitoring of systems—be these legal, migratory, or employment—allow for the establishment and exacerbation of criminal networks which seek to exploit the vulnerable for profit.

Conflicts generate refugees and IDPs whose vulnerabilities are already high because of their lack of secure accommodation. However, when this is coupled with weakened nation states, they are faced with severe desolation. The lack of support provided exacerbates poverty, and the displaced are left with little or no governmental support, no social services, and few employment opportunities, alongside poor living conditions. As they begin to strive for the same desired conditions as one another, they must compete for resources—including paid work—which provide the ideal conditions for perpetrators of slavery to exploit these desperate individuals with false promises of job opportunities.

Conflict and its aftermath also have a disproportionate effect on women, and demobilisation efforts commonly overlook any members of armed forces who did not hold combat roles, where women and girls are often used in auxiliary positions. Those who are excluded from these programmes are disadvantaged as they are omitted from reintegration efforts, leaving them with little choice other than to return to their captors or try to survive alone. Again, should they try to provide for themselves, they become a prime target for perpetrators of slavery but if they return to their captors they are often equally resigning themselves to severe exploitation.

Overall, this section has demonstrated that there is a multitude of methods through which conflicts make people vulnerable to slavery, even once the conflict is over. It emphasises that the risk of slavery does not end when the conflict does, but the vulnerabilities conflict generates continue to put people at risk of slavery for an immeasurable length of time.

3.4 Modern slavery related to conflict beyond war

Sections 3.1, 3.2, and 3.3 summarise the extant literature that explicitly links conflict and modern slavery. This relates to victims (predominantly discussed in terms of child soldiers), perpetrators (where the focus is on peacekeeping troops), and post-conflict zones. However, a key flaw here is the tendency to conflate conflict with war. The broader definition of conflict offered in chapter two encourages a move away from this narrow understanding of conflict, reinforcing that it does not always equate to war and, in fact, it can exist separately to violence entirely. However, there is a tendency in the literature to consider the notion of conflict only in terms of violence and, as such, there is a possibility that other authors may discuss issues of modern slavery that link to broader iterations of conflict, but where they do not explicitly define the situation as one of conflict. In recognition of this possibility, after summarising the literature that covers modern slavery or human trafficking while explicitly using the term conflict, I went on to broaden the search terms.

As noted in chapter two, using the key term 'non-armed conflict' in a search of academic literature is futile and returns only results relating to 'armed-conflict' or 'non-international armed conflict.' As an alternative, I broadened the search to look for publications that link issues of modern slavery, human trafficking, or exploitation to issues including 'disagreements', 'arguments', 'divorce', and 'support breakdown'. These are terms that could equate to the definition of conflict provided in chapter two, but where authors may not have made that same connection. This section briefly summarises the literature that engages with these search terms, but determines that these concepts remain widely absent from the research relating to the causes of modern slavery.

3.4.1 Disagreement and modern slavery

A search of 'disagreement' alongside 'trafficking', 'modern slavery', and 'exploitation' yielded two main outcomes with limited relevance to this study. It led to publications that discussed disagreements in terms of definitions of different forms of trafficking and exploitation and what should and should not be covered under the rubric of modern slavery (Haynes, 2014; Bonilla and Mo, 2018). The majority of the literature on this issue concentrates on how, and whether, sex work and sexual exploitation overlap (Bruch, 2004; Lobasz, 2009; Chacon, 2017), with debate between those who are sex-work abolitionists and those who support sex-workers' rights (see Quirk et al., 2021). The term 'abolitionists' refers to those who consider all forms of sex work to be exploitative and thus seek for an end to both sex trafficking and sex work, while those who support sex-workers' rights argue that sex work is legitimate work and look for a way to end sex trafficking while allowing sex work to continue (Dempsey, 2010). The latter argue that sex trafficking and sex work should not be conflated and that it is important to recognise sex work as legitimate work as opposed to a form of exploitation.

The other key finding from this search related to disagreements regarding the extent of the problems of modern slavery and human trafficking (McGough, 2013; Haynes, 2014; Bonilla and Mo, 2018). This is a widely discussed issue which considers the difficulty of being able to accurately measure a hard-to-reach population such as victims of modern slavery. Relatedly, these references consider the methodologies of quantitative data collection regarding victims and survivors of modern slavery and human trafficking (Gallagher, 2014; Broome and Quirk, 2015), again incorporating debate around different forms of exploitation and whether it is appropriate to incorporate them under the term modern slavery. While these findings are all useful in accessing broader contexts, understandings of, and approaches towards modern slavery, the search returned no results which considered disagreements as a causing factor for modern slavery in any form—the issue upon which this title is focused.

3.4.2 Arguments and modern slavery

Searching the literature for issues relating to 'arguments' and modern slavery, human trafficking, or exploitation came up with a lot of hits. However, perhaps unsurprisingly, the vast majority of mentions of 'arguments' linked to the argument the author was making or citing in their publication as opposed to whether arguments might be considered a potentially conducive environment that may lead individuals into situations of exploitation. In fact, a long and detailed trawl of this literature indicated that thus far there has been no engagement with the concept of arguments constituting a possible determinant of situations of modern slavery, human trafficking, or exploitation, therefore reflecting the lack of consideration around disagreements, as outlined in section 3.4.1.

3.4.3 Divorce and modern slavery

As discussed in chapter two, the term 'conflict' often holds connotations of violence, and yet violence is not a necessary requirement for a situation to be one of conflict. Divorce is an example of this, where there is a conflict between parties within a marriage leading to the ending of the relationship, but where violence is not (always) a component of the conflict. There is scant literature which directly speaks of divorce in relation to modern slavery, human trafficking, or exploitation, although there are publications which allude to the impact that divorce could have on increasing vulnerabilities to exploitation. This literature gives particular consideration to the prospect that divorce can negatively impact someone's economic standing: 'a divorce will have severe economic consequences, and newly divorced are overrepresented among the poor in many countries' (Tyldum, 2013:110). While this is not explicitly expanded upon, the author implies that those economic consequences could, in turn, push individuals into precarious situations whereby they may become more vulnerable to exploitation. Other publications draw upon the idea that the strength, number, and nature of a person's relationships can influence the likelihood that they would become vulnerable to trafficking (Oppong, 2012), suggesting that those separated by divorce could be at higher risk of becoming victims. This expands beyond the idea that divorce increases vulnerabilities only of the partners once separated, to suggest that the vulnerabilities extend to wider family members including children because of the resultant weakened family relationships.

3.4.4 Support breakdown and modern slavery

Section 3.4.3 links with the final search term I used: 'support breakdown', engaging the idea that a collapse in a person's social network—potentially as a result of a conflict—could increase their vulnerability to becoming exploited. Again, perhaps unsurprisingly, the results from this search term, alongside 'modern slavery', 'human trafficking', and 'exploitation' led to a number of publications, but where the focus was on the support needs for victims and survivors of modern slavery and human trafficking, as opposed to whether a breakdown in support may have increased their vulnerability to becoming victimised.

There was very limited work addressing whether there may be any direct link between a breakdown in support networks and exploitation in the forms of human trafficking or modern slavery. Rosenblatt's (2014) research was one exception, however. This investigated the sex trafficking of American children, and one of the findings of the research indicated that American children who have suffered a familial breakdown are at increased risk of being trafficked for sex because they are left without appropriate coping and conflict resolution skills.

In literature which is broader, but which still connects to the possibility of a breakdown in support increasing the risk of trafficking, there is discussion of how support breakdowns could lead to homelessness (Veale and Dona, 2003; Hebblethwaite et al., 2007; Ward and Seager, 2010; Kassaw, 2019). While these publications do not all directly make the connection between homelessness and an increased risk of victimisation, the links between homelessness and modern slavery/human trafficking is something well established in the broader literature (see for example The Passage, 2017; Kassaw, 2019; Avis, 2020; Jagpal et al., 2020; Murphy, 2020).

3.4.5 Summary

After summarising the literature that explicitly links the term 'conflict' to issues of human trafficking and modern slavery, it was clear that conflict is used almost exclusively in relation to armed violence. This section looked beyond this understanding of conflict to employ the broader definition outlined in chapter two. This involved searching with broader terms of examples of conflict which do not necessarily involve violence, including the search terms: 'disagreements', 'arguments', 'divorce', and 'support breakdown'. The findings of this literature search indicated that there have been publications relating to modern slavery that incorporate these terms, but that very little research has been undertaken to overtly identify how these issues might increase a person's vulnerability towards becoming victimised. 'Disagreements' tend to be used to refer to the debates around what forms of exploitation should be understood as modern slavery, and 'arguments' turn up results of the point the author is making or citing in their publication. The findings from the searches of 'divorce' and 'support breakdown' link a little more clearly with the intentions of this title in trying to establish how conflict could lead to modern slavery. Publications relating to these issues imply that divorce and support breakdowns could lead to homelessness and a lack of coping skills which could, in turn, increase a person's vulnerabilities. Overall however, this literature search reiterated that there has been a lack of research looking directly at how forms of non-violent conflict could lead towards situations of modern slavery.

3.5 Conclusion

Academic studies that consider the convergence between conflict and modern slavery are rare, and those that explicitly refer to conflict consider conflict only in the sense of war, overlooking broader understandings.

Although it is possible to draw conclusions from the literature as to how war could relate to modern slavery, there are few pieces that explicitly address the link, and those that do tend to be made as part of discussions about children during war, gender issues resulting from war, the plight of refugees, conflict interventions, and demobilisation and reintegration programmes. Within the literature that does overtly consider the link between conflict and modern slavery, the focus rests predominantly on victims or perpetrators of modern slavery linked to conflict, or on post-conflict zones. There is even more specificity once these topics are considered in detail, in that discussions of victims relate principally to child soldiers and discussions of perpetrators focus on peacekeepers.

This review summarises three key areas identified in the literature as drawing a relationship between conflict and modern slavery: victims, perpetrators, and post-conflict zones. Before and during a conflict, discussions of slavery generally link to the recruitment of child soldiers. Immediately after the conflict, the focus on slavery turns to the release of the child soldiers and the introduction of peacekeeping forces, but much of the focus remains on women and girls forced into sexual exploitation. Discussions relating to post-conflict slavery consider a variety of issues from refugees and internally displaced persons to demobilisation and reintegration efforts, alongside the corruption caused by the breakdown in law and order as a direct result of conflict. A broader literature search using examples of non-violent conflict to understand whether such iterations of conflict may have been studied without explicitly defining them as such revealed that while some attention has been paid to forms of non-violent conflict (such as divorce), little research has been undertaken to identify whether there is a direct causal link between such forms of conflict and an experience of modern slavery.

Although there is a wealth of literature relating to refugees and the precarious methods by which people travel in the hope of seeking safety in foreign countries (Brekke and Brochmann, 2015; Crawley et al., 2016; Kaytaz, 2016; Kuschminder, 2017; Stevens, 2017), little consideration has been given to how people may become vulnerable to modern slavery during these journeys. Commentary is provided on the fact that trafficking and slavery do occur in these situations (Salt and Stein, 1997; Koser, 2000), but there is a lack of focus or understanding on how.

Such oversight extends to the time frame of vulnerabilities. The literature accepts that people become vulnerable to conflict-related slavery before a conflict has begun, especially in the case of the recruitment of child soldiers.

It recognises that people remain vulnerable as the conflict occurs, and it appreciates that people continue to be vulnerable once the conflict has finished. However, literature relating to post-conflict vulnerabilities focuses almost exclusively on slavery within the immediate period once the conflict has ended. There is mention of ongoing insecurities, of refugees who continue to be at risk until they find safety, of men and women who must find methods of providing for their families, and of children who seek work outside of their communities because they are unable to reintegrate. However, little consideration is given to whether these conflict-initiated vulnerabilities ever actually end, or whether the impact of conflict ever truly abates.

It is significant that the literature focuses exclusively on the in-country experiences of modern slavery during conflict. There have been calls upon the UN Secretary General 'to address and prevent trafficking in conflict' (The Freedom Fund, 2016:no pagination); however, little attention is paid to situations in which people suffer modern slavery as a result of a conflict, but after they have left the conflict situation. This overlooks circumstances in which people have managed to reach a new destination in relative safety, but where a lack of knowledge of this new location may leave them vulnerable to people who seek to profit from their exploitation. An obvious example of such a group would be people arriving in the UK and claiming asylum after fleeing a conflict in their home country. Without knowledge of this new country, the language, or the asylum system, they may be at risk should they be approached by strangers who appear to be offering support.

The Freedom Fund (2016) has highlighted how this flawed focus extends to politics, indicating how in Europe, billions of dollars have been spent on curbing immigration and asylum seeking, yet very little concentration has been placed on trying to increase safety and security for those who are moving and are in desperate need. While there is literature on the struggles facing refugees and asylum seekers once they arrive at their destination, there is little to link the specific experiences of those who then go on to be exploited in contemporary forms of slavery, though this is discussed in chapters five and six. The literature that does exist looks at the lack of support provided by the UK asylum system that puts asylum seekers at risk of labour exploitation (Lewis et al., 2013) and at the methods through which governments shift focus from their policies that exacerbate opportunities for slavery by championing other aspects of their work (see for example, Quirk, 2015b; O'Connell Davidson, 2016). Again, this is discussed further in chapters five and six.

One final major concern throughout the literature is the tendency to focus on the systemic impact of conflict to the detriment of understanding the agentic processes at play. The literature concentrates on a top-down approach, identifying how conflict affects large-scale structures (such as politics, economics, and corruption) which then go on to impact individuals. This approach overlooks the vast intersectionality of the people who are living through the conflict and how structural inequalities already experienced by individuals (such as gender, religion, ethnicity, etc.) may be exacerbated by the conflict, causing their vulnerabilities to be heightened. While this top-down approach is important in understanding how structures in conflict may lead to modern slavery, this work simultaneously approaches the link from the bottom up in order to understand the impact that agency has on situations of modern slavery.

The most fundamental flaw of the literature is its failing to understand conflict in any context outside of war. As outlined in chapter two, I define conflict as a set of conditions whereby parties identify and act on mutually incompatible goals. While this act may be violent, the presence of violence is not necessary in order for the situation to be defined as conflict. It is possible to be affected by a conflict without being an active participant. Using this wider definition of conflict allows for a deeper and more nuanced approach to the interaction between conflict and modern slavery, and will offer vastly more insight into situations of conflict that are currently overlooked in academia.

Chapter four
Fleeing conflict to modern slavery

Chapter one included a brief summary of the process of undertaking the research for this title. It outlined the methods of reaching out to gatekeepers to identify respondents from three separate categories:

1. Those who had fled conflict
2. Those who had fled conflict and experienced modern slavery
3. Those who work with either of the above groups

As outlined in chapter one, I encouraged contact from individuals who self-identified as having experienced conflict. While initially I had expected this to lead to respondents who had fled war zones, it became clear that the respondents' understanding of conflict was far broader than just armed violence. Coupled with a review of the literature in chapter three which identified that research which explicitly links the terms 'conflict' with 'modern slavery' or 'human trafficking' is limited to understanding conflict only in terms of war, this led to the development of a new and broad definition of conflict which includes but is not limited to war. The definition employed in this title then is reflective not only of the definitions within dictionaries, research, law, and fields of practice (such as policing and social work), but which also, importantly, incorporates broader iterations of lived experience.

Reaching out to gatekeepers led to twenty-four in-depth, face-to-face interviews being conducted. Eleven of these interviews were with individuals who had fled conflict (some of whom had also experienced modern slavery), thirteen were with agency workers, and the stories of another sixteen clients were elicited through these interviews with agency workers. More details on these respondents can be found in chapter one.

This chapter discusses the findings from the interviews where individuals had fled conflict and gone on to experience modern slavery, considering their experiences and the methods by which they became victimised.

From Conflict to Modern Slavery. Alicia Heys, Oxford University Press. © Alicia Heys 2023.
DOI: 10.1093/oso/9780192846549.003.0004

The chapter is divided into three sections to cover: first, experiences of slavery within the conflict situation; second, experiences of slavery after fleeing the conflict situation to the UK; and third, experiences of slavery after fleeing the conflict situation but before arriving in the UK.

Following the approach of grounded theory, after completing each interview, I generated transcripts, subsequently coding and analysing them in order to identify recurring themes. It was clear from the outset that no two people's stories were the same; however, there was a common thread running through many of the stories, that conflict had generated two specific vulnerabilities: a lack of viable options and a reduction in support networks. Those fleeing conflict situations are commonly so desperate to leave that they are willing to take risks that they would not normally take and are often left in situations where their choices are so restricted that they must choose the option that appears to be the lesser evil. While for some these risks might be beneficial and lead them into more secure situations, for others they may lead to situations of modern slavery. Further, displacement, disruption, or disagreements as a result of conflict can lead directly to a breakdown in support networks, meaning individuals are often unable to rely on people they know and trust and may need to turn to strangers for support.

Due to some of the interviews requiring interpreters and some stories being provided by agency workers rather than the subject of the story themselves, there is some discrepancy regarding the use of pronouns in quotes from the interviews. All interviews are quoted verbatim and, unless stated otherwise, pronouns used in quotes are indicative of the subject of the story. Further, for clarity, throughout the rest of the title, where interview respondents (or the person whose stories they are retelling in the case of many of the agency workers) are referenced, their names will be emphasised using bold text. All names are pseudonyms and more information on the respondents can be found in chapter one.

4.1 Victims of modern slavery in conflict

This chapter considers those who have experienced both conflict and modern slavery. In this section, attention is paid to the respondents who became victims of modern slavery while still in a situation of conflict, demonstrating how these conflict-induced vulnerabilities of reduced options and reduced support networks led them into situations of exploitation.

4.1.1 Chiku

Chiku was a young female who became a victim of modern slavery as a direct result of conflict changing her living circumstances and pushing her towards a situation of vulnerability. **Chiku** was from Sierra Leone and she and her father were the only family members that survived the civil war. **Chiku** was the youngest of four daughters and was still a child when the war ended, but with no one else to support them and a lack of job opportunities in the wake of the war, her father sold her to a man who was to become her husband.

> When the war ended, and she had been raped quite a number of times during the conflict, there was not very much left and her dad decided that the best thing to do for both of them would be to have her married to a man she described as being very old . . . she described him as being incredibly unpleasant and very violent towards her and kept her in his house as his wife and also as his slave.

It is not possible to identify the intention behind her father's choice to have **Chiku** marry a much older man; perhaps he sold her to this man purely for the money, but it is equally possible that he believed she would be safer with a husband if he was without the means to care for her himself. However, the reasons that **Chiku** became a victim were larger than just her father's actions and related back to the circumstances caused by the civil war. The war had led to a limiting of the options available to her and her father. Job opportunities were severely impacted by the conflict, leaving them with few options to be able to support themselves. Further, there were no other family members left alive who they could have turned to for help. While it is impossible to know with certainty, it is perhaps unlikely that **Chiku**'s father would have made the same decision to marry her to a violent older man if conflict had not left him without viable alternatives.

4.1.2 Mahal

Mahal's story is another that demonstrates how conflict can increase vulnerabilities to modern slavery. **Mahal** was a girl, about fifteen years old, from the Democratic Republic of the Congo, living in an area that was badly affected by war. One day on returning from school, she discovered that her parents had been killed. Due directly to the loss of her parents, **Mahal** found herself as a child with no family and no one to support her. With the assistance of a non-governmental organisation (NGO) that supported refugees in the region, **Mahal** moved to Kinshasa to live with extended family there. When she arrived at Kinshasa, a member of her family offered to support her in going to school. **Mahal** had always gone to school and was very proud of her achievements; she had always wanted to be a teacher, so she gratefully accepted this offer. However, it transpired that this offer of schooling was merely a method of deception and she was, instead, forced into a situation of sexual exploitation. **Mahal**'s story exemplifies how the impact of the conflict—in her case war—put her at risk by generating the specific vulnerabilities of a lack of options and a reduction in her support network. Without the conflict, Mahal would not have been faced with the limited options of either staying in her home town as a child with no family or moving cities, and nor would she have become reliant on extended family because her trusted support network was no longer there. These new vulnerabilities caused by the conflict pushed her into a situation where she became exploited by a member of her extended family, someone she would likely never have had to rely on if not for the impact of the conflict.

4.1.3 Louise

Louise's experience of modern slavery further exemplifies the way that conflict can generate the vulnerabilities that increase the likelihood of experiencing modern slavery in terms of reducing both the available options and a person's support network.

Louise was an ethnic Armenian living in Azerbaijan and, when she was about ten years old, violence towards ethnic Armenians in Azerbaijan became widespread.

> She described that one evening a mob of people arrived outside her house, shouting that all ethnic Armenians should be killed, and that they were going to cleanse the country of Armenians. And she said that her dad looked at this mob of people with weapons outside, burning neighbours' houses and said they were our neighbours, we've always lived with them. He went out to try and talk to them and they killed him.

Evidently, this left **Louise** and her mother, a doctor, in a very vulnerable situation, knowing that they were also at risk of being killed. They put all their trust in a neighbour who helped them escape the house and they sought refuge with one of this neighbour's contacts, an Azeri woman and her violent son, where **Louise** and her mother undertook domestic chores. It soon became clear that the woman and son had no intention of paying **Louise** and her mother for the work they were undertaking, and the exploitative nature of the situation became particularly evident when they tried to leave.

> Eventually, the mother said we're going to have to leave. We're going to have to get out of this and tried to leave the house and was very badly beaten up by the son of this woman, who wanted to prevent them from leaving.

Unable to escape, this situation of domestic slavery continued for six years and was a huge life change for a woman who had been a doctor and was now, with her ten-year-old daughter, exploited and controlled.

For **Louise** and her mother, a significant point of their experience of this ethnic conflict was when their neighbours killed **Louise**'s father and left her and her mother without support and at risk of meeting the same fate. If the ethnic discrimination had not existed, **Louise**'s father would not have been killed, and **Louise** and her mother would not be at risk of targeted threats. The conflict left them with no choice other than to stay where they were certain they would be murdered, or leave in the hope that they could find safety but with no one they could confidently trust to help them. They chose the latter option, but the structural ethnic discrimination meant that their support networks were extremely limited and they were quickly trapped in a situation of modern slavery.

4.1.4 Summary

These examples of **Chiku**, **Mahal**, and **Louise** all demonstrate very different stories of exploitation: an exploitative marriage, sexual exploitation, and domestic servitude. However, there are two common factors that contributed towards causing slavery in all three stories: the loss of family support and a lack of viable alternative choices. **Chiku** and **Mahal** both lost family to armed conflict, and **Louise** lost her father because of ethnic conflict. This meant a reduction in their support networks and limited the number of people they knew they could confidently rely on for support. All three also found themselves in situations where conflict left them with limited options, and yet they did continue to have some degree of choice. **Chiku** had the 'choice' of marrying the older man or living with no one to support her, **Mahal** had the 'choice' of living alone as a child with no support or moving to be with family, and **Louise** had the 'choice' of staying in her home which her neighbours were attacking or risking accepting support from others. All faced significantly limited options, meaning that their choices were no longer autonomous, but were entirely influenced by the impact of the conflicts on each of their situations and they were each faced with making a choice that represented the 'lesser evil'.

4.2 Victims of modern slavery in the UK

Section 4.1 summarises the experiences of those who suffered modern slavery in the same country in which they experienced conflict. This section moves on to illustrate multiple cases from the findings where people had fled conflict to the UK, but whose experience of modern slavery did not occur until after they arrived. Although none of the cases are the same, there is, again, a clearly identifiable theme that conflict generates two specific vulnerabilities which increase the likelihood of experiencing modern slavery: a reduction in options and a breakdown in support networks.

4.2.1 Beth

While this section relates to those who experienced modern slavery in the UK, **Beth**'s experience must be highlighted here as she suffered slavery both during conflict, and after arriving in the UK.

Beth was from Uganda where her family had been farmers who were very badly affected by conflict. The Lord's Resistance Army (LRA) had come to their village and taken all the children: the boys to be soldiers and the girls to be 'wives' to commanders. Beth was one of the children abducted and she was held as the 'wife' of an LRA commander for about four years.

Relating back to the extant literature discussed in chapter three, **Beth**'s experience of being held in sexual exploitation by a commander of an armed force is one that is, unfortunately, commonly cited by young girls in

Uganda. She was kept in this situation of modern slavery for around four years before she was able to escape and move to Kampala, the country's capital. While the other examples of modern slavery discussed so far have highlighted that the exploitation was caused by a lack of viable options, for **Beth**, her situation constituted an almost complete removal of options; she had no agency in joining the LRA as she was kidnapped rather than deceived or coerced (notions of agency are addressed further in chapter seven).

However, after escaping this situation of slavery, **Beth** was exploited again. When **Beth** moved to Kampala, she found accommodation living with someone she met there. This person then suggested that they could find **Beth** some work in the UK where she would be better paid. With no support, a very low level of education, and few opportunities to earn a wage other than through sex work, **Beth** felt fortunate to have been given this opportunity. She agreed to the offer and was brought to London; however, when she arrived she was forced into sexual exploitation, receiving no pay. **Beth** was kept in this situation for two years before she managed to escape by climbing out of a window.

For **Beth**, both of her experiences of modern slavery linked back to conflict. Her experience being held as the 'wife' of an LRA commander after being kidnapped by armed forces was undoubtedly so. While the cause of her experience of modern slavery in the UK is perhaps less direct, it also links back to the same conflict in which she was kidnapped. If she had not been kidnapped by the LRA, she would not have lost her family support network. However, she was removed from her family and, after escaping the LRA commander, had to find somewhere to live where she could remain hidden. Therefore, because of the initial conflict, she was left in a situation where she was living in a new city without anyone she could rely on for support and with few options where she would be able to earn enough to support herself. This left her vulnerable to an offer of work which was exploitative. Again, for **Beth**, the conflict had limited her choices and it was as a result of this lack of options coupled with the lack of trustworthy support that led her to experience modern slavery. While her experience with the LRA in Uganda exemplified a situation of modern slavery in which she had practically no choice at all, the offer of a job in the UK represented an active choice, but not an entirely autonomous one. In Kampala, **Beth**'s options were to stay in the city where she had no support network and no job opportunities, or to accept this offer of work abroad. While she may have anticipated that the latter held some risk, it was a situation in which there was realistically no valid alternative.

The remaining stories from the interviews that exemplify people fleeing conflict and experiencing modern slavery in the UK continue to reflect **Beth**'s experience of conflict increasing existing vulnerabilities by affecting available options and support networks.

4.2.2 Andrea

Andrea was born in Uganda where her parents were killed during war. 'She had moved to Kampala on her own. Was living in some kind of church-type community, but she didn't have any family and was just told I can help you get a job abroad.' Like **Beth**, **Andrea** was in a desperate situation, displaced because of the war and left without support. For both of them, an offer of work provided a positive way out of their situations. **Andrea** was told that the job would be secretarial work in the UK, and she was keen to start. However, upon arrival, there was no job and she was instead kept in a situation of domestic servitude. She was held in this exploitation for six months before a friend of the family exploiting her helped her to escape.

Andrea's support network broke down because of the war. Her parents were killed, leaving her with no one she could trust for help. Her choices were also limited directly by the conflict. She could stay in Uganda and do whatever she could to make enough money to survive, or she could accept this rare opportunity of an offer of a job abroad. This job offer was highly appealing because it offered the opportunity both to earn more money and to escape the conflict. **Andrea**'s caseworker described her situation as a 'perfect combination of problems, of conflict plus family being killed plus having no other support network. This just made her extremely vulnerable to this offer'. Moving to the UK only exacerbated her vulnerabilities because she knew no one in the country and did not know who, if anyone, she could trust to help her out of the exploitation.

4.2.3 Zoe

Zoe's story is another that highlights how escaping conflict can lead to modern slavery. **Zoe** grew up in South Sudan before it gained independence in 2011. Her parents were killed in the war and, as a result, at seven years old, **Zoe** and her siblings fled to Uganda to live with an aunt. The aunt was strict with the children, encouraging them to forget their Sudanese lives, their Islamic religion, and their Arabic language and to do everything they could to become Ugandan. The aunt highlighted the importance of learning English. When **Zoe** was about eighteen years old, this aunt then sold her to a man who brought her to the UK and forced her into sexual exploitation where she was held for about eighteen months. Because of this, **Zoe** became pregnant and, towards the end of her pregnancy, found the opportunity to escape out of a window.

Zoe's story highlights again how conflict triggered her experience of modern slavery. As a result of the war her parents were killed and, at seven years old and the oldest of her siblings, she was not able to care for herself and her remaining family and there was no one else to support them. Without her parents and as a young child, **Zoe** had little choice but to travel to Uganda to live with the aunt who was meant to care for her, but who sold her into slavery.

4.2.4 Tara

Tara's story reflects **Zoe**'s. She grew up in the north of Nigeria during a war and, because of the conflict, became a refugee in the south of the country. She had left everything behind in the north of Nigeria and had travelled alone with no one to support her. When she was living as a refugee, she was approached by an older woman offering her work; **Tara** accepted the offer and worked for this woman as a cleaner for a few months. 'And then the woman said I'll send you to an aunty in England and you can earn a bit more money from going abroad.' Like for **Beth** and **Andrea**, this offer of a job abroad was appealing to **Tara** who had no support and limited ways of making a living in Nigeria. She accepted the offer of work, was granted a visa, and travelled to the UK to meet with the person who was to employ her. However, upon arrival, she was forced into a brothel where she was made to work for around nine months. Like **Zoe**, **Tara** became pregnant because of this situation, and eventually one of her clients took pity on her and helped her to escape.

Tara's story again emphasises the impact that conflict has on choice. While it might seem that she had agency to make the decision between whether to stay and work in Nigeria or move to the UK, those choices would not have presented themselves if not for the conflict. If the conflict had not occurred, she would still be living in the north of Nigeria within a community that she knew and who supported her; she would not have become a refugee in the south, faced with the option of earning very little as a cleaner or with the opportunity to move to another country for a better salary. Like **Andrea**, **Tara** continued to suffer in the UK where she had no support network and no one to turn to for help when her situation became exploitative.

4.2.5 Padma

Padma was another woman who fell victim to modern slavery because of conflict. **Padma** was from the Ivory Coast and was Dyula, an ethnicity that has been badly targeted in the Ivory Coast civil war. Her husband was a political activist who was murdered for expressing his views. Without her husband, **Padma** was left with no support. She had no children and no other family, and was directly at risk both because of her ethnicity and by association with her husband. Picking up on this vulnerability, she was approached by a man who offered to assist her in escaping the Ivory Coast, explaining that he could get her into the UK if she acted as his wife. The ethnic conflict and civil war had left **Padma** with little other choice; her options were to stay in the Ivory Coast where she knew she would likely be killed, or take a risk by accepting the offer of this man. She took the risk and posed as this man's wife, but when they arrived in the UK, it became clear that he had never intended to help her. The man locked **Padma** in a house and sexually exploited her for two years. If not for the conflict targeting her ethnicity and causing her husband's death, **Padma** would not have needed to escape the Ivory Coast. Although she was already vulnerable because of her ethnicity placing her as a target during the conflict, it was the exacerbation of this vulnerability by the murder of her husband that left her with no support and led her to accept the assistance of this stranger who went on to hold her in a situation of sexual slavery in a country where she had no contacts and therefore no one to turn to for help.

4.2.6 Hattie

Hattie was another young woman who fled conflict to the UK but became trapped in sexual exploitation. **Hattie**'s distress when retelling her story was evident during our interview. She provided a lot of detail about her experience, and to reflect that the retelling of her experience below is more comprehensive than the stories summarised above, incorporating much of her account in her own words. **Hattie**'s experience of conflict was not of war, but of conflict with her employer after she fought for better workers' rights for her and her colleagues. **Hattie** experienced modern slavery after arriving in the UK, but had also been victimised in an interim country though, as explained below, she did not know where that was.

Hattie had grown up in a poor family in Vietnam but had managed to gain a college education. Despite this, she was unable to find any relevant work, so became a factory worker.

> Our salary was low and we didn't get paid enough for the hours we worked so we, the workers, often striked, put on strikes. There was a workers' union in the company, the factory; however, we didn't get a lot of support from the union at all. They didn't do anything. Through a friend, a colleague in the factory who actually belonged to a Vietnamese labour worker organisation that supports workers' rights and fair treatment, and through this I realised that this organisation could help the workers.

Hattie joined this organisation and encouraged a number of her colleagues to do the same.

> I also offered support and help and took part in some negotiations from the workers to the factory owner asking for increased salary and fairer treatment and working conditions. However, most of the meetings did not go very well. They often ended with someone being fired ... I was requested by the factory security guards to attend a meeting as a representative for the workers to negotiate some deals. But when I attended, the Director wasn't like what they promised me for the meeting, but it turned out that inside of the office I was told I was fired and my case would be referred to the police to deal with me. And my case was sent to the police to be dealt with and I was charged with affray and opposing the local authority, causing public disorder. I was charged for encouraging the workers to form demonstrations. I received the form where the charges were put out to me, together with a letter from the other workers and my father had to bribe the police. I was released two days after. And I was released on bail with the condition that I had to report every Monday of the week, once a week on a Monday, and that they would carry on investigating the matter and they would prosecute me with those offences.

Hattie went to report twice, but then heard that one of her friends who was in the same situation had not been released after reporting on the third week. **Hattie** was afraid and fled to another region of Vietnam. As a result, a warrant was issued for her arrest.

> I went to the south of Vietnam and stayed with some relatives at their home for about five months and also during that time I talked to some of my friends who also informed me that some of my friends were arrested and not released at all so they advised me that I go abroad because I couldn't hide like this for long in Vietnam and I wouldn't be able to do anything.

However, **Hattie** came from a poor background and could not afford to pay for a journey out of Vietnam. She confided this to her friends, and they told her of an agent they had heard about who could help her leave the country and she could pay off the debt by working once she arrived at the destination. **Hattie** contacted the agent and asked about the kind of work that would be expected of her when she arrived. She was told she would be caring for children or for the elderly or disabled. **Hattie** was happy to do such work and signed up to an arrangement with the agent. A week later, she crossed the border into China and then was loaded into the back of a lorry where she stayed for around a month as it travelled through Europe, though **Hattie** was unaware of the countries she was transiting through. She eventually arrived at a house, still with no knowledge of which country she was in.

> I was told to work and the work I was forced to do was sleep with different men but I didn't want to do it. I had to after a few weeks . . . When I refused to carry on doing that I was assaulted, beaten up and I was left to go hungry. Then I was locked into a room in the basement . . . And after a few weeks a man came along and told me I would be moved somewhere else where I would be able to do another job and the job wouldn't be like the one I was forced to do, so I agreed to go. And then I was put into a lorry inside some wooden compartments, boxes, and I was told to stay silent, not to make any movements or noise. Because at that time I didn't want to stay in that house any longer so I agreed to follow the man. So when I arrived in the UK I was forced to do the same job again but I didn't want to. So I asked the people who controlled me to speak to

> that man and they told me that I was sold to them by that man now [the man who had offered her a different job]. And then of course I wanted to leave, I wanted to run away but I was threatened by these people that if I dared to run away they would chase my family and kill my family. And so I had to work for at least two years for them, paying off the debt which was 25,000 euros.

This threat of hurting a victim's family is a technique commonly used by perpetrators of modern slavery to keep their victims compliant (Hopper and Hidalgo, 2006). In the case of **Hattie**, she was confident that these people knew where her family lived and she was terrified that a lack of compliance on her part would lead to violence against those she had left behind in Vietnam.

After over two years of suffering rape on a daily basis and realising that this debt was never going to be repaid, **Hattie** discovered that she was pregnant. When she disclosed this information to the perpetrators, they moved her to another house where she was left to care for babies. In this job, **Hattie** was left unsupervised and was able to climb a wall to escape. She kept running until she found strangers who spoke Vietnamese and she asked them for help.

Hattie's story is clearly incredibly distressing and is one that demonstrates the extreme exploitation of a vulnerable and desperate individual. It is also a story that exemplifies the devastating impacts of conflict. The conflict highlighted in **Hattie**'s case uses the broader definition as clarified in chapter two and was a conflict between herself and the factory owners when they became displeased at her attempts to fight for better wages and workers' rights. Due to this conflict, and after she learnt of others in her situation being arrested and not released, **Hattie**'s options were severely restricted. Her choices were then to stay in Vietnam and be arrested, with the expectation of not being released, or find a way to leave. She chose the latter. To avoid the unfair arrest, **Hattie** had to remove herself from her support network, and she escaped the conflict by employing the services of an 'agent' who led her to believe she would gain a legitimate job upon arrival. However, this led **Hattie** unwittingly into a situation where she was trafficked into sexual exploitation and trapped in debt bondage to pay off her debt. Her story exemplifies the direct correlation between conflict and modern slavery. **Hattie** would not have had to flee the country, or employ a person to help her do so, if not for the conflict.

4.2.7 Francine

Francine was another person whose experience of conflict was not of war; she grew up in a very strict family in Gambia and when her father organised an arranged marriage for her which she did not want, she experienced familial conflict. **Francine**'s sister was living and studying in the UK and **Francine** had told her father that she wanted to do the same because she did not want this marriage, but he was adamant that it was to go ahead.

After visiting her sister in the UK, **Francine** returned home where she met a Nigerian man who was visiting Gambia on holiday. She told him about her sister studying in the UK and how she wished she could do the same to avoid the marriage that her father had planned.

> He befriended her. He started over a period of several months... meeting her in secret. He told her not to tell her family about them. And said that he could get her to the UK and he could find a place for her to live and he could help her to study. So she developed a friendship with him over time. And then she agreed to go to the UK with him. She was told not to tell anybody about where she was going. So she essentially fled her family to get away from this arranged marriage. And she went to the UK. She must have been about eighteen when she fled. Eighteen or nineteen. She came over to the UK and his sister met them at the airport. They went and stayed with his sister for a while. Everything was all right. And they then moved into a place of their own and were in more of a relationship at that point.

For **Francine**, the main reason that she accepted the offer of this man to bring her to the UK was to escape the arranged marriage that her father was organising for her. If not for the conflict caused by this intended marriage, she would not have been so eager to leave Gambia. Once they were in the UK, the man told her:

> that he wanted to marry her and that he wanted her to convert to Christianity. So she said, because she loved him, she would convert. So she converted to Christianity and then he told her she had to tell her family what she'd done, so she phoned up her family in Gambia and her dad was furious because everybody in Gambia was Muslim, her family was Muslim, so she said that her dad disowned her. She said that he said she could never come back to the country.

This conversion from Islam to Christianity caused further conflict between **Francine** and her family to the extent where she was no longer able to return home and her connection to her support network was severed. This meant that remaining with this man in the UK was her only viable option. However, she described how once she had told her family of her conversion and witnessed the resulting fall out, this man changed towards her.

> He started being violent towards her and he raped her several times a day. And then on her birthday he said that he'd got a surprise for her and he got three other men to come to the house and they all raped her as well. And then she said that there was a lot of money around and that [people were paying him] ... and that continued for ten years ... He locked her in so she couldn't get out. He went to work, I think he had a job in London, but he would continually bring men back who paid but would rape her.

Again, employing the broad definition of conflict outlined in chapter two, **Francine**'s initial experience of conflict related to her going against her father's wishes. This led to a limiting of options in that she must either go ahead with the arranged marriage, or accept the invitation from the man who offered to bring her to the UK; she felt that there was no other alternative and she was desperate not to go ahead with the marriage. However, another conflict situation arose when she informed her family that she had converted to Christianity. The main impacts of this conflict were a removal of both familial support and of legitimate options. Without her family to turn to, **Francine** had little other choice than to remain with this man in the UK. As such, without the initial conflict, **Francine** would likely not have been so eager to pursue the relationship with this man who had intended to exploit her, and without the second conflict **Francine** would not have experienced such a dramatic reduction of agency. It was a combination of these two issues that caused her to become caught in a situation of modern slavery.

4.2.8 Ifra

The discussion so far has provided illustrations of how individuals fleeing conflict have come to experience modern slavery in the UK as a result of that conflict, be it war or broader understandings of the term such as familial or employment conflict. **Ifra**'s story is another example of this, though her experience of exploitation calls for us to understand how structures in the UK can also generate risk; this is a topic discussed further in chapter six. Like **Hattie**, **Ifra** found it particularly distressing to recount her experiences, but provided considerable information in our interview. **Ifra**'s story is provided in detail below, with much of the account told in her own words.

Like those discussed above, **Ifra** came to the UK because she was fleeing conflict, but for her, the conflict was political. **Ifra** was a politician in Bangladesh and had a disagreement with her political opponents. As a result, she was physically beaten by members of the opposing party who threatened to kill her. Here, **Ifra**'s support network broke down as her husband divorced her because of the trouble her situation was causing.

> She used to be harassed all the time in Bangladesh by the other party saying you need to withdraw the case otherwise we'll kill you and do this to you so she couldn't actually go anywhere. Because obviously her husband didn't help so she didn't know where to go because there was no one to help her.

Ifra knew she needed to leave Bangladesh but did not know how. She went to her father's village in the hope that someone there could help her, and a person she knew offered to take her to Dakar where he introduced her to someone who could help her leave the country.

This man arranged a visa for **Ifra** and organised a flight, explaining that she would be chaperoned by a man who would help her find housing and work when she arrived in England. However, when they arrived, this man disappeared, leaving **Ifra** alone in a country she was unfamiliar with, unable to speak the language.

> So then she was crying [in the train station] and she had no one and she was lost and this Bengali person said why are you crying for? And she told him her story and he said come on I'll take you to the job centre and maybe they can help you. So that person was really nice and took her to job centre. When she went to job centre they said you have got a visa so would you work and she said yes. But when her visa ran out they couldn't keep her because the visa expired.

When the job centre informed **Ifra** that they were no longer able to continue working with her, they offered her no advice as to what an expired visa meant, how she might go about applying for asylum, or which other agencies might be able to offer her advice. As a result, **Ifra** remained wholly unaware of what overstaying her visa meant and was oblivious to the asylum system. Not knowing what else to do, she returned to the train station where she had originally met the man who introduced her to the job centre.

> When she was there she saw some Bengali people and asked if they knew of any jobs going, I really need a job. And they said you can come to my house and do some work at home and you'll get food. So she went and did that for a month and got free food and somewhere to stay. While she was in that house doing the housework, the person's brother rang her one time and said do you want to work and I said yeah I do.

Ifra explained to me that she hadn't known how to get a job after the job centre told her they could no longer help her, but she knew no one in the UK and she was certain she would be murdered if she returned to Bangladesh. She felt her only option was to approach strangers to ask for help and she felt fortunate when this opportunity became available to her. She worked in this stranger's brother's house cooking, cleaning, and doing all the domestic work for around six months without pay before she was asked to start working in their restaurant as well.

> She was then in this habit that he wanted her to go to the restaurant every day, so she'd get up and work in the house from eight till four and then go to work in the restaurant four till two in the morning. Then she didn't know what to do. She didn't want to be in the house any more. She asked to get dropped back at the job centre but they wouldn't. They said if she carried on they'd go to the police.

These people threatened **Ifra** by explaining that, because her visa had expired, she was in the UK illegally, and that if the police found out she would be returned to Bangladesh. Because she was so certain that she would be murdered if she returned to Bangladesh, these threats kept **Ifra** compliant. She also explained how the man controlling her would quickly lose his temper and become violent towards her, leaving her with permanent scars that she showed during the interview and which by recalling caused her to become uncontrollably upset. After the beatings, **Ifra** would beg for a day off to let the cuts and bruising heal, but she was allowed no respite and was forced to continue working these eighteen-hour days.

One day she refused to go to the restaurant and cook. When the man controlling her found out:

> he took his belt off his trousers and started beating her with it ... He was bruising her, kicking her. Then he was dragging her saying come on, I'll take you to the police station now and she said no don't take me, I'll work.

Ifra lived in fear of this man and his family because of both the physical threats and violence, but also through the psychological control of threatening her with being returned to Bangladesh. This kept her compliant for three years, where she worked these eighteen-hour days without pay. The situation finally became so distressing that **Ifra** decided she would rather take a risk with the police than continue to live in these conditions. She left the house, walked to the nearby post office and told them of her story; the staff at the post office called the police who came to meet **Ifra** and supported her through an investigation and into long-term support.

Ifra's story of exploitation is one that can be traced back to her experience of conflict in Bangladesh, but it also indicates that modern slavery can actually be unintentionally encouraged by government agencies. At the beginning of her time in the UK, **Ifra** was in the country legally and the job centre—a statutory organisation—was willing and able to help her. Once her visa ran out, however, they no longer had a duty to support her. Although not their main remit, they were aware that she had overstayed her visa and yet offered no advice or signposting as to where she could or should go for support. As such, she was left unsupported. As a result, **Ifra** turned to strangers for support and became vulnerable to deceitful offers of help which transpired to be a situation of modern slavery comprising labour exploitation and domestic servitude which she suffered for three years.

While **Ifra**'s situation of modern slavery was triggered by a breakdown in communication with an agency that should have taken—even minimal—steps to provide her with information to help keep her safe (or even report her for overstaying her visa), her story also further demonstrates vulnerabilities caused by conflict. For **Ifra**, fleeing Bangladesh would not have been a consideration, let alone a necessity, if she had not experienced conflict with the opposing political party; however, the conflict led to a lack of options for her: stay in Bangladesh where her political opposition was threatening to have her killed, or find a way to leave the country. This occurred in a context where her support networks had broken down in terms both of her husband leaving her, and in her needing to leave behind everyone she knew in order to find safety in another country.

4.2.9 Summary

This discussion of people experiencing modern slavery after arriving in the UK links several stories which, on the surface, may appear very different, but on closer inspection hold some distinct similarities. All these stories highlight that conflict generates two specific vulnerabilities that increase the likelihood that a person will become a victim of modern slavery: conflict limits the legitimate options available to each individual, and causes a breakdown in support networks. All the respondents discussed in this section were left in situations where there were choices (other than in **Beth**'s experience of kidnapping), but where these choices had been limited to only undesirable or risky options. When the conflict also reduces a person's support network, it means that they have fewer people to turn to for help or advice, leaving them more likely to turn to strangers for support. All the stories outlined in this section highlight how that interplay of reduced options and reduced support networks increases the likelihood of experiencing modern slavery. For the respondents, this lack of support also continued after arriving in the UK where the individuals knew either no one, or very few people in the country, and where ties with family and friends back home were severed. Again, this increases the likelihood of becoming reliant on strangers whose intentions are unknown.

4.3 Victims of modern slavery in interim countries

The discussions so far in chapter four have focused on those who experienced modern slavery either in the same country they experienced conflict or after fleeing conflict to the UK. However, there are also examples from the interviews demonstrating how some people have fallen victim to modern slavery after fleeing the conflict, but before arriving in the UK. **Edan** and **Catherine**'s stories exemplify this, and both their experiences of modern slavery continue to emphasise how conflict generates specific vulnerabilities that encouraged their exploitative situations: a lack of options and a breakdown in support networks.

4.3.1 Edan

Edan was from Afghanistan and he and his father were the only family members that survived the war, highlighting an immediate and significant reduction in his support network. With his father, he fled the conflict in the early 2000s, seeking safety in Iran when their only alternative option was to stay in the conflict zone. However, when they arrived in Iran, they became trapped in a situation of bonded labour in a factory where they were prevented from going outside. They were kept in this situation for around four years until **Edan**'s father fell ill and subsequently died. Upon his father's death, **Edan** was told that he was to be sent to Syria as a fighter. He was desperate not to let this happen and with no one else to turn to, managed to find a way to escape on his own before he was sent away. After hearing people talking about the UK offering a place of safety, **Edan** chose it as his destination and began his journey to get there. He is currently in the UK, waiting on the outcome of his asylum application.

The conflict was the sole reason that **Edan** fled Afghanistan. If not for the conflict, he would not have lost his significant support network and nor would he have been faced with the limited options of either staying in the conflict zone and risk being killed, or fleeing to Iran. However, these vulnerabilities were exacerbated because of the high rate of refugees in Iran who have fled the war in Afghanistan. This means that structural changes have led to situations in which the exploitation of such refugees through labour is not uncommon and, for many, is the only viable option when their alternative is to reject the work but then have no way to support themselves.

For **Edan**, conflict removed the voluntariness of his choice. While he and his father made an active choice to move to Iran, they would not have considered doing so if it had not been for the conflict in Afghanistan and the immediate danger and lack of support that threatened them as a result. If their choices had not been limited in this way, then it is unlikely they would have found themselves in a situation of modern slavery.

4.3.2 Catherine

Like **Edan**, **Catherine**'s experience of modern slavery occurred in an interim country. She grew up in Albania in a close, supportive family where she gained a high level of education including a university degree. Although

Albania is recognised as a particularly patriarchal society, her upbringing showed her a form of family life that was different from the norm. When she did get married, her experience of married life was neither what she had expected, nor what she had hoped. Once she was married, she moved with her husband to live with his parents in Greece, but unlike her parents' marriage, there was no equality in her relationship.

Catherine described how there was so much societal pressure on women being in relationships that it was expected that women should accept the way their husbands treated them—no matter how unfairly—because the shame of being divorced was far worse. **Catherine**'s husband treated her badly. She was shamed for giving birth to a daughter, and she was expected to do all the domestic work for her husband, daughter, and for her parents-in-law. Finally, 'she left her husband because there was another woman who claimed to be his wife. The relationship had been quite emotionally neglectful. She'd been unsupported and isolated'. Having seen relationships differently because of her upbringing, **Catherine** was not willing to continue to accept this mistreatment from her husband, despite the societal pressure to tolerate it, and she left him.

Because **Catherine** had left her husband and her support networks had been severed, she needed to find a job to be able to support herself. She found work in a café where she began to make friends with a man who became a regular customer. Over time they became friendlier and the relationship became romantic. **Catherine**'s situation of being a divorced woman meant that she found herself flattered by the attention of this man when her divorced status was something generally frowned upon by society. She described the man as kind and charming. He knew she would be earning a low wage at the café and offered her a job where she would be able to earn more and, because she felt she now knew him well enough to trust him, she gratefully accepted. Unfortunately, this man had no intention of helping **Catherine** and the forging of this relationship was simply a way of deceiving her into a situation of modern slavery in which **Catherine** was taken away from Greece back to Albania and forced into sexual exploitation. 'So men would come. And it was very high-powered men. So it was people in government. People in the police.'

Because of the types of people who were paying to rape **Catherine**: police officers and government officials, she felt there was no one she could turn to for help or to report the situation to. She had to find her own way out and eventually managed to escape in the back of a lorry. She has been in the UK since, but has not tried to contact her family out of fear thatthe people who trafficked and raped her will use these communications to find her. **Catherine** continues to wait for a decision about her asylum application in the UK, an issue which also causes her distress, as is discussed further in section 6.2.2.

Catherine's story is one of marital conflict which caused her to leave the relationship, resulting in her experiencing a lack of support, but the societal expectation of women being subservient to their husbands exacerbated her vulnerability. If not for the conflict with her husband, she would not have needed to find work in a café to support herself, but if not for the structural disapproval of single, divorced women, she would have been unlikely to be so quick to accept the advances of the man in the café who went on to exploit her. This highlights the way that the interaction between conflict and social structures can make someone vulnerable to a situation of modern slavery, but it also emphasises how a lack of legitimate choice heightens those vulnerabilities. **Catherine**'s choices were to remain in an abusive relationship, or to leave and receive societal judgement for doing so. If not for the pressure caused by these choices or, more accurately, lack of choices, then **Catherine** would not have been recruited into a situation of modern slavery.

4.3.3 Summary

Edan and **Catherine**'s stories highlight the ways in which the result of conflict can interact with pre-existing social structures to an extent that leads to migration and heightens people's vulnerabilities towards becoming victims of modern slavery. While they experienced different types of conflict—war and marital conflict—and different forms of slavery—labour and sexual exploitation—there are similarities between their stories. Both experienced limited choices because of the conflict, both found themselves lacking support (both within and after fleeing the conflict) and both chose to leave the conflict to try and find safety. Without the conflicts, neither would have needed to leave their current situations, but social structures exacerbated the vulnerabilities caused by the conflicts. For **Edan**, fleeing conflict in Afghanistan led him to Iran where the structural inequalities of refugees meant he had little choice but to enter into a situation of slavery in order to get by. For **Catherine**, fleeing marital conflict resulted in her needing to find work to support herself, but the patriarchal structure of women being expected to rely on support from men meant that she accepted the advances and offers of a man who went on to force her into sexual exploitation. It was the result of the conflict limiting the choices and support available to them that pushed both **Edan** and **Catherine** into vulnerable situations but these vulnerabilities were then further exacerbated by pre-existing social structures.

4.4 Conclusion

This chapter discusses the findings from the research that identified situations of modern slavery. It includes examples in which the slavery occurred in the country of conflict, after arriving in the UK, or in an interim country. While all those who suffered modern slavery had vastly different experiences, there were two key vulnerabilities that conflict had generated for all the respondents, regardless of the form of exploitation or the country in which it occurred. These were a limiting of choices and a lack of support. The limiting of choices meant that all the respondents were in situations where they had to make decisions which were all imbued with risk, leaving them to choose the option that appeared to be the lesser evil. This demonstrates how these individuals still have some level of agency, but their agency is severely restricted. As discussed further in chapter seven, this means that individuals are still able to make active choices, but these choices are significantly restricted by the context in which they are made.

In terms of the reduction in support, for some this came about directly because of the conflict, such as those whose family members were killed during war. For others, the lack of support came after arrival in the UK. In some instances, this related to familial rejection causing a break of ties with family and therefore preventing the ability to return to family and potentially to safety. In other instances, the lack of support related directly to situations in which UK statutory agencies could have reasonably been expected to provide assistance which could have prevented these individuals from experiencing modern slavery.

Chapter five moves away from those who experienced modern slavery to examine the findings relating to those respondents who fled conflict to the UK but without suffering such exploitation. It considers interventions which helped people stayed safe from modern slavery, and whether these were as a result of successful government interactions, or due to the support of non-governmental organisations or strangers.

Chapter five
Fleeing conflict to safety

Chapter four discussed the findings from the research that relate to those who fled conflict but went on to experience modern slavery, and it identifies some of the key vulnerabilities generated by conflict that put people at risk of such situations, namely a reduction of legitimate options and a breakdown in support networks. This chapter focuses instead on those who escaped a conflict and fled to the UK without experiencing modern slavery. It considers whether their safety was a result of successful government systems, or in spite of their failings.

5.1 UK government intervention: stories of success

The UK's Modern Slavery Act was introduced in 2015 by Theresa May shortly before she became prime minister in 2016. Once prime minister, she claimed that her government would 'lead the way in defeating modern slavery' (May, 2016), and the UK government continues to state that tackling modern slavery is one of its priorities (Hesketh and Balch, 2021). Some of the respondents in this research provided stories that made it clear that interaction from the UK government did successfully prevent them from becoming vulnerable to situations of modern slavery. There were three main methods highlighted in the interviews through which the UK government successfully supported people. These are: the safety provided by resettlement programmes, the input of the Border Force, and the lack of chartered removal to certain countries. These topics are discussed in this section using examples from the interviews. Section 5.2 then moves on to consider non-governmental responses which kept people safe, including support offered by NGOs and strangers.

From Conflict to Modern Slavery. Alicia Heys, Oxford University Press.
DOI: 10.1093/oso/9780192846549.003.0005

5.1.1 Resettlement programmes

The United Nations High Commissioner for Refugees (UNHCR) advocates three long-term, durable solutions to support refugees: voluntary repatriation, local integration, and resettlement. The intention of all these solutions is for the long-term self-reliance of refugees (UNHCR, no date a).

Voluntary repatriation is suitable for those in a situation where it is safe for them to return home. Local integration may be appropriate for those who have fled their home to a nearby country and are able to settle there. Resettlement is for those who are in a situation where it is unsafe to return home (e.g. a conflict is still ongoing, or they may be at risk of persecution), and who are unable to integrate into another local area (e.g. unable to claim asylum, or have specific needs that the area is unable to support). Resettlement is often the only way for refugee families who have been separated to be reunited in safety. 'Resettlement is the transfer of refugees from an asylum country to another State that has agreed to admit them and ultimately grant them permanent settlement' (UNHCR, no date b:no pagination).

The UN resettlement programmes involve identifying refugees who are most at risk in the country where they have sought protection, and moving them to one of the countries that participates in the programme. The preconditions to be considered for resettlement are:

1. the applicant is determined to be a refugee by UNHCR; and
2. the prospects for all durable solutions were assessed, and resettlement is identified as the most appropriate solution. (UNHCR, no date c:5)

The process to be submitted for resettlement involves a referral to the UNHCR, where resettlement staff will verify the registration and refugee status of the person(s) and organise an appointment for a resettlement interview which involves all the family members in the case and can last up to six hours. After the interview, the staff member will submit a Resettlement Registration Form, which outlines the biographical information of every person included in the case, and provides a summary of the claim and the UNHCR's decision for each adult on the case. This will detail any specific needs or vulnerabilities which will assist in determining the most suitable country for resettlement. Each resettlement country has its own methods regarding resettlement and may then conduct its own interviews. As soon as the state responds to the UNHCR with a decision, the UNHCR will ensure the applicants are informed of the outcome. Should they be accepted, they may be expected to undertake medical screening depending on the resettlement country's requirements. The new host country will provide some level of orientation for the refugees, whether this be printed or video materials, or orientation courses. Travel for the refugees is arranged and funded by the resettlement country (UNHCR, no date d). Most resettlement programmes offer participants permanent resident status but a refugee can only qualify if it is not possible for them to safely return to their home country or settle in the country of asylum. Between January and August 2022, UNHCR submitted the files of 64,415 refugees for consideration by resettlement countries. In that time frame, UNHCR assisted 32,289 departures for resettlement (UNHCR, no date e).

Resettlement is intended to be a durable scheme, allowing the refugees to gain long-term self-sufficiency. For this reason, it is important that the resettlement process involves more than just the movement of a refugee from one state to another. As such, the receiving states are expected to provide support to help the refugees integrate into their new society. The resettlement programmes expect that any refugees taking part in the schemes will be afforded the same rights as any other citizen of the receiving state. It is beneficial not only for the refugees that they integrate, but also for the receiving state. By assisting the refugees to become independent, working members of their new society, the state then benefits through their social and economic outputs and helps to prevent a divide between members of society. To ensure integration into the new state, the resettlement programmes provide cultural orientation programmes as well as assistance in training and accessing education and employment.

Between 2004 and 2020, the UK had a resettlement programme called the Gateway Protection Programme (GPP) in collaboration with the UNHCR with a quota to resettle 750 refugees per year.

> The Gateway Protection Programme (GPP), running since 2004, is the UK quota refugee scheme providing assistance to refugees designated as especially vulnerable by the United Nations High Commissioner for Refugees. It is co-funded by the UK Border Agency and the European Refugee Fund (ERFIII). (Platts-Fowler and Robinson, 2011)

The GPP worked via the UNHCR identifying refugees who required resettlement and sending details of potential candidates to the British government which then decided who would be accepted. Once the successful refugees had been notified, flights and visas were organised and they were brought to the UK, greeted at the airport, and taken to their new home. Support in the form of vocational training, education, assistance in applying for employment, cultural programmes etc. continued for a year to help the refugees to settle into their new community. The GPP offered refugees indefinite leave to remain, meaning that they were able to start their life anew without worrying about when they would have to move away again.

The UK also ran a specific resettlement scheme in order to support people fleeing Syria. This was the government's Vulnerable Persons Resettlement Scheme (VPRS), established in 2014, which offered five years' protection to those in the greatest need, such as survivors of torture, or those with urgent medical needs. The UK government hoped that, because of the short amount of time that Syrians had been displaced, they would be able to return home at some point in the future. In 2017, the scheme was expanded to support those who had fled conflict in Syria but were not of Syrian nationality. This resettlement programme worked via:

> the selection and transfer of refugees from a country in which they have sought protection—usually somewhere with a large number of refugees who are living in camps or urban settings—to a third country which has agreed to admit them as refugees and where they can rebuild their lives. (Refugee Council, 2018)

During the Covid-19 pandemic, the resettlement of refugees through this scheme was temporarily paused, but it restarted in December 2020 and the final refugees on the scheme arrived in the UK on 25 February 2021. The final number of refugees who were resettled in the UK under the VPRS was 20,319 (UK Visas and Immigration, 2021).

The British government had intended to merge the Gateway Protection Programme with the UK's other resettlement programmes in 2020 in order to establish a new, single resettlement scheme. The Covid-19 pandemic delayed these plans and the UK's various resettlement programmes were put on hold (Gower, 2021). However, on 25 February 2021, the UK Resettlement Scheme was launched. This is accessible to refugees who have been assessed for resettlement by UNHCR (Refugee Legal Aid Information, 2021).

Resettlement programmes offer a great degree of protection that is not afforded in cases of asylum (Refugee Council, 2018). Those who come through the programmes are supported for a year after they have arrived in the UK, while those seeking asylum receive minimal assistance, as discussed in more detail later in this section. Two of the respondents in this research, **Barak** and **Nadim,** were Syrian nationals who received support through the government's Vulnerable Persons Resettlement Scheme. Because of the scheme, their lives settling into the UK were drastically different from a number of the respondents who did not receive equivalent support.

Barak recalled the extreme violence in Syria. He had lived there all his life and brought up a family, but it soon became so dangerous that he sent his wife and children out of the country so that they could be safe. **Barak** stayed in Syria and continued to work. He described how civilians were protesting against the president, Bashar al-Assad, and government soldiers were sent to retaliate. The soldiers looted from people's homes and set up check points in the town which made it both difficult and unsafe for people to come and go. 'They [the government soldiers] got an order from the officer that anyone who was Muslim, kill them. It doesn't matter how old he is, or a man or a woman, it doesn't matter.'

The soldiers gradually became more violent, indiscriminately killing men, women, and children by shooting them in the street. **Barak** was shot twice and survived, but his twelve-year-old cousin was killed by the soldiers. The war had meant there was no water, electricity, medical supplies, or hospitals, and injured people had to rely on voluntary doctors or nurses. Because of the lack of medical support and the likelihood of being shot again, he took his chance to escape by crawling for seven hours through a tunnel that was used to bring in aid supplies.

Barak reached the border to Lebanon, but there were guards protecting the checkpoints, preventing anyone from leaving because they may have been able to help fight against the president in Syria. He managed to circumnavigate the checkpoints and enter Lebanon illegally. The rest of **Barak**'s family had fled to Saudi Arabia and they had all arranged to meet in Jordan. However, to be able to enter Jordan, **Barak** needed to prove that he had entered Lebanon legally, so returned to the border to bribe the officials to stamp his passport, making it appear that he had entered legally. 'They take the money, they give you a stamp, and then you have entered legally from both sides. And that way he can fly to Jordan.'

Once they then legally crossed the border into Jordan, **Barak** and his family were automatically registered with the UN. This registration doubled as an application for resettlement, and **Barak**'s family were required to renew this application every six months. It is not possible to apply to be relocated to a specific country, so the family did not know where they would be resettled if they were successful. In 2015, after three years of waiting, **Barak** got a phone call notifying him that his family had been accepted onto a resettlement scheme. **Barak** was asked: 'Are you happy to travel to America?' He explained, 'The first choice [option] was to travel to America. I want to go wherever! Even Somalia!'

Resettlement officers took **Barak** for an interview where he had to bring identification to prove he was Syrian. Following this, his wife and three children were required by the resettlement system to attend an interview to corroborate his story. **Barak** described how lucky he was that both interviews were within a month of each other, when some of his friends had to wait nine months between interviews. After the second interview, he received another phone call to inform him that they were entitled to travel to the UK. The family accepted the offer, received visas, and were travelling within fifteen days.

Nadim's story is heavily reflective of **Barak**'s. **Nadim** was also from Syria and had brought up his family there. He had run a successful business and owned his own home, but after the war destroyed them, he and his family fled to neighbouring Lebanon. However, **Nadim** described a similar problem to **Barak** in that there was no way for him to legally cross the border into Lebanon. Eventually, Nadim and his family 'paid money for the government in Syria as well Lebanon' for them to be able to cross the border and have their passports stamped to make it appear that the crossing was legal. It was at the point of this 'legal' border crossing that Nadim and his family were registered with the UN and, simultaneously, for a resettlement programme.

While **Nadim** was working in Lebanon, he received a phone call to invite him for a resettlement interview 'where they asked him [about his life] from the date he was born to the current day'. Later in the week, **Nadim** received another phone call asking the whole family to come for an interview. After this interview, the family were assigned a place in the UK as it was the most appropriate destination country that was able to offer support for the medical conditions that **Nadim** suffered. It was three months between being accepted on the resettlement programme and boarding the plane; in that time, the family were taught about life in the UK including its laws, cultural traditions, and way of life.

Barak and **Nadim** both described how lucky they felt to have been accepted onto the scheme, stating that they knew people who had been waiting much longer than they had. They were provided with visas and flights to the UK. On arrival they were met at the airport and taken to their new, funded, fully furnished homes. Their children had school places waiting, and the adults had English for speakers of other languages (ESOL) lessons and vocational training sessions organised for them. A support worker was assigned to each of their families to work with them for the first year to ensure that their resettlement ran as smoothly as possible. This support worker was there to answer any questions, interpret letters they received, and keep the families informed of their entitlements. Both **Nadim** and **Barak** had a very comfortable transition from life in the interim country to life in the UK and feel settled in the UK.

Barak and **Nadim**'s stories highlight a clear flaw in the system for registering for resettlement programmes. Both **Barak** and **Nadim** were automatically registered for a resettlement programme once it appeared that they had legally crossed a border. However, neither of them made the border crossing legally, but bribed officials to stamp their documents. It was this bribing of officials that allowed them and their families to be registered with the UN and the resettlement scheme, when thousands of others in the same situation who could not afford bribes could not register for the programme.

Nadim describes how easy life has been for him since arriving in the UK. His children are in school and he attends ESOL classes three times a week. He engages well with the community and attends the local mosque once a week, making friends with people there and people he meets in the street. Similarly, **Barak** feels settled in the UK and has made friends. He has booked to take his driving theory test in the hope that he will be able to find work as a taxi driver. Both **Nadim** and **Barak** stated, in relation to life in the UK, that 'this is my country now'. They both feel settled with their families in the UK and hope that they will be able to find jobs and continue providing their children with a good education.

However, the experiences of **Nadim** and **Barak** who arrived in the UK through a resettlement programme differ drastically from the experiences of the respondents who claimed asylum, as evidenced by several of the agency workers I interviewed. **Jane**, whose job is to help welcome and provide orientation for refugees arriving in the UK discussed how the resettlement programmes create:

> a two-tier system because, like, clients that come through the resettlement programme, they're met at the airport straight away, they've got a friendly face, support and they're allocated a project worker who supports them through the whole [process]. They've got people to work with them to help find school places. They're given a house straight

> away. They've got support with access to benefits. Any issues to do with the house or school they can go and see them. All kinds of support there that doesn't exist for anyone that makes the journey themselves because they rock up in a town, then they've got to find everything out for themselves, which is completely different.

Gloria, who works with refugees, corroborated this.

> The Syrians are so well provided. When they come, they immediately have a house, access to benefits. We are obliged to provide ESOL classes, whereas anyone else is almost prohibited from joining them. So obviously that makes a huge difference to how quickly they're going to adjust and settle ... I mean it's incredible support really. Compared to a refugee from anywhere else in the world.

This difference in treatment for those on a resettlement programme compared to those claiming asylum was also highlighted by **Fadi**, who works for a refugee advice service.

> I still feel like it's a two-tier system. It's like you've got good refugees and bad refugees. Sometimes I say to myself ok it's a good model don't get me wrong. I like the model but why don't we do this for everyone? ... You've got people who have got nothing at all, that are going through all this horrendous situation then you've got some people who come and everything is ready for them.

Fadi notes how the difference between the two systems is not only unfair for those who do not get supported through a resettlement programme, but that it can cause a strain within communities that contain both people claiming asylum and people on a resettlement programme.

The consensus among the agency workers is that the resettlement programmes are excellent and provide much-needed support to help people fully integrate into their new society. However, by providing such a high level of support, the programmes cause disparity between groups of people who are leaving the same countries and the same situations (Basedow and Doyle, 2016; BBC, 2017; All Party Parliamentary Group on Refugees, 2017). Evidently, it would be too costly to provide this service to every asylum seeker that arrives in the UK, but the effect of this two-tiered system should be considered in relation to how it impacts communities of refugees.

It is also important to note here another fundamental flaw with the resettlement programmes: corruption. There are brief mentions in a small number of sources about corruption in resettlement programmes. Hilhorst et al. (2012) discuss how people living in border camps have recounted stories of aid workers requesting bribes to work on resettlement programme applications. Without the bribes, the applications are put on hold for an unspecified amount of time while the aid workers focus on progressing the applications of those who can afford to pay. Corruption among the agency workers has also been identified by Hayden (2018) in a report based on interviews with refugees in Khartoum undertaken over a ten-month period. The research found that 'individuals working with the Sudanese branch of the UN agency responsible for resettlement engage in corrupt practices, and that life-changing decisions are often made based on bribes rather than eligibility' (Hayden, 2018:no pagination). Like the findings discussed by Hilhorst et al. (2012), this report noted how UNHCR workers asked for bribes in order to advance applicants' resettlement applications. The price of the bribe was in the region of $15,000 per person. To gather such huge sums of money, applicants were borrowing from family members across the world. However, the pressure of needing to pay this money back puts these individuals in a precarious situation where they are most likely to have to work in order to pay off a debt that they should not have had to pay in the first instance. Of course, this makes them vulnerable to exploitative labour when they are looking for work with employers who are willing to let them work beyond the legally stipulated maximum working hours.

Of particular interest is the fact that the UNHCR makes public the punitive measures in place should an applicant be found attempting to bribe a UNHCR officer. They will either have their resettlement processing suspended for three to ten years, have their application terminated, or be considered for referral for criminal prosecution (UNHCR, 2008). However, it suggests little equivalent should it be the officers that are culpable, simply offering claims that accusations of misconduct are investigated (UNHCR, 2013). This indicates a belief that asylum seekers are more accountable for their corrupt actions than the officials who place them in a position where they have no option but to succumb to the corruption or give up on resettlement.

Both **Nadim** and **Barak** had accessed the resettlement programme in a corrupt way, but their experience is not one identified in the literature. While the literature covers the concept of corruption and bribery in advancing the progress of a resettlement application, **Nadim** and **Barak**'s experiences relate to making a border crossing appear legal. Both respondents had fled Syria to Lebanon but had crossed the border illegally. They had later returned to bribe border officials to stamp their documents so it appeared that their crossing had been legal because it is only with a legal border crossing that an individual becomes eligible for a resettlement programme. They were both accepted onto a resettlement programme and were provided with a place in the UK. Of all the respondents in this research project, **Barak** and **Nadim** were the only two who suggested that life for them had been easy since arriving in the UK.

Despite these flaws, resettlement programmes are highly effective at supporting individuals into safety and they offer assistance that is incomparable to that offered to other refugees and asylum seekers in the UK. The resettlement programmes ensure that there is support from the point of departing whichever country the refugee is leaving, and this support continues in the UK for a year. The assistance provided, especially in language lessons, vocational training, support looking for a job, and in a named support worker is invaluable in helping those refugees to settle and integrate into their new society.

As outlined in chapter four, conflict generates two specific vulnerabilities which can increase the likelihood that an individual will go on to be exploited in a situation of modern slavery: a reduction in the options available to them, and a breakdown in support networks. For those benefitting from resettlement programmes, the structured and reliable support offered to them offsets some of these vulnerabilities, particularly in relation to the breakdown in support networks. The comprehensive assistance provided by resettlement programmes means that individuals placed on them do not need to turn to strangers for advice or offers of work or accommodation, because they have long-term assistance in place. Although their choices may be limited to the extent that their accommodation is chosen for them, overall, they maintain their agency in making decisions because they are not placed in a situation of desperation where they need to find employment or accommodation via any means in order to survive. However, this is a situation faced by many asylum seekers who do not receive support comparable to the resettlement programmes and must do what they can to survive and which, for some, will result in situations of modern slavery. This is discussed further in chapter six.

This discussion of the success of resettlement programmes in comparison to the asylum system when it comes to effectively assisting people to integrate in and contribute to their new society emphasises how pre-empting mass migration would be more beneficial in preventing modern slavery than focusing on preventing immigration. As Solomon and Thibos (2017:no pagination) describe:

> Obviously, yes, we want to prevent—not in the sense of preventing migration, but the factors that force people to have to move. But we also have to proactively look at migration as one of the adaptation strategies. So if we know a particular area, or a particular region, or even an entire country may become uninhabitable, let's not wait until there's a disaster to deal with the migration. Let's plan ahead! By anticipating, you get people out of harm's way and allow them to live safe and productive lives.

If governments were to use such foresight to prepare for a likely resulting mass migration out of an area, then provisions could be put in place to ensure that these migrants do not need to rely on smugglers or traffickers to get them out of their country, or on strangers to help them find housing or employment once they have reached their destination.

Once potential situations of mass migration have been identified, then the responsibility to protect could be invoked in order to provide support to the citizens of the state in question. The responsibility to protect is a political commitment to end and prevent some of the worst forms of violence and persecution (UN, no date). The responsibility to protect highlights how:

> the primary responsibility for the protection of its people rested first and foremost with the State itself. However, a 'residual responsibility' also lied with the broader community of states, which was activated when a particular state is clearly either unwilling or unable to fulfil its responsibility to protect or is itself the actual perpetrator of crimes or atrocities. (ibid.)

In cases where high numbers of people are displaced, the state at the source of the displacement is accountable to do what it can to protect its citizens from human rights violations. This is particularly important because displaced persons have a higher mortality rate than any group, other than perhaps those who remain where the violence occurs (Bellamy, 2017). However, where states are unable or unwilling to provide this protection, there is an expectation that the international community will provide support.

While the resettlement programmes are arguably one method through which this responsibility to protect may be fulfilled, the proportion of people it helps in relation to those in need is very small. UNHCR (2018) describes how in 2017, there were 1.19 million refugees in need of resettlement yet there were only resettlement places for 75,188 refugees, just 6 per cent of those in need. Instead of creating a hostile environment for those in desperate need, to reduce the risks of exploitation for those fleeing dangerous situations, destination countries should consider being more accommodating. When physical safety is a person's priority, they cannot be expected to put their lives at risk by waiting for visa applications before fleeing. By reducing the hostility facing those arriving in the UK and increasing the support and communication that they receive, the UK government would be simultaneously decreasing the likelihood that such people would end up in situations of modern slavery, and the likelihood that they would try to remain hidden from authorities. After all, 'there may be no easier way for the international community to meet its responsibility to protect than by providing asylum and other international protection on adequate terms' (Barbour and Gorlick, 2008).

5.1.2 The Border Force

Nadim and **Barak**'s stories highlight how the UN resettlement programmes provide support to refugees that is significant enough to help prevent the development of vulnerabilities that may lead to situations of modern slavery. **James**'s journey to the UK was very different to that of **Nadim** and **Barak**, and yet he also benefitted from the input of statutory systems that kept him safe when he could have otherwise become vulnerable to slavery. His story is one that involved the intervention of the Border Force upon his entry into the UK.

James grew up in Iran with a good education and was a member of the national wrestling team. He had been wanting a tattoo, but described how some Sunni Islamists consider it to be against Islamic law. Despite having always contested religion and having a disregard for Islamic laws, it was simply not possible for him to get a tattoo in Iran. However, when one of his wrestling tours took him out of the country to Georgia, he was able to get the tattoo.

> But when I got back to Iran for another competition, there was a team of supervisors to make sure that everything in the competition was happening according to Islamic means, they call it. One of the people who was controlling came to me noticing the tattoo I had and said you understand it is against Islamic law to have a tattoo that was in public. I said I don't believe in that stuff and that's why I got it and I like the tattoo. But he carried on, saying that you can't and you're not supposed to have a tattoo, you can't have a tattoo in Iran. So things got bad, they arrested me and kept me in custody and detention basically, a detention centre. They were torturing me, questioning me.

During the interview, **James** rolled up his sleeve to reveal a tattoo on his upper arm, covered by a large burn where he explained the guards had attempted to burn off the tattoo. Realising the situation **James** was in, his father managed to find the money to pay **James**'s bail which equated to around £14,000, but 'after a month of my release I found out that they had been back to my home and were asking for me and my whereabouts, saying stuff like there was a sentence for me to be hanged because I was offensive towards Islam'.

James realised then that it was not safe for him to stay in Iran as, should he be found, he would receive the death penalty for getting his tattoo. For **James**, his conflict was not one of war, like **Nadim** and **Barak**, but was a conflict with religious law. The conflict then limited his choices: his options were to remain in Iran where he would be hanged, or to find a way out of the country via illegitimate means in order to circumnavigate being identified at the border. His family managed to put together enough money to pay a smuggler to get him out of the country; this smuggler took **James** illegally from Iran to Turkey, where he was then left to find his own way.

After arriving in Turkey, **James** paid another $500 to get a boat to Greece, but found he could not get status there, so walked until he reached France where he stayed in Calais for approximately nine months. **James** described how he spent the whole time in Calais living in a small tent, even when the temperature dropped well below zero. There was nowhere to shower, he didn't have enough food, and he had to rely on candles to provide light. He explained how there were large numbers of 'agents' operating from Calais, claiming that they were able to assist people in crossing the border. Sometimes they would deceive people who could not afford to pay, offering to help them cross the border but, in reality, simply using them as a decoy. The agents would give them instructions but were essentially sending them into a trap to be arrested as a distraction so the agents could assist those who were paying to covertly get around the guards. **James** also described instances where agents would separate husbands and wives, telling them it was safer to travel separately; they would help the husbands onto the back of lorries in return for cash, and then keep the wives behind, holding them in sexual exploitation. He found it extremely difficult to talk about the time he spent living in Calais, and explained that there were occasions when he and others tried to intervene in some of the situations where he saw people being exploited, but that this always brought violence in retaliation, so he had to be very careful in deciding whether or not to put himself at risk.

Along with wanting to escape the terrible conditions he was living in and the constant exploitation he witnessed, **James** described how he desperately wanted to get to the UK because he was able to speak the language and without those language skills, he felt he would really struggle anywhere else.

> I had to find my way to hide in the lorry obviously. Unfortunately, I had to make an incision. I tore the cover of the back of the lorry in order to get into the lorry. Obviously once the driver found out, when we were in the UK, that there was a tear in the back of the lorry, from there he informed the immigration officers who came and removed me from the lorry and took me to a deportation centre in Portsmouth and [I] was kept for a while then in a hostel in Cardiff. I was arrested by the immigration officers.

Although **James** was initially arrested by the immigration officers, they helped him to begin the asylum process and, because of his experiences in Iran meaning he could not safely return, he was granted leave to remain in the UK.

James faced similar issues to those who did go on to experience modern slavery such as those discussed in chapter four, including living through conflict and experiencing the resulting limitation of choices and lack of support network. This was particularly evident when he was faced with the choices of either staying in Iran and facing the death penalty or trying to find a way out of the country. While he was lucky in that he managed to find a relatively safe route to the UK, upon arrival, his choices were removed almost entirely after being identified and arrested by immigration officers. For **James**, unlike other respondents, despite the removal of choices, he ended up in safety. The immigration officers successfully engaged with **James** and supported him to begin the asylum process. Their recognition of his situation, coupled with successful partnership work helped to ensure that **James** remained safe and did not need to seek employment or accommodation through illegitimate routes which could have left him vulnerable to exploitation.

5.1.3 Restricted repatriation

James fled Iran because he was sentenced to be hanged. After arriving in the UK, he was granted leave to remain because of the danger he would have faced if he was repatriated. However, there are many whose asylum claims are unsuccessful and, with a negative asylum decision, are returned to the country that they fled. With the knowledge that repatriation is always a possibility, many live in constant fear of being repatriated and are unable to settle or integrate into their lives in the UK (discussed further in chapter six). To comment on the choice of terminology, 'repatriation' or 'removal' are used throughout this title where others may use 'deportation'. In legal terms, deportation is a process of repatriation used only in cases where the person in question poses a danger to the public.

This fear was something that **Nadia** and **Ofira** faced, but because they were both from Eritrea where there is forced military conscription, the Home Office rarely repatriates Eritrean nationals. In Eritrea, everyone is subject to a draft to the military service. Children—both boys and girls—begin to get called up in the last year of school. They will go on to finish their education at the military camp, which is in the middle of the desert. **Kafu**, a legal caseworker supporting asylum seekers explained that, unlike other countries with forced military conscription, there is no time limit on serving in Eritrea. 'You do military service for a number of years and then they are on the reserve list for life, but [the time served] can be extended and extended and extended.' Some children will drop out of school in order to avoid the draft, but without finishing their education they find it difficult to get employment.

Ofira was recruited in Eritrea to undertake domestic work for a family in Qatar and saw the job as an opportunity to avoid the military draft. The family brought her to London with them to work as their maid. **Ofira** did not like the family and was unhappy with the way she was treated; however, she feared returning to Eritrea because she was subject to the draft. In this case, conflict with her employers caused **Ofira** to flee her employment, but the structures in place in her home country meant that she was too afraid to return home. Although **Ofira** was not sure of her employment rights when she arrived in the UK, the description she gave implied that she held an overseas domestic worker visa, or 'tied visa' meaning that she did not have the option to easily change her employer (overseas domestic worker visas are discussed further in chapter six).

Overseas domestic workers in private households are exempt from numerous UK labour regulations including a maximum weekly working time and restrictions on the duration of night work. Further, a legal loophole means they are often paid under the national minimum wage (Demetriou, 2015). In 2012, the UK government introduced the 'tied visa' for domestic workers which further compounded the restrictions imposed on them. The tied visa means that the employee's legal status is tied to a named employer, therefore restricting their ability to leave their employment if it becomes exploitative. An amendment was made in 2016 which means that workers could change employers but only if their original six- month visa was still valid, meaning there is little time for an issue to arise, the worker to report the abuse, then commence and conclude the legal action against the employer. Further, the worker would require their passport to prove their identity, and passports are commonly confiscated by employers (Kalyaan, 2021).

In this sense, this visa system limited **Ofira**'s choices, as her legal options were either to stay with her employer where she was being mistreated, or return to Eritrea. Neither of these were outcomes that **Ofira** wanted and both would have left her in a situation of exploitation. However, because of the military draft in Eritrea, the UK Home Office rarely repatriates Eritrean nationals and, while **Ofira** was still waiting for an asylum decision at the time of my interview with her caseworker, it is likely that she will be able to remain in the UK. As such, a lack of chartered removal to Eritrea was a government policy that prevented **Ofira** from being returned to her home country where she would be exploited, and it allowed her to circumnavigate the restrictive and potentially exploitative aspects of the tied visa system.

While **Ofira** was not repatriated after leaving the employer to which her visa tied her, many others under this visa system are not so lucky. Under the tied visa system, employees do not have the option to change their employers (other than through the limited means offered by the 2016 amendment), meaning that should they become unhappy with their employment, for example if it becomes exploitative, their only options are to remain in the exploitative employment, or return to their home country where many may face exploitation. This system is one way through which the UK government risks encouraging exploitative working conditions and is an issue covered in more detail in chapter six.

Like **Ofira**, **Nadia** was also from Eritrea. She had the choice of accepting the conscription or looking for a way to flee Eritrea; she chose the latter option and managed to escape the country to Italy. However, once she was in Italy, she was raped by an Italian police officer and fell pregnant with his child. Out of fear, **Nadia** felt unable to stay in Italy and continued her journey until she arrived in the UK. It is unlikely that **Nadia** will be returned to Eritrea because of the military draft; however, at the time of my interview with her caseworker, she was awaiting a decision on whether she would be returned to Italy, even though she was raped by an officer of the law there. This is due to the Dublin Regulation, adopted in 2003, which allows EU countries to require another country to accept responsibility for an asylum claim if the person has entered that other EU country or made a claim there. It is important to note that these regulations ceased to apply in the UK from the end of 2020 as a result of Brexit.

Nadia's initial reason for fleeing was to avoid conscription, a structural issue that is inextricably linked to conflict, be it in response to immediate conflict or in preparation. Fleeing caused her to become vulnerable as she was no longer in a country that she knew, she had no support, and she did not speak the language. The lack of chartered removal to Eritrea from the UK means that it is unlikely that **Nadia** will be returned there, and this is a positive step as it would mean that the government was not returning her to a situation of military exploitation. However, should the Home Office choose to remove **Nadia** to Italy, they would be putting her at risk of repercussions relating to her rape. Although **Nadia** has not suffered modern slavery, her vulnerabilities were taken advantage of by the police officer who raped her, and should she be returned to Italy, her experience of the police there may encourage her to avoid anyone in a position of authority. Such a situation would leave her to rely on strangers for assistance, a position in which she would be highly vulnerable to exploitation, and whereby her fear of authority would limit her options for seeking statutory support.

This section has referred to stories from the interviews in which the respondents fled to the UK after experiencing conflict, but who did not suffer modern slavery. It relates to those who could have been at serious risk of modern slavery, but where the intervention of UK government systems and agencies successfully reduced these risks (although, at the time of the interviews, **Ofira** and **Nadia** were currently safe, they were awaiting the outcome of the Home Office's decisions which could still put them at risk).

5.2 Searching for safety in the wake of failing systems

This section reviews more respondents who fled conflict and came to the UK without experiencing modern slavery. However, it concentrates on those respondents whose risk of slavery was reduced *despite* UK government policies placing them in vulnerable situations. It considers how strangers and NGOs stepped in to assist in situations where the UK statutory agencies failed to provide sufficient support to keep these individuals safe. By outlining these findings, I demonstrate how in some situations, government systems put individuals at direct risk of modern slavery, and it is only with the intervention of others—strangers or NGOs—that they are kept safe. This is particularly prominent through the asylum system which removes agency and leaves asylum seekers in a precarious position whereby, if they conform to the rules of the asylum system, they have no control over their own futures.

5.2.1 The support of strangers

The following examples are of respondents who remained safe in the UK due to the assistance of complete strangers. For **Sakti**, this assistance came both in fleeing conflict and after arriving in the UK, while for **Oscar**, the assistance came purely after arriving in the UK. The assistance received by both respondents helped to significantly reduce the danger they faced, but particularly for **Oscar**, this assistance reduced vulnerabilities to modern slavery.

Sakti was Serbian. She grew up in Bosnia and was working as a surgeon when the war broke out in 1992. She recalled growing up in a calm and peaceful country until the war started and it became dangerous for anyone living there.

> Then suddenly here all Serbs are taken on [to a] stadium. Half of them is killed. There were some of my professors who were Serbs. They were brought, killed. They, there were things which were awful you know.

There were huge amounts of casualties due to the war and not enough surgeons, with most of them fleeing the conflict. Although it was extremely dangerous, **Sakti** stayed in Sarajevo to work in the hospital.

> Most of the doctors had left and they didn't have enough so they made three shifts ... I work forty-eight hours meaning I spent all twenty-four hours in trauma centre dealing with everything, children and adults, and then another twenty-four hours I would go on paediatric ward. In between I was the one who had to go with the bandages and you know do all the review of all wards. And you know it was very dangerous because you're going between hospitals and shelling is all the time. You never know when something can come down and kill you. I survived.

Sakti recalled one time working in the hospital when there was no water or electricity and it was below freezing. She described there being an abundance of journalists harassing the hospital staff and taking photos of operations, to the point where **Sakti** chose to operate by lamp light so as not to attract their attention. However, there was one journalist 'who really helped us a lot. And then he started bringing us food and he looked after us and he was the one who told me that it's after two years he said you really don't have to stay any more, your life is in danger'. It was at this point that **Sakti** began to realise that there was not much more she could do for the people she was helping. People were coming to the hospital less often, and the situation had improved since the beginning of the war.

The journalist offered to help **Sakti** to leave the country, but her mother still lived in Sarajevo and she refused to leave without her. She applied to the government twice for permission for her mother to leave, but both times was refused on the premise that if her mother left, **Sakti** would likely leave too, and the government wanted her to stay and work. Here, **Sakti** realised that the war had restricted the options available to her: she could stay in Sarajevo, working in danger in the hospital, or accept the assistance of this stranger to escape, a possibility that would likely never occur again.

Sakti wanted to accept the assistance of this journalist, but explained to him that she could not leave without her mother. In response to this, the journalist managed to smuggle **Sakti**'s mother out of the country in the back of his car, returning the next day to collect **Sakti**. He drove her straight to the airport, despite the fact they had to drive through gunfire. **Sakti** described how there was an empty plane that had been used to supply aid to the area, and the journalist managed to convince the pilot to take **Sakti** back with him. The plane flew to Italy and from there **Sakti** travelled on to London where she had friends. She explained that did not think she would ever have been able to leave Sarajevo without the help of this journalist.

Once **Sakti** arrived in the UK, a reference provided by this same journalist counted towards her being granted indefinite leave to remain (thus being granted permanent status and not being subject to immigration control). However, after receiving leave to remain, **Sakti** received no support or guidance from any statutory agencies. She had a skilled profession but had to turn to strangers for advice on where she should look for work and how to apply. She was lucky that she was able to find legitimate work, but it is clear to see how other people in **Sakti**'s position might be more vulnerable. Relying on strangers to help find work could easily lead to exploitative situations if those offers of help are not genuine.

Unlike **Sakti**, **Oscar** did not rely on anyone's help to get him to the UK. However, once in the UK, he found himself in a vulnerable situation and it was the assistance of a stranger that helped to keep him safe. **Oscar** was from Gaza and had moved to the UK to complete a master's degree. He then returned to Gaza to take up his old, high-status job, but was refused the position he had previously held and was unable to find alternative employment. Along with struggling to find work, **Oscar** and his family had no safe housing. He described how he had a house, but because of the bombs, it was safer to live in a tent in a refugee community. He recalled going back to his house and narrowly escaping before it was bombed.

> I went to my home to bring some things [back to the tent] and I got a call on my landline to say you have to leave your home within five minutes. Leave everything and just go. And I said ok and I did that and in five minutes it was destroyed.

Oscar knew that he and his family could go and stay with his parents, but he commented that he felt uncomfortable asking for help in the long term, and that even though they had housing, it was still unsafe. 'I have parents and they invited us [to] go but we already went there and it was very dangerous, there were car bombs everywhere, so I preferred to stay in a tent so I lived there.'

Oscar was left in a very difficult situation where he had to decide whether to stay in Gaza where he had no safe home and no prospects of work, or flee the country in the hope of a safer life. He chose to flee Gaza, leaving his wife and children living in a tent in the hope that he could come to the UK, find safe housing and employment, and bring them across to be with him. He had previously been a student in the UK, meaning that his English was fluent and he knew a few people in the country. However, he described how his priorities had drastically changed when he came to the UK for the second time.

> For me, because I came here like asylum seeker this time. So when I first came [when he was coming to be a student] my hope was to finish my study and get my qualification and that happened and I was hoping to come back again for PhD but it's different now. I don't want PhD now I want to get documents, because if I get documents I can find a job and work and invite my other family. Otherwise I will stay here for unlimited time and have nothing. I can't leave. I can't. So the first important thing for me was to get documents.

Oscar was clear that his previous goals were irrelevant when he arrived in the UK for the second time. This time all that mattered to him was that he found work so that he could bring his family out of danger and that they could all be reunited.

Oscar managed to secure a visa to the UK and organise travel with the intention of applying for asylum once he arrived. After he had arrived in the UK, he was able to ask around through informal networks for information on what was required of him, which led him to contact the Home Office straight away to apply for asylum. After his asylum interview, he was provided with documentation that allowed him to live in the UK for five years, 'but once I've got my document from the Home Office, just go.'

Oscar was provided with no advice on where he should go or information on any agencies that may have been able to offer him support, reflective of **Sakti**'s experience. He was lucky that he spoke English and had lived in the UK before, because he had acquaintances that he was able to contact; however, he was only able to find somewhere to stay for two nights before becoming homeless. He continued applying for jobs, both those which were relevant to his master's degree and those that were not, but he continued to be unsuccessful. While he was applying for jobs, he encouraged his wife and children to make the journey so that they could join him in the UK, with the hope that he would have sorted housing and accommodation by the time they arrived.

> They know nothing about the situation here. They knew nothing that when they came here they'd be homeless like me. And I needed them to come, to help me be not homeless . . . And when I collected her from the

> airport I had nowhere to go, even with children. So I collected her [his wife] with a warm welcome and then take them, with no place to go.

His wife and children made the journey, but **Oscar** was still unemployed and homeless when they arrived, six months after being granted asylum by the Home Office.

> I had nowhere to go with luggage, with children, no. And she [Oscar's wife] . . . was crying but I had nowhere to go. And we were there an hour, two hours, three hours, then there was a lady who just came two or three times and she asked us what are you doing here? I've seen you here for hours now. And I said we have nowhere to go. She took me to a masjid, a mosque.

The people at the mosque showed **Oscar**'s family generosity, with some offering money and others offering a place to stay for the night. The family went home with one of the men from the mosque who provided beds and food for them all overnight and took them to the council the next day so that they could apply for housing. From this meeting, **Oscar** and his family were granted space in a homeless shelter.

Because **Oscar** had been given no information when he received his documents from the Home Office, he knew nothing about applying for housing until this stranger offered him support and assistance. It was only because of the chance meeting with the woman in the street taking the family to the mosque that **Oscar** and his family eventually found accommodation in this shelter. Frustratingly, with fluent English, **Oscar** felt confident that he would have been able to have had this meeting with the council himself straight after receiving his documents if only he had known that was what was required of him. If he had been informed of this upon receiving asylum, he would have been able to go straight to the council offices and apply for housing instead of spending so long homeless. Because he was offered no information with his documentation from the Home Office, without this intervention from a stranger, **Oscar** would have remained unemployed and homeless even though the Home Office had recognised him as a refugee and granted him asylum.

The shelter that **Oscar** was housed in then assisted him in applying for his own house, which he was eventually successful in achieving. His children were accepted in local schools, his wife attends college, and **Oscar** now has a job supporting other refugees who are going through similar situations to his own. **Oscar**'s story exemplifies how having refugee status does not necessarily equate to safety in the UK. Although his language skills meant that he could communicate with ease, he still struggled, not knowing where he could go for assistance, and finding himself homeless even though he had interacted with government agencies and was recognised as a refugee. Being homeless and looking for work is a position in which many may become vulnerable to offers of labour which risk becoming exploitative (discussed further in chapter six). **Oscar** was fortunate that the stranger who offered to help him provided him with legitimate assistance, but this is not always the case, as **Ifra**'s story exemplified in chapter four. He was lucky to have received help from the strangers in the mosque, but the fact that he needed to rely on these strangers highlights a real flaw in the asylum process. **Oscar** had been granted asylum without being provided with adequate information or support which led directly to him being unaware of his entitlements or where to go for help, and which then left him homeless.

5.2.2 Non-statutory support

Section 5.2.1 focuses on the stories of **Sakti** and **Oscar** who benefitted from the support of strangers when government systems failed to keep them safe. This section considers those respondents who turned to non-statutory agencies for support in the UK when the statutory agencies were failing to provide the assistance they required.

Verity was from Somalia and was of Bajuni—an ethnic group that faces severe discrimination in the country—ethnicity. **Verity**'s caseworker described that there are often cases of 'majority clans coming by boat to their territories and saying this is now our land, you're coming to work for us. Or being taken from traditional Bajuni territory back to other bits of Somalia'. **Verity** had been raped approximately 100 times by members of these majority clans, and her family had been badly attacked. She had a relative who had managed to escape Somalia to Europe and knew of the terrible situation that remained there. Because **Verity** was the oldest daughter in the family, she was deemed to be the most at risk, and this family member paid for her to leave Somalia and get to the UK. For **Verity**, this meant leaving the rest of her family, including her child, back in Somalia.

Like many of the stories, **Verity**'s highlights a lack of choice. Her options were to remain in Somalia with her family, where she would continue to suffer repeated rapes and extreme violence, or leave and try and make a life for herself in the UK. After weighing up the risks of leaving, **Verity** decided that it was safer to move than try to stay in Somalia, and this option would not have been available to her if not for this offer of assistance from her relative.

However, once she reached the UK, she had a hard time making government authorities believe her story. 'She claimed [asylum], was comprehensively disbelieved, and told you're Kenyan, we don't believe a word you're saying.' **Verity** turned to a legal charity to support her through her case. **Kafu** was **Verity**'s caseworker and recalled **Verity**'s story being particularly harrowing. **Kafu** noted that:

> [T]his woman appeared and said she was Bajuni from one of the Bajuni islands, her family had been very badly attacked, she had been raped about 100 times by members of one of the majority clans . . . She had horrific scarring. Kind of burns everywhere.

Kafu explained how in **Verity**'s initial Home Office interview, she was provided with:

> a male translator from Kenya who had tried to claim that Bajuni is the same as Swahili [Bajuni is a specific dialect] . . . and [she] had felt very, very inhibited about talking in front of a man and particularly about bits that had happened to her.

This lack of understanding or empathy from the Home Office caused **Verity** further unnecessary stress after she had fled a horrific situation in the hope of finding safety. Eventually, with the support of **Kafu**, **Verity** got through the legal process and was successful in claiming asylum in the UK. **Verity**'s vulnerabilities were evident, yet the inappropriate actions taken by the Home Office in their choice of interpreter, along with the culture of disbelief, only served to cause more distress and confusion relating to her story. If the statutory response had been more suitable, **Verity** would not have had to rely on an NGO to assist her in gaining legal status.

Gamba, **Fredrika**, and **Isaac** were all also reliant on support from NGOs. They received support from drop-in centres and were clear in their interviews that without this support they would be very vulnerable because they were struggling to survive on the assistance provided to them by the UK government.

Gamba was from Cameroon and his father had been a university lecturer and part of a political dissident group that **Gamba** was also a member of. **Gamba** was preparing to go to the UK to study at university and had applied for a visa when his father was taken into hospital. When **Gamba** went to visit, his father told him that, for his own safety, he must get the next flight to the UK, leaving him with no time to say goodbye to anyone. After being in the UK for two weeks, **Gamba** got news that his father 'died in the hospital under military guard, making sure that he was not administered [treated] until he died'. His mother fled to Nigeria and warned **Gamba** that he was also wanted for his political activism.

Gamba was able to pay for his own plane ticket to leave Cameroon, but he raised a pertinent point. He commented that for many, money may not be the problem when it comes to leaving a perilous situation, the issue is legality. Where **Gamba** was able to obtain a visa to travel to the UK, several of his friends were denied visas, which meant that they could not buy a plane ticket. As a result, they must either pay a substantially higher price to risk the hazardous journey across the Mediterranean by boat, or simply try to hide.

> I could say for sure that me flying to England was the cheaper option. The people who take the Mediterranean Sea pay four or five times what I have paid. So if you are not well off you can't make these journeys and you actually trek to the next village or to the next country if it's close by. If not you might just find yourself hiding in Cameroon or somewhere.

This means that those who cannot obtain a visa are more likely to suffer exploitative conditions as they do everything they can to leave their country under the radar via illegitimate methods. For those who can afford it, like **James**, discussed in section 5.1.2, this may mean an upfront fee for smuggling, while those who cannot afford this fee might, like **Hattie**, discussed in chapter four, make a deal to work to pay off the debt and become trapped in situations of debt bondage, trying to pay off a debt that never decreases.

After hearing of his father's death and receiving the warning that he was also in danger, **Gamba** applied for asylum so that he could stay in the UK after his visa expired, knowing that if he went back to Cameroon he would likely be killed for his involvement in the same political dissident group. He discussed how difficult it is to be an asylum seeker in the UK. Although he is fluent in English, and this has no doubt eased the process, he had no family or friends to meet or support him when he arrived. His mother had fled Cameroon to Nigeria for her own safety and, although they tried to keep in touch, sometimes this was very difficult.

> [As asylum seekers] we are given a budget [£40.85] per week. That is for breakfast, lunch, and dinner and whatever else you might need, so . . . at times you might need to sacrifice food to call her.

Gamba described how he was grateful to be safe from the trouble he faced in Cameroon, but that he felt that the asylum process was there simply to try and find flaws in claimants' accounts. This reflects **Verity**'s description of the culture of disbelief. **Gamba** stated:

> At least I'm safe, but to say that it's been fine is a lie . . . You still have many people going through the asylum process which is a fault-finding mission where your caseworker is supposed to be there to help you but just picks faults up in what you said and whatever you say you need to prove it. Now who runs away from their home and thinks about carrying proof along? . . . That would be the last thing you think about bringing along. But whatever you say you need to prove it. And the burden of proof is so high unlike court where you are innocent until proven guilty. In asylum you are guilty of telling lies until you prove yourself telling the truth.

Gamba highlighted how the home countries of many asylum seekers do not have welfare systems, and many are unaware of UK social policy. The asylum seekers' priorities are to escape danger and find a safe place to live where they can then find work to support themselves; the concept of a benefits system is unknown to them. **Gamba** discussed how difficult it was to be an asylum seeker in a system that assumes claimants are lying and which considers their motivation for being in the UK as simply to apply for benefits.

> We don't come from a system where we have a welfare system in our own countries, so you have to work to earn whatever you have to eat. So there is no one coming here hoping. We are not travelling here knowing you get free money. If anyone is coming here they are coming for safety first and then they will look at ways to better their lives. So it's really hard to be honest.

At the time of our interview, **Gamba** had been in the asylum process for six years as his claims keep getting rejected. He knows that he will be killed if he returns to Cameroon, so is not willing to give up, and would rather be homeless and destitute in the UK than risk going back. Under UK rules, it is prohibited for him to work or return to his education in the UK, which means that he has learned to survive on the small government stipend. However, after being detained recently, **Gamba**'s government support was revoked, meaning that he is no longer provided with money or housing and, as a result, was set to become destitute and homeless.

Gamba discovered a local drop-in centre and attends for the support and advice that he requires, but which he has been denied by the statutory agencies that he has approached. The lack of support provided to **Gamba** has resulted in him relying fully on this drop-in centre, and he is even living with someone who volunteers there. When asked where he would be without the support of the drop-in centre and this individual, **Gamba** stated:

> I would be homeless. I would depend on charity ... There are a lot of people like that, especially people that come from places like Iraq, Iran, Syria, Afghanistan. The Home Office knows that they can't support them. They reject their claim and kick them out of accommodation ... If you are caught working you go to jail.

Gamba went on to describe how communities of asylum seekers tend to work together to support each other in finding work when they struggle to make ends meet on the government stipend. As most asylum seekers are prohibited from working in the UK, this work is likely to be precarious and poorly paid with no opportunity to negotiate conditions. However, for those receiving no statutory support other than £40.85 per week, or nothing at all if their claim has been rejected, then it is clear to see how these offers might be tempting. Of course, there is always the risk that these offers of work are not legitimate and, like **Ifra**, may lead them into situations of modern slavery. However, should these individuals find themselves being exploited, because they are not meant to be working they then have no way to report or request help without facing punitive measures (discussed further in chapters six and seven). Yet, for those who are homeless and destitute and too afraid to return to their home country, such a risk might appear to be their only option.

Fredrika's experience of being in the UK is very similar to **Gamba**'s. She was from Uganda and originally came to the UK to study, but once in the

UK faced family expectation to get married. Despite **Fredrika**'s protests, her family arranged the marriage and **Fredrika** was married to a man for around four years, during which time he was aggressive and abusive towards her. She eventually left this marriage and disclosed to her family that she was homosexual. Her family rejected her because of this admission; homosexuality is illegal in Uganda and she was considered to have shamed the family. Because of this reaction, and because of the illegality of homosexuality and the stigma and violence experienced by those in Uganda who identify as such, **Fredrika** was too afraid to return to Uganda and instead claimed asylum in the UK.

Fredrika's initial asylum claim was rejected, which was devastating for her as she knew that it was unsafe for her to return to Uganda. Although the main reason she wanted to claim asylum was because she is homosexual and, as such, her life would be at risk in Uganda, she did not include this information in her initial claim.

> Well my first claim was not initially being gay because I was really scared to come out, so now that I have to put in a fresh claim. I have to say that it's part of everything, it's part of my initial application [is] my sexuality and I need to put that out there because I feel like I was trapped in something because coming out in my country and my culture is unheard of and I come from a Christian background so it's a bit tricky. Initially I was scared to come out because you never know what will happen to you.

When I interviewed her, **Fredrika** had been in the asylum system for four years, waiting for a decision. She fills her time by volunteering to support other asylum seekers and refugees which, although she enjoys, can sometimes be frustrating and disheartening as she helps people with their applications and watches them get accepted while she continues to wait for a decision.

> You'd be helping somebody which is coming to the country and got their status in like a month and . . . you've been waiting four years, nearly five and you have to deal with people like that. Well I help them with a big smile on my face but sometimes it's still frustrating because their lives are going to move forwards and mine is stuck.

However, this frustration is only a small part of the emotional turmoil that **Fredrika** faces every day as she lives her life completely uncertain of her future.

After **Fredrika**'s asylum application was rejected, all statutory support was withdrawn. She became homeless and was prohibited from finding employment or continuing with her education. With these restrictions, **Fredrika** was desperate. She had nowhere to live and needed money to survive but was unable to access legitimate employment. These vulnerabilities made her a prime target for people seeking to benefit from her exploitation. Fortunately, she was identified and taken in by a local women's shelter and now survives on £10 a week that she is given by a local charity; she regularly visits a drop-in centre for company and is in the process of reapplying for asylum. As in **Oscar**'s story, this reflects the kindness of people who have no statutory responsibility to help, but who provide support in a way that significantly reduces the vulnerabilities caused by flawed government policies.

Isaac was another respondent who was supported by a drop-in centre when he was left unsupported. His father was a diplomat in the Democratic Republic of the Congo (DRC) where he faced trouble because of his job. As a family, they fled to Russia where they stayed together for several years. His mother died in Russia, and his father did not want to take **Isaac** and his sister back to the DRC. In 2011, **Isaac**'s father told him and his sister that they were going on holiday to the UK and sent them to stay with someone he knew; **Isaac** had no choice in the matter. That was the last time he saw or spoke to his father. **Isaac**'s sister is still young, and he has had a son since arriving in the UK; he feels a lot of pressure to try and support them, but while in the asylum system he was prohibited from finding employment.

Because **Isaac** has a son and sister in the UK, it was incredibly important to him that he was able to stay in the country; his only other family is his father and he has no contact with him and is uncertain if he is even still alive. When **Isaac** was told he needed to claim asylum, he was unaware of what this meant. He had no knowledge of the system, but his desperation to stay in the UK meant that he felt pressure to provide a version of events most likely to allow him to remain. In doing this he provided false details to the Home Office.

> The day [at] the Home Office, I don't know what is asylum and when I came ... I didn't give my real name. I said I came from Congo straight away, but I came from Congo, Russia, here. I said all this, but they found out and stopped everything, because when they got my son's paperwork it came out, my fingerprint which showed when my dad's job finished. We didn't have any choice and gave the fingerprints and they found out

> everything—that I was lying, this and that, and they got my real name. I told them what they found out but by then they wanted a reason.

Because **Isaac** had been given no information prior to his Home Office interview, and was unaware of the purpose or potential outcomes, he was wary of the system and it was this reluctance to put his trust in strangers that caused him to give false information. Now he is aware of the asylum system, what it means, and what is required of him, he has since put in another claim and is waiting for the outcome. Both **Isaac** and **Fredrika** found themselves reluctant to tell the Home Office the true version of events straight away, partly because they had no real understanding of why the Home Office needed this information and how they might be treated as a result (especially for **Fredrika** who had already suffered after sharing with her family that she was homosexual), and partly because they wanted to provide a backstory that they thought the Home Office wanted to hear. This reflects Christie's notion of the ideal victim (1986) and how individuals are more likely to be classed and treated as victims if they were weak and passive in the situation that befell them. This is discussed further in chapter seven.

When I interviewed him, **Isaac** had been waiting for over seven years to get status in the UK and is rarely provided with any information on the progress of his case. After making his applications, **Isaac** received no information on what he was entitled to or of any organisations that may have been able to assist him. He described how he uses his weekly government stipend to support himself, his sister, and his baby, but that the money is not enough and he is desperate for more, but prohibited from seeking legal work.

Isaac noted how he knew plenty of people who were working while they waited for their asylum decision, but that because he had previously been detained and released with no explanation as to why, he was not willing to take a risk in working, even though any extra money would be a huge benefit. He described that many people were willing to help others from their country into finding illegitimate employment. These comments are resonant of Bloch's findings from research with undocumented migrants living in England (2013). In studying the experiences of seventy-five young respondents, Bloch found evidence of co-ethnic networks of undocumented individuals supporting each other to find work. Interestingly, Bloch's research also indicated that those most at risk of exploitation were those who were unable to speak English and working in a co-ethnic enclave, and who therefore had the greatest dependency on others. This reflects **Ifra**'s experience (described in chapter four) of looking for help from strangers who spoke her language. She was unable to speak English but found work with a fellow Bengali family who went on to exploit her for three years.

When there are people like **Isaac** who has survived on the government stipend (currently £40.85 per week) for seven years, it is easy to understand why some may choose to accept work while waiting for an asylum decision. In these situations, a choice must be made between respecting the law and surviving on this small amount of money, or taking a risk in accepting offers of work which must remain hidden from authority. With the latter, there is an inherent risk that this work could be exploitative as the employers hold all the power and there would be no recourse to report it or get support if the conditions were poor. This is an issue which is further addressed in chapters six and seven.

Like **Gamba** and **Fredrika**, **Isaac** is supported by a drop-in centre which he attends regularly to get the support and advice that he is not provided by statutory organisations. He has relied on this non-statutory service to discover information about the asylum system, his entitlements, and what he should expect from the system. These are all issues that should have been provided to him upon his asylum application and, without the support of this drop-in centre, **Isaac** would have been unaware of his rights or the restrictions placed on asylum seekers. Without this knowledge, he may have even sought employment which could have resulted in detention, exploitation, or both.

5.3 Conclusion

This chapter has considered those who have fled conflict and come to the UK but who have not experienced modern slavery, and it has reflected on whether these respondents have remained safe because of UK government policies, or despite them. Two methods have been highlighted through which the respondents who did not experience slavery were kept safe from it: the support of the government and statutory agencies, and the support of strangers and NGOs. While the former exemplified ways in which government structures had been successful in identifying and protecting potentially vulnerable people, the latter related to situations in which those systems had failed and the respondents remained safe only through interventions by strangers or NGOs.

Those who were kept safe because of government policies were those who were granted permission *and* support to remain in the UK. For some, this was via a UN resettlement programme where successful applicants received a level of support far beyond that offered to other asylum seekers. Others who were kept safe through governmental intervention included **James** who was identified by the Border Force upon his illegal entry to the UK and supported to begin the asylum process. His story illustrated a successful intervention by this statutory body which identified him and effectively worked with partners to maintain his safety. The final group of people kept safe by government policies related to those from countries to which the Home Office has no chartered removal. This meant that structures were in place to ensure that these individuals were not repatriated to a country where they would likely face extreme exploitation. However, on this last point, while the Home Office prevented exploitation occurring in the home country, it was not indicated through the interviews what support these individuals had been provided with and whether UK government policies had successfully kept them safe in the UK.

While some respondents were kept safe because of the input of government systems, there were also plenty of examples from the interviews in which government systems put people at risk; this was particularly true of asylum seekers who received support wholly incomparable to that received by those on a resettlement programme. For these individuals, regardless of whether they had received asylum or were still waiting on a decision, there was a significant lack of support from statutory agencies. This lack of support increased their vulnerabilities towards modern slavery, and it was only the assistance of strangers or NGOs that kept them safe and informed of their rights.

This chapter has highlighted the failings of government policies to support the most at risk and emphasises how even those who have received a positive asylum decision are often not provided with enough information or support to keep them safe. Chapter six goes on to discuss these risk factors in more detail, looking at how some UK policies could actually serve to increase the likelihood of some individuals going on to experience modern slavery.

Chapter six
Generating the conditions for risk

Chapter four addressed the vulnerabilities caused by conflict and how these vulnerabilities may lead someone directly, or indirectly, into modern slavery. Chapter five considered the ways that individuals have stayed safe from slavery after fleeing a conflict situation to the UK. This chapter turns to look at how risk factors, both to modern slavery and in a more general sense, can be generated and exacerbated by UK policies.

This chapter first considers intersectionality and structural dynamics to understand the interplay between personal characteristics and situational contexts in driving modern slavery. I argue that there is no single or intersecting identity trait that is always responsible for increasing the likelihood that one person will become more vulnerable to modern slavery than another. Instead, it is the context of the situation that should be prioritised in order to identify risk. Contexts that limit people's choices and reduce their agency are those that are most likely to generate a risk to modern slavery; this is regardless of the identity of the person in question.

Second, I consider how some of the UK's restrictive policies significantly increase the risk of individuals suffering exploitation and modern slavery by generating these specific vulnerabilities. I illustrate these points with examples from the respondents. In section 6.2.1 I consider the modern slavery response in the UK and some of its strengths and weaknesses, focusing on how modern slavery has been conflated with immigration crime, and how the long decision-making process can impact those who have already suffered modern slavery. I then go on to look at the asylum system in section 6.2.2 as a context which generates vulnerabilities for those seeking safety in the UK, including giving thought to the long wait for decisions to be made, why people might be encouraged to lie about their experiences, how a lack of information about the system can increase risk, and the psychological impact of the system on those seeking asylum. Section 6.2.3 then gives consideration to the overseas domestic worker tied visa system and how it can generate risk by tying someone's status to their employer. Section

From Conflict to Modern Slavery. Alicia Heys, Oxford University Press. © Alicia Heys 2023.
DOI: 10.1093/oso/9780192846549.003.0006

6.3 brings all these discussions together to emphasise how these systems in the UK limit people's choices and support networks, leaving them to make risky decisions which may lead them into exploitative situations and thus mirror the vulnerabilities generated by conflict which can push people towards situations of modern slavery.

6.1 Intersectionality and structural dynamics

The simplest thing to derive from the findings discussed in chapters four and five is that no two people's experiences of fleeing a conflict situation are the same, and that it is simply not plausible to make generalisations. Different backgrounds, choices, and identities lead to different experiences, and it is here that notions of intersectionality should be discussed.

Intersectionality was developed in response to feminist discourses which grouped women by gender alone. Such a grouping was criticised by black feminists for failing to understand how the experiences of race significantly separated black and white women's struggles where, like white women, black women were subordinated by their gender, but also, unlike white women, by the colour of their skin. Their claims were that feminism suggested that all women's experiences were the same, citing the white woman's experience as representative, and overlooking the further struggles faced by non-white women.

Crenshaw (1989) highlighted that black women's experiences were different to white women's and that, as such, they should not be categorised together. Instead, she argued that the experience of black women was to be found where racism and sexism intersected. This began the conception of intersectionality whereby gender is no longer considered an isolated category, but attention is now given to the way it intersects with other categories of identity as a method of understanding inequality (Conaghan, 2009). The purpose of intersectionality was to show that people could have multiple identities at the same time—such as being young, black, female, and living with a disability, for example—rather than each of these identities existing in independence of the others. By understanding this coexistence of identities within one person's experience, intersectionality is able to go beyond analyses of discrimination that are based only on a single identity trait.

Intersectionality is no longer concerned only with the experiences of women, but is used to highlight how the intersections of different identities can lead any group to experience inequality. To relate intersectionality to the research undertaken for this title, it can be used to highlight the intersections at which people are most likely to experience inequality to an extent that leads them into a situation of modern slavery. However, when considering who may be vulnerable to situations of modern slavery, the literature tends to stay vague, claiming that people become victims of modern slavery because they had previously been vulnerable 'in some way'. This is not a helpful assertion and fails to highlight any specific vulnerabilities.

Modern slavery studies often tend to focus on the end result of the slavery rather than the root causes (e.g. Craig et al., 2007; Bales and Trodd, 2008; Kara, 2009; Murphy, 2014; Human Trafficking Foundation, 2015, 2016; Anti-Slavery International, 2017). They concentrate on individual forms of slavery, such as child slavery, sexual exploitation, or labour exploitation, meaning that the reasons that the slavery occurred are often overlooked. There is, of course, also literature that focuses predominantly on root causes (e.g. Phillips, 2015; LeBaron et al., 2019). However, there is a dearth of research about conflict as a driver of modern slavery, especially notions of conflict that extend beyond war, as discussed in chapter three. The research in this title overcomes this flaw by looking at conflict as a start point of the development of vulnerabilities as opposed to using the end point of the experience of slavery as the focus.

In academic literature on modern slavery, intersectionality is rarely a key focus. Prominent exceptions are Yea (2015) and Strauss (2016) whose work respectively provides an overview of how intersectional identity markers can create a distinction between trafficked and non-trafficked persons, and insight into how social and political categorisation can lead to vulnerabilities. These examples focus on labour exploitation; however, most references to intersectionality relating to modern slavery refer to the sexual exploitation of women and notions of victimhood. Baker (2013) and Russell (2014) both consider intersectionality in reference to the usefulness of the victimhood placed on those who have experienced slavery in the form of sexual exploitation. Baker focuses on paternalism and rescue narratives, highlighting how the implication of the word 'rescue' inevitably implies that the 'victims' are passive and lacking agency. Russell mirrors this point with regards to the use of the term 'victim', and both authors indicate how this passive victim terminology clouds the other aspects of each individual's identity, instead grouping all 'victims' as women with the same experience. These criticisms highlight how framing women in this way serves to overlook the vastly different constituent parts of their identities and is a clear reflection of Crenshaw's criticism of white feminism (1989). Agency and the impact of victim terminology are issues discussed further in chapter seven.

To use intersectionality in the context of this research involves considering the intersecting identities of the respondents in order to understand what it was about their identities that led them to be discriminated against in such a way as to become victims of modern slavery. To consider the individuals in simple categories such as gender, race, ethnicity, or religion alone would be to consider only one aspect of their identities and therefore would overlook any other facet which may have also had an important impact on their experiences of inequality. It would also suggest that all those of the same broad category, women for example, would have similar experiences in leaving their conflict and would be just as likely to experience modern slavery as one another. As the findings from this research show, that is not the case. Eighteen of the victim stories accessed through interviews were those of women, all of whom had fled conflict, and yet some of them had experienced modern slavery while others had not. This exemplifies how considerations that focus only on how the vulnerabilities of being a woman might lead to modern slavery are flawed and, to truly understand the situations, analyses must delve much deeper than this.

Intersectionality encourages the researcher to take each individual and assess how different aspects of their identity intersect. A comparison can then be made between individuals with the same identity intersections to consider whether they had similar experiences. To take the example of women, from the interviews **Ifra** and **Mahal** were both women fleeing conflict and both experienced modern slavery. However, this does not mean that being a woman fleeing conflict necessarily makes someone vulnerable to modern slavery; intersectionality encourages such an analysis to be taken further to consider other aspects of an individual's identity that could cause them to be vulnerable. **Ifra** was a woman with a high-status job as a politician who fled conflict. **Louise**'s mother was also a woman with a high-status job (a doctor) who also fled conflict; both these women experienced modern slavery. However, **Sakti** was a woman who had a high-status job (a surgeon) and fled conflict, yet she did not experience modern slavery. Again, this implies it would be invalid to claim that women with high-status jobs fleeing conflict are necessarily vulnerable to modern slavery. These examples highlight how important it is to recognise that correlation and cause are not the same. We might see a correlation between those fleeing conflict and experiencing modern slavery, but without the combination of a motivated perpetrator, a suitable target, and a conducive environment, then the vulnerability caused by fleeing conflict will not always translate into a situation of modern slavery (Barlow, 2019). A person fleeing conflict is not necessarily going to be exploited, but their vulnerability to exploitation is increased due to the lack of a protective environment or support network, combined with the way that conflict reduces the options that are available to them.

It is clear from these examples how easy it could be to keep adding more aspects of identity into the comparison in order to identify precisely which intersections cause people to be most at risk of modern slavery. However, such comparisons would quickly reach saturation and lose comprehensibility. Ehrenreich (2002:267) refers to this issue as the 'infinite regress problem: the tendency of all identity groupings to split into ever-smaller subgroups, until there seems to be no hope of any coherent category other than the individual.' As discussed by McCall (2009), intersectionality can get caught between scale and coherence. This occurs when, in order to fully compare people's experiences, the intersections of multiple aspects of people's identities must be considered, but doing so can quickly lead to incoherence when those categories become so specific and include lengthy lists of constitutive categories of identity such as race, ethnicity, religion, class, age, gender, education level, etc.

It is not possible to identify which specific intersections might cause vulnerability in a small-scale research study such as this, as there is restricted potential for comparison. While a larger-scale qualitative study of the experiences of people who have fled conflict and suffered modern slavery may help overcome this issue of comparison, it would still struggle with the issue of scale versus coherence. This research suggests that it is not possible to generate specific enough categories that both incorporate all the intersections of a person's identity while keeping the intersections broad enough to make valid comparisons.

Even though inequality continues to be complex, the practicability of intersectionality can be limiting when considered in isolation. It faces the restrictions of being unable to provide both scale and coherence, and it overlooks the impact of external factors. To consider only the vulnerabilities established due to intersecting aspects of a person's identity is to overlook some of the significant differences experienced by members of the same groups in relation to context and structural dynamics. It is only by considering all these aspects together that a true understanding of any one person's story can be fully grasped. This will mean that it will rarely be possible to make direct analytical comparisons between people's stories, because the likelihood that individuals will have the same intersecting aspects of identity and live through the same contexts and structural dynamics is extremely limited.

Conaghan (2009) argues that discussions of identity and experience should be mirrored with those of systems and processes in order to provide a balanced approach that does not overestimate the impact either of identity categories or of context or structural dynamics. She suggests that the aspects of identity and structure are inseparable and consideration must be given to them both. While the findings of this research support this to some extent (as is discussed further in chapter seven), it must be recognised that identity categories are influenced by structural issues. Hunter and de Simone (2009) argue that, in fact, it is more productive to concentrate on the context or structural dynamics of a situation than on identity categories (an idea corroborated by Cameron and Newman, 2008; and Blazek et al., 2018). Such standpoints claim that while aspects of people's identities may make them more susceptible than others to situations of modern slavery, it is the overarching structures of society that are most responsible for generating those vulnerabilities in the first instance. This is one of the key findings of this research, particularly in relation to the impact of conflict and of UK government systems in limiting choices and leaving people in situations where they must make risky decisions. The respondents who experienced modern slavery represented hugely different identity categories, but all suffered similar vulnerabilities generated by overarching structural contexts. It is therefore not possible to understand risks to modern slavery using intersectionality alone. There is no single or intersecting identity trait that is always responsible for increasing the likelihood that one person will become more vulnerable to modern slavery than another. Instead, it is the context of the situation that should be prioritised in order to identify risk.

As outlined in chapter four, conflict generates two specific vulnerabilities which increase the likelihood of a person experiencing modern slavery: reducing the options available to a person, and breaking down their support network. This chapter demonstrates that these vulnerabilities are not exclusively generated by conflicts and, in fact, there are policies in the UK that generate the same vulnerabilities and are responsible for increasing the risk that a person might become a victim of modern slavery.

6.2 The restrictive policies of the UK government

As noted in section 6.1, while advocating the importance of considering context and structural conditions alongside intersecting identities, it must also be recognised that intersectionality is contextual in the sense that inequalities caused by identity are often due to structural conditions. However, it is common that the identities of foreign nationals in the UK are overlooked. While migrants' identities are vastly different, ranging in age, gender, ethnicity, nationality, religion, and any other number of factors, once they have reached the UK they are regularly referred to as a homogenised group, as 'refugees', 'asylum seekers', or 'migrants'. This highlights the way that the UK's immigration system is essentially generating a new class of (non-) citizen (Sales, 2002). The focus here is on their identity after arriving in the UK, an identity which is limited purely to their migration status. While foreign victims of modern slavery who are identified in the UK are also commonly branded by their victim status as opposed to by their identities, when aspects of their identities are considered, they are usually in reference to their pre-exploitation selves: their levels of education or economic standing for example. In referring to these individuals' identities in this way, emphasis is placed on how vulnerabilities may have existed before their arrival in the UK, and attention is drawn away from the ways in which the UK government's systems generate new identities and contexts which encourage vulnerabilities and put people at risk of modern slavery.

The rest of this chapter investigates some of these UK contexts and how they can generate risk and thus questions how the UK government can claim that it holds modern slavery as a priority issue when it continues to perpetuate structural conditions which encourage exploitation. This section considers the specific modern slavery response in the UK and how there are still flaws in the system which continue to generate and exacerbate vulnerabilities.

6.2.1 The modern slavery response

This section outlines the current UK approach of identifying and supporting victims of modern slavery. It provides an overview of the National Referral Mechanism (NRM) and offers insights into how this has changed over time. While there was a brief interlude for two years where the modern slavery decision-making process was not divided by the immigration status of the victim, there is a clear pattern indicating that the UK's response to modern slavery is heavily tied in with its anti-immigration stance.

Conflation of modern slavery and immigration crime

As mentioned in chapter three, across Europe there has been a significant focus on limiting immigration. The Freedom Fund notes how $17 billion has been spent within Europe since 2014 (article published November 2016) on curbing immigration and asylum seeking. In the UK, this focus and money is placed on reducing the number of immigrants entering the UK as opposed to trying to identify and support those who have already entered; the government uses this approach to frame its anti-immigration efforts as a way of tackling human trafficking. As O'Connell Davidson and Howard (2015) outline, as newspapers report tragic events of migrant boats capsizing, politicians refer to them as victims of smugglers who are trafficking people across borders.

Although these claims are clearly incorrectly confusing smuggling and trafficking (both defined in section 2.1.2), approaching these situations in this way allows the politicians to suggest that migrants moving without the state's consent are putting themselves at risk of trafficking, and therefore, by limiting illegal immigration, the state is offering them protection. It could also go some way to explaining the government's tendency of conflating modern slavery with immigration crime. This conflation of modern slavery with immigration crime has become a focus of the UK government over recent years as can be seen from the development of the Modern Slavery Police Transformation Unit into the Modern Slavery and Organised Immigration Crime Unit, with the introduction of the 2022 Nationality and Borders Act (whereby an entire Part of the Act is dedicated to modern slavery), and with the very recent reclassification of modern slavery as an 'illegal immigration and asylum issue' where the brief has been removed from the minister responsible for safeguarding (Dugan, 2022). This reframing is a simple way in which the government is able to exhibit its policies as paternalistic while it simultaneously fails to accept accountability for the ways in which its restrictive policies create the perfect environment for modern slavery to thrive among those who search for safety in the UK (O'Connell Davidson, 2013a, 2013b, 2016; Kidd et al., 2019) and who are too afraid to make themselves known to authorities because of the potential repercussions (discussed further in 6.2.2).

Focus on source countries

Perhaps this also goes some way to explaining the government's tendency to look elsewhere for the root causes of modern slavery while overlooking its own impact and failing to hold itself accountable (O'Connell Davidson and Howard, 2015). The UK government's focus surrounding modern slavery continues to be placed on structural issues in source countries as opposed to structural issues in the UK, as highlighted by the inaugural Independent Anti-Slavery Commissioner who stated that:

> Truly effective prevention must start in countries of origin to prevent vulnerable people from being exploited in the first place. Often this will mean working in collaboration with international partners to develop effective and targeted prevention projects. (Independent Anti-Slavery Commissioner, 2018)

However, inspection of statistics suggests that this is misguided and much more emphasis should be placed instead on how environments in the UK encourage modern slavery. The NRM statistics provide information determining the numbers of people referred into the system who are believed to be potential victims who experienced modern slavery in the UK, in the UK and overseas, or overseas only. In 2021, 58 per cent of people referred into the NRM experienced modern slavery only in the UK, with a further 11 per cent experiencing it in both the UK and overseas (Home Office, 2022a). Further, UK nationals are repeatedly identified as the most common nationality of victims referred into the NRM, suggesting that efforts should be more significantly focused on how the UK presents conducive environments for modern slavery to occur.

This emphasises a serious flaw with the UK government's tendency to look to source countries as responsible for causing modern slavery when, in practice, the majority of victims identified in 2021 suffered their exploitation in the UK. To focus on source countries is to move attention away from the failings of the UK government when instead it should be held accountable for the vulnerabilities it causes. It also serves to allow the perpetuation of UK systems that create and encourage the environment for modern slavery to thrive.

If it is the case, as evidenced by respondents such as **Ifra** who did not know how to navigate the asylum system and who was provided no information in how to do so, that vulnerabilities towards modern slavery are exacerbated by strict and confusing migration policies after arrival in the UK, then it is counter-intuitive for the UK government to state that tackling modern slavery is a priority (Hesketh and Balch, 2021) while simultaneously advocating a hostile environment for illegal immigrants. As Quirk asserts, these political agendas are not aligned (2015a) and, as O'Connell Davidson states, it is hollow for a government to claim it wants to lead the way in defeating modern slavery, when it encourages systems that deny large groups of people their basic rights.

> [T]he liberal democratic states that are so eager to combat 'the scourge of modern slavery' in the form of THB [trafficking in human beings] are equally if not more enthusiastically engaged in depriving many groups of migrants of their freedom through (often for-profit) immigration detention, denying them basic rights, forcibly moving them across borders through deportation, and sustaining a flourishing industry in the prevention and control of human mobility. In other words, whilst seeking to suppress one form of traffic (THB) on grounds that it leads to restrictions on human freedom, liberal states sanction other forms of movement and trade, or traffic, that produce precisely the same effects. (O'Connell Davidson, 2016)

Gamba evidenced this situation in his interview. He described how, for him, travelling safely by aeroplane was a cheap route to the UK, but it was only available to him because he was able to get a visa to study. Without visas, his friends were having to pay four to five times more than him to a smuggler who would sail them across the Mediterranean. If they could not afford a smuggler, the only options available to them were to migrate on foot or stay in hiding in their home country for the rest of their lives. This affirms how strict government policies on immigration are directly pushing people into dangerous situations. It is not the case that these migrants are so desperate to get to the UK that they will risk the perilous journey, but that they are so desperate to survive that they know they must leave their home country by whatever means possible; yet it is often only the rich that can afford these life-risking journeys. If legal restrictions mean that they are unable to travel via safe means, then the only option left for them is to risk their lives with smugglers. Thus, by placing restrictions on the movement of people in dire need, governments are encouraging movement via unsafe means; movement that, without statutory support on arrival, could well result in situations of modern slavery.

The National Referral Mechanism

The National Referral Mechanism is the UK's system for identifying, counting, and offering support to victims of modern slavery and human trafficking. Although the NRM is flawed in many ways, it provides the most reliable non-estimated set of figures relating to modern slavery in the UK.

To be entered into the NRM, there is no rule as to where the reported exploitation must have taken place. This means that people who have fled a situation of slavery and come to the UK, people who have been enslaved along the journey, and people who have been victims of slavery in the UK are all, supposedly, granted the same protections.

The NRM is a two-step process whereby a specific list of first responders have the authority to complete an NRM form on behalf of a potential victim (reflecting the discussion regarding the conflation of modern slavery with immigration crime, it is insightful that the UK Border Force, Home Office Visas and Immigration, and Home Office Immigration Enforcement are all first responders and yet the National Health Service is not). The first responders refer the case on to one of two competent authorities which are part of the Home Office (discussed further later in this section). The competent authority then gathers all the information they can on the case in order to make a two-tiered decision as to whether the individual meets the criteria to be confirmed as a victim of modern slavery. Newly released Home Office guidance states that the competent authority has five days to make a Reasonable Grounds decision that there are 'reasonable grounds to believe, based on objective factors but falling short of conclusive proof' that the person referred is a potential victim of modern slavery (Home Office, 2023). Note that this guidance created a stricter threshold for Reasonable Grounds decisions where previously there was no call for objective factors and a potential victim's own testimony was sufficient. If the Reasonable Grounds decision is positive, then additional information is gathered on the case in order for the competent authority to make a Conclusive Grounds decision. This Conclusive Grounds decision states that 'on the balance of probabilities, there are sufficient grounds to decide that the individual being considered is a victim of modern slavery' (Home Office, 2023). Potential victims are entitled to a recovery period while this Conclusive Grounds decision is made. Previously the entitlement offered a minimum of a forty-five day recovery period. This has recently been reduced to a minimum of thirty days (Home Office, 2022c), but in reality the recovery period lasts as long as it takes to make the Conclusive Grounds decision, with the most recent NRM statistics showing that the mean length of time to make a Conclusive Grounds decision was 666 days (Home Office, 2022b). The uncertainty experienced by potential victims of modern slavery during this period of waiting, reflecting the wait for an asylum decision as outlined in section 6.2.2, can negatively impact the physical and mental health of those waiting for a decision, and has been shown to worsen trauma (Heys et al., 2022). In situations of modern slavery, the victim reports that they have been a victim of a crime. They must then wait over a year and a half for their case to go through two stages of investigation in order to determine whether they are to be believed, and this is relating only to their own status as a victim—entirely separate from any criminal investigation that may be pursued against the perpetrator. It is not clear why victims of modern slavery are treated this way, with an air of testing and disbelief, when it is so different to the treatment of those presenting as victims of any other form of crime, but perhaps it allows us some insight into the government's stance regarding victims of modern slavery.

It is worth noting that since the NRM has existed, it has been based on this two-tier decision-making process, with 'expert decision-makers' employed to make the Reasonable and Conclusive Grounds decisions. Nevertheless in 2021, a legal case called into question both whether the decision-makers really have any level of expertise, and how detailed the investigations into cases of modern slavery for these decisions really are. *R v Brecani* was a 2021 case in which a seventeen-year-old boy was convicted of conspiracy to supply cocaine, a Class A drug, and sentenced to three years in detention. He raised the section 45 defence, which is a statutory defence written into the Modern Slavery Act for victims of modern slavery who commit a criminal offence because of their slavery experience. The defendant received a positive Conclusive Grounds decision while the trial was in progress, with the competent authority therefore acknowledging that he had been a victim of forced criminality. However, the prosecution gathered significant evidence from the appellant's phone which was not available to those making the Conclusive Grounds decision. This evidence appeared to undermine his claims of having been trafficked, indicating that, instead, he was a willing co-conspirator. As a result, the case held that a positive Conclusive Grounds decision is not admissible in evidence at a criminal court, because the decision is made by individuals who are not experts, and decisions may be made on partial evidence, as appeared to be the case here.

This is reflective of the comments made by the Crown Prosecution Service (CPS) in a previous case: *R v DS*, which stated that 'the evidential bar to be designated as a victim of modern slavery, often made before any evidence is heard or tested, was a low one and can be untested, self-serving, and based on hearsay evidence' (Crown Prosecution Service, 2020). These cases highlight some of the flaws in the NRM decision-making process whereby the decisions are based on limited evidence.

As a result of *R v Brecani*, NRM decisions are still acceptable in court as a method of indicating that a person may have been a victim of modern slavery or human trafficking, but they are not deemed robust enough to be relied upon as *proof* of modern slavery or trafficking. In summary, it means that a Conclusive Grounds decision from the NRM is admissible in court, but is not weighted as expert evidence because of the flaws in the decision-making process highlighted by this case. These cases question how robust the NRM decision-making process actually is, and they bring to light the possibility that it may well be more difficult to find evidence around the case of a non-EU national than EU or UK nationals (simply because of the professional networks that are in place to gather such evidence) and it must be considered whether this impacts the likelihood of receiving a positive Conclusive Grounds decision.

Prior to 2019 there were two competent authorities that NRM referrals were sent to depending on the potential victim's immigration status: The National Crime Agency's Modern Slavery Human Trafficking Unit (MSHTU) and Home Office Visas and Immigration (UKVI). Perhaps it is unsurprising that of these two previous competent authorities, the MSHTU made decisions regarding any UK national or any European Economic Area (EEA) national without a live immigration issue, while any non-EEA national, or any EEA national with a live immigration issue would be referred to UKVI to make the Reasonable and Conclusive Grounds decisions. Perhaps equally unsurprising were the results of these decisions.

In the UK in 2018 (the last full calendar year that used these two competent authorities), there were 6,933 individuals referred into the NRM (National Crime Agency, 2019). In 2019, the National Crime Agency released an end-of-year summary to summarise the statistics from 2018; this included a data table that showed the case decision status at 12 March 2019 (National Crime Agency, 2019:79). Almost two thirds of referrals into the NRM in 2018 were for non-EU nationals, while 36 per cent were EU or UK nationals (4,506 and 2,483 respectively). Yet EU and UK victims were almost six times more likely to receive a positive Conclusive Grounds decision than their non-EU counterparts (35 per cent and 6 per cent respectively).

This is not necessarily to say that the remaining 65 per cent and 94 per cent received negative Conclusive Grounds decisions, as some will have been withdrawn, received negative Reasonable Grounds decisions, or the decision may still have been pending; however, it is still indicative of a bias. In 2014, the Anti-Trafficking Monitoring Group published a five-year review of the NRM which identified that the percentage of positive Conclusive Grounds decisions made for British and EU/EEA nationals was 80 per cent whereas for those with a live immigration case it was less than 20 per cent (Anti-Trafficking Monitoring Group, 2014) therefore indicating a significant bias within the system. Rhys Jones (2013) draws attention to another interesting fact that, from 2009 when the NRM was established, until 2013 when his article was published, every judicial review conducted regarding NRM decisions was in reference to a decision made by the Border Agency (later replaced by UKVI as a competent authority) regarding potential victims with a live immigration issue; none were made against the other competent authority whose decisions did not concern those with live immigration cases. This emphasises, again, bias and poorly formed decisions against non-EU citizens, and implies that immigration status was prioritised without thorough attention being paid to the reported modern slavery experiences.

Considering the vast differences between positive Conclusive Grounds decisions for EU nationals set against non-EU nationals, it is not a big leap to suggest that the drive to curb immigration and the unlikeliness of receiving a positive Conclusive Grounds decision as a non-EU citizen were linked. It is clear then that the government's priorities of tackling modern slavery and reducing immigration are incompatible (O'Connell Davidson, 2013a).

When UKVI was responsible for making Reasonable and Conclusive Grounds decisions for potential victims of modern slavery with live immigration issues, but was also responsible for the UK's visa system, there is an undeniable conflict of interests and the vast difference in decision outcomes is arguably a result of this. These issues have been raised previously to the formation of UKVI, when the UK Border Agency was responsible for making Conclusive Grounds decisions and it was identified that '[n]ational efforts to fight trafficking are undermined by requiring a potential victim to describe their personal situation to the agency who may at the same time be considering their immigration status' (Rhys Jones, 2013). Equally, any immigration offence was likely to be considered a priority over the fact that the person was a victim of a crime.

In 2019, the Home Office changed this segregated decision-making process so that all decisions, regardless of the immigration status of the potential victim, were made by the newly formed Single Competent Authority. This indicated a move forward, away from the misguided blurring of lines between immigration and modern slavery. However, despite the fact that NRM data sets are made publicly available at the end of every calendar year, the publications tend to include different sets of data, making it impossible to use direct annual comparisons to see the impact that this change has made. The breakdown of statistics by whether potential victims are EU or non-EU nationals is one such data set which is not comparable over time. In 2021, for example, we know that 12,727 potential victims were referred into the NRM (Home Office, 2022a), but information is not provided as to how many of these were EU nationals, or what the outcome of decisions by immigration status was, which makes it difficult to see whether the change to a Single Competent Authority helped to overcome some of the biases outlined here.

While the move to a Single Competent Authority was widely celebrated in marking a move away from focusing on immigration status over victimhood, it was short lived. Just two years later, in 2021, the Home Office, without consultation, created a new competent authority: the Immigration Enforcement Competent Authority, which sits alongside the now confusingly-named Single Competent Authority. The Immigration Enforcement Competent Authority's remit is to make NRM decisions for 'many adults who are subject to forms of immigration control, including any adults in respect of whom deportation is being pursued and those who are held in administrative immigration detention' (FLEX, 2021). There was very little warning about the introduction of this new competent authority and Detention Taskforce took the lead in producing a letter signed by over thirty organisations to call upon the Home Office to reverse the introduction of the Immigration Enforcement Competent Authority, stating that its introduction 'is a retrograde step returning us to a discriminatory two-tier system, in which many victims of modern slavery in the UK who lack secure immigration status will not be appropriately identified, protected or supported, and will therefore fear coming forward to the authorities to seek help' (FLEX, 2021).

Impact of decision-making

The likelihood of receiving a negative Conclusive Grounds decision could also have a detrimental impact on encouraging other victims of modern slavery to consent to referral into the NRM. If they become aware of people who have lived through a situation similar to their own, but who have received a negative decision and who, without referral into the NRM, would not have come to the attention of the authorities, then it is evident why some victims may choose not to make their situation known. This wish to remain hidden is surely only further strengthened by the obvious discrimination that faces immigrants (Parker, 2015). Especially for those who have fled a dangerous situation, if they believe that making their story known holds the potential to result in their detention or repatriation, then it may be in their best interests to try and remain hidden from the authorities.

Further, it can be argued that there is limited benefit to any victim of modern slavery being referred through the NRM. Although there is an offer of safe housing with support while the Conclusive Grounds decision is being made, it is common that these decisions take an inordinate length of time, with the most recent statistics showing the mean length of decision-making times sitting at 666 days (Home Office, 2022b). While at the outset this may appear beneficial—a long time in safe accommodation—those in the NRM are made aware that, should they receive a negative decision, they have nine days to exit the safe house, regardless of how long they have been there. Up until the beginning of 2021, a positive Conclusive Grounds decision offered similarly limited support with the requirement of leaving the supported accommodation two weeks after receiving the positive decision. In these circumstances, regardless of whether individuals were receiving positive or negative decisions, they were living on the edge, aware that they may suddenly have to pack up their lives and move on. The extended waiting times have a negative impact on both physical and mental health (Heys et al., 2022). The waiting also limits how settled a person is able to become in this accommodation and reduces the likelihood that they will want to learn about the local area or invest in friendships. In these situations, it could reasonably be considered that individuals could believe they would have been better off if they had circumnavigated the system and avoided the NRM; if they had been able to find work and accommodation through others then they may indeed have had better security than that offered through the NRM. However, as discussed in chapter four and in section 6.2.2, turning to other people for assistance in finding work is a key method through which someone can become trapped in a situation of modern slavery.

Frustratingly, despite recognising a person's vulnerabilities, a positive Conclusive Grounds decision through the NRM does not put a person in priority need for housing. The UK Housing Act 1996 states that:

(1) The following have a priority need for accommodation—
   (a) a pregnant woman or a person with whom she resides or might reasonably be expected to reside;
   (b) a person with whom dependent children reside or might reasonably be expected to reside;
   (c) a person who is vulnerable as a result of old age, mental illness or handicap or physical disability or other special reason, or with whom such a person resides or might reasonably be expected to reside;
   (d) a person who is homeless or threatened with homelessness as a result of an emergency such as flood, fire or other disaster.
   (e) a person who is homeless as a result of that person being a victim of domestic abuse.

Some advocates have successfully argued the case for victims with a positive Conclusive Grounds decision to be considered in priority need of accommodation under section c: for some 'other special reason'. However, without such priority being explicitly stated in the Housing Act, this is not a guarantee, and without an advocate who knows the system on hand to support the victim through the housing application process, it is unlikely that they would be successful. This would leave them homeless and, ironically, at increased risk of modern slavery as they seek work and accommodation through strangers they meet on the street.

Similarly, a positive Conclusive Grounds decision does not automatically grant the recipient discretionary leave to remain (DLR); the Home Office is simply required to *consider* whether people with such a decision should be granted DLR. This is an issue picked up by Burland (2017) who noted of the 2016 NRM statistics, that:

> Only 384 of the 2563 people who received a positive CG [Conclusive Grounds decision] in 2014, 2015 and 2016 were granted discretionary leave to remain in the UK. This statistical evidence is not found in the NRM data, but it highlights the limited value of a positive CG and the reality of the UK's short- term and limited response to its support for trafficked persons.

So then, through the UK's NRM, if a person who has been a victim of modern slavery in the UK must live precariously as they wait months to receive a Conclusive Grounds decision which is then not guaranteed to benefit them, we must ask whether the government's claim that tackling modern slavery is a priority really stands up to scrutiny. We should also consider that many may view circumnavigating the NRM as a more likely means to be able to start living their lives with immediate support from friends, acquaintances, and strangers as opposed to limited (if any) support, with no specified timeline, if they choose to wait for help from the government.

Positively, from the beginning of 2021, the system of support offered by the NRM has changed through the Modern Slavery Victim Care and Coordination Contract (MSVCC). The MSVCC has introduced a Recovery Needs Assessment which offers follow-on support to victims of modern slavery who received a positive Conclusive Grounds decision through the NRM on, or after the 4 January 2021. It offers a 'reach-in' service for at least forty-five calendar days, which:

> is designed to keep a survivor's transition to independence on track if they have any emerging or reactive requirements for support or advice. It can include links to activities and places where they can get help including finding a job, counselling and other therapies, ESOL classes and translation services. (The Salvation Army, 2021)

This is a significant improvement from what was previously termed as the 'cliff edge' that victims experienced as they received a positive Conclusive Grounds decision and their support simultaneously abruptly ended. Although this is certainly a progressive step forward, there have already been issues identified, for example, how British nationals are often missing out on the support offered by the new contract (Heys et al., 2022).

6.2.2 The asylum system

While section 6.2.1 considered the specific response to modern slavery in the UK, this section builds upon some of the concerns raised and considers the asylum system and how it generates an environment which is conducive to encouraging modern slavery.

In the UK, public tension surrounding migration has increased in correlation with both the rise in immigration itself, as well as the increasingly uninformed and uninhibited political discussions on the subject (Crawley, 2006). While those in the asylum system are provided with £40.85 per week on which to live, the treatment of asylum seekers in the UK is increasingly punitive, with the prohibition on working, the dispersal of refugees, and an increase in detention (Vickers, 2015).

A person cannot claim asylum in the UK until they have arrived at the border, and there are no safe, legal, guaranteed ways to do this. As such, many often experience long and dangerous journeys in the hope that they will be granted asylum upon application. However, while those who seek asylum may receive a cash stipend and a bed while they wait for the outcome of their decision, they receive little other support or advice, and once asylum has been granted, little changes. Once granted asylum, they have their weekly stipend stopped and may have to leave their accommodation. While they are then entitled to apply for welfare benefits or seek employment, they have no support worker to advise them through these processes. The government has identified such refugees as vulnerable enough to warrant asylum yet does not offer support to ensure that those vulnerabilities do not result in the exploitation of people left unassisted in a country that they do not know. There is clearly a risk that these people will be vulnerable to offers that may transpire to be situations of slavery when they are left in such a position of uncertainty. They must find a way to support themselves but may not know where to go to find out their entitlements or to apply for legitimate employment, and they may be too afraid of repatriation to seek assistance. As such, offers of cash-in-hand work or a place to stay may be tempting, but may equally be an entry into exploitation. However, it is also important to note that by failing to take accountability and offer support to refugees, the government not only allows them to live at risk of exploitation but is depriving itself of the social and monetary input that the refugees would provide if they had support in settling quickly into the community. If asylum seekers were permitted to work, this would benefit the UK economy by an estimated £97.8 million each year (Lift the Ban, no date).

The asylum system was discussed in detail by several respondents involved in this research. This section investigates these findings and discusses how the asylum system can generate risk; this is discussed particularly in terms of the vulnerabilities that can be generated through the lack of clarity on how the system works, the long waiting times for decisions to be made, and the impact that a lack of effective communication and support can have on those in the system.

Lack of clarity

Contrary to the assumption that all immigrants come to the UK because they think 'the streets are paved with gold' and the welfare state is an enticing opportunity (May and Cazeneuve, 2015), there were respondents who simply did not know about the asylum system, and the lack of clarity about the system caused them to become vulnerable.

Catherine arrived in the UK 'illegally' after escaping a trafficking situation in Albania and, knowing nothing about the asylum system: what it was, how to claim, or how it might assist her, she found casual work and accommodation in the UK. However, upon hearing about the asylum system, she applied straight away, but her delay in applying counted against her and her claim was denied. This is an issue that has been identified in wider research, whereby a delay in accessing support has been seen to undermine the credibility of those making a claim for asylum (Lewis et al., 2013). For **Catherine**, a lack of information on the asylum system when she arrived in the UK directly affected her chances of getting a positive decision. If she had access to this information when she arrived in the country, she would have begun the application process immediately; instead **Catherine** is on her third application and has been waiting six years to be granted asylum.

Ifra's story highlights how a lack of knowledge of the asylum system can actually encourage a situation of modern slavery. Having fled Bangladesh after her political opponents threatened to have her killed, **Ifra** moved to the UK and found work. After her working visa expired, the job centre informed her they were no longer able to support her. She left the job centre unaware of any agencies that could support her, or of the asylum system, despite the fact that she was an ideal candidate due to the risk to her life should she return to Bangladesh. This resulted in her turning to strangers to look for support and accepting an offer of work from a stranger that transpired to be a situation of modern slavery that lasted for three years.

If people in situations such as **Ifra**'s and **Catherine**'s were to be made aware of the asylum system on their arrival to the UK, even if arriving with a visa, their vulnerabilities could be drastically reduced. It is also fundamental that statutory organisations interacting with individuals who may not know about, but may be in a position to apply for, asylum accept a degree of accountability for at least signposting such individuals to organisations that may be able to offer them support and advice. Had **Ifra** received such advice it is unlikely that she would have turned to strangers for help and found herself in such extreme exploitation where she was held for three years.

These examples show that clear information on who should apply for asylum, how the process works, and why they need to apply is not successfully reaching those who would benefit from such material. They illustrate how, without clear information being provided on the asylum process, those who continue to be unaware are at an immediate disadvantage, be that in regard to the likelihood that their asylum claim will be accepted, or in the potential that a lack of knowledge of the asylum system could lead to modern slavery.

There are, of course, practical issues that prevent such information being made directly available to this hard-to-reach group. Primarily, if people are entering the UK by circumnavigating border checkpoints and statutory authorities, then there is no easy route to make sure this information reaches them. However, that is not to say that providing such information is impossible, simply that more onerous methods must be considered (discussed further in chapter eight).

However, this lack of clarity around the asylum system is something not only experienced by those unaware of the mechanism, but even by those who are successfully granted asylum. **Oscar** applied for asylum in the UK after fleeing conflict in Gaza. He described how he was granted asylum, and how he was given the documentation and then told 'just go'. **Oscar** speaks English fluently but was provided no information on what the next step was for him, what he was entitled to, or where to go for information or support. As a result of this, he quickly found himself homeless. While homelessness has been well researched as a vulnerability that can increase a person's likelihood of experiencing modern slavery (see for example The Passage, 2017; Kassaw, 2019; Avis, 2020; Jagpal et al., 2020; Murphy, 2020), **Oscar** was lucky to have been supported by a stranger who explained that he needed to apply for housing with a council. If he had been informed of this upon receiving asylum, he would have been able to go straight to the council offices and apply for housing instead of spending so long homeless. Because he was offered no information with his documentation from the Home Office, without this intervention from a stranger, **Oscar** would have remained unemployed and homeless even though the Home Office had recognised him as a refugee and granted him asylum.

Environment of distrust

The immigration system generates an environment of distrust as is evidenced by the Windrush scandal, where people who had every right to be in the UK were being told they must leave the country. With such issues facing those with legal status becoming public, those who are in the UK illegally would likely, rightly, identify themselves as in a very vulnerable position. If those in the UK legally are being told they must leave, then 'illegal' immigrants are faced with little hope (Bulman, 2018a). Such an environment generates distrust and fear which makes asylum seekers reticent to provide accurate accounts to authorities, or to lie because they are reluctant to tell their sensitive stories of hardship to people who have a vested interest in repatriating them (Herlihy and Turner, 2006; Stepnitz, 2012). Further, with a predisposed unlikeliness of receiving a positive Conclusive Grounds decision simply because they are not from the EU, victims of slavery who fit this category may automatically be discouraged from applying to the NRM for support.

This distrust was highlighted repeatedly by respondents who discussed how the lack of clarity on the reasons for some of the probing questions, plus the fear of repatriation, meant that they were guarded in disclosing their personal and traumatic stories to those they believed were inclined to repatriate them to countries they felt terrified to return to. A number of the respondents described how they had lied in their initial asylum claims. Some explained that they were simply unable to remember or got confused over some of their answers. For example, **Catherine**'s claims have been rejected twice as they are considered unreliable, but she suffers severe Post-Traumatic Stress Disorder (PTSD) because of her slavery experience and this is widely acknowledged to impact upon memory (Nejati et al., 2018). Others admitted to lying or altering facts because they were fearful of the authorities making the decisions, or because they wanted maximise the likelihood of a positive decision because of their fear of being repatriated.

Fredrika recalled how her main reason for wanting to claim asylum in the UK was because she was homosexual and feared being killed or imprisoned because of her sexuality if she returned to Uganda. However, because of the hostile reactions of her family to her telling them that she was homosexual, she was extremely reluctant to disclose this information to a stranger in the asylum interview, not knowing if their response would reflect that of her family's. As a result, without the disclosure of her sexuality, her claim did not have enough merit to warrant a positive decision, and **Fredrika** was denied asylum.

Isaac lied in his asylum claim. He had no knowledge of the asylum process or what was expected of him, but his desperation to stay in the UK where his child and younger sister were meant that he felt extreme pressure to provide a version of events most likely to lead to a positive decision. However, immigration agencies are under pressure to reduce immigration and, as such, decisions may err on the side of the negative and discrepancies in a person's story will likely encourage a negative decision, as was the case for **Isaac** when it was discovered that he had not told the truth. The lack of clarity around the asylum system was exacerbated for **Isaac** after he was detained by immigration officials. He was detained and released without being given any information as to why he had been detained. This clearly caused him a great deal of distress, but also led to a lack of trust in the authorities. Their inability to communicate with him on the issues surrounding his detention, or to take accountability for his welfare, made him reluctant to engage or put his trust in organisations of authority going forward, and reticence to open up to authorities is often construed as an attempt at deceit (Herlihy and Turner, 2006).

This reluctance to engage with officials in authority was further exemplified by both **Catherine** and **Nadia**. Before applying for asylum in the UK, **Catherine** had been exploited by police and government officials in Albania, and **Nadia** had been raped by a police officer in Italy. The lack of clarity they were offered around how the asylum system works meant that they feared their disclosures making it back to those who had mistreated them. As such they were disinclined to disclose the truth for fear of who else would hear of their stories and the potential retribution as a result.

These examples indicate how fear and distrust of authorities can lead asylum seekers to lie or withhold information during their claims. The result of this is that their claim is likely to be rejected and their support will end, as was the case for **Fredrika** and **Isaac** after officials had discovered flaws in their disclosures. However, neither were willing to give up and would have taken the risk of being homeless and destitute in the UK rather than risking their lives by returning to their home countries. **Gamba** had a similar experience and described how he felt the asylum system was there to try and find discrepancies in applicants' accounts. His initial asylum claim had been rejected but he had reapplied in the knowledge that he would be killed if he returned to Cameroon where he was wanted for his political activism, the same reason that his father had been murdered. **Fredrika** and **Gamba** both became homeless and destitute after the government ended their support; however, they were both fortunate to receive assistance from charities, which undoubtedly reduced their vulnerabilities. While, at the time of our interviews, they were living in precarious situations, they had both opened new claims for asylum because they were of the strong belief that they would be killed should they return 'home'.

Such examples demonstrate how the lack of clarity provided to claimants as to the necessity for honesty in their claims, coupled with the environment of distrust generated by the hostile immigration environment, can encourage people to avoid authorities, withhold information, or lie during their asylum claims. However, this is likely to lead to the applicants receiving a negative decision which can result in destitution for those who are simply too fearful to return to their home country. At this point, asylum seekers become vulnerable to offers of illegitimate and potentially exploitative labour as a method of survival.

As such, clarification is necessary for those undertaking asylum interviews on the reasons that asylum seekers may withhold the truth. However, clarification on the asylum system, the reasons for the interviews, and all the potential outcomes should also be provided to those applying in order to emphasise to them the importance of providing truthful accounts.

Psychological impact

The fear of repatriation outlined in the previous section is a constant threat for asylum seekers and can have a significantly detrimental impact on their mental health. An 'illegal' status can permeate every aspect of a migrant's life as the threat of detention becomes a constant source of fear and anxiety (Sigona, 2012).

Isaac indicated how the asylum system detrimentally impacted him as he was taken in and out of detention with no explanation as to why, and continued to wait for a decision on his asylum application while being forbidden from getting work or an education. This point is emphasised by Thibos and Topouzova (2017:no pagination) who state that:

> [t]he threat of being caught in these nets [detention], and the dire consequences that can result from doing so, are one of the main reasons why many remain at risk in countries of transit and destination.

The fear of repatriation is an issue that was highlighted in multiple interviews. Although several respondents mentioned that they would love to return home if it was safe to do so, many described how returning home is simply not an option for them because of the risks associated with their return. A number of respondents were certain that, should they return to their home countries, they would be killed. Waiting on the outcome of their asylum claim then generated high levels of stress as, to them, the result was not simply whether or not they would be granted rights to remain in the UK, but was potentially a genuine life or death decision.

At the time of our interview, **Fredrika** had been in the asylum system for four years and, as a homosexual woman, fears being returned to Uganda where she is certain she would be arrested, if not killed, because of her sexuality. Her life centres around waiting for the outcome of her asylum application and she has been unable to pursue much of a life during the long waiting times. For her, her entire future rests on the result of this decision, and this has significantly impacted her mental health. She has struggled to make friends in the UK, stating that she prefers to be alone, and that being destitute makes it very difficult to maintain any type of relationship, because asylum seekers are unable to afford to go anywhere and have no home to invite friends into.

> If you were in my situation, you don't even think about meeting people. When people meet you have to go somewhere, have a cup of coffee. But if you don't even get £10. I get £10 from a charity organisation for a week. How am I going to start to afford bringing people to my . . . I don't know, it's hard.

Fredrika described how once she starts to think about her emotions, she can quickly spiral into despair as she worries about her future, not knowing if she will be permitted to stay, get a job, and resume a normal life or if she will be returned to Uganda where she is fearful that she would be arrested or killed.

> You can't work. You just can't do anything. You basically go through phases and things that you'd never experience. You get depressed. Becoming suicidal, which has happened to me about three times. And then you start thinking about your sexuality, and then you start thinking oh what's going to happen tomorrow. Because when you go to sign at [name of office], you might or you might not come back. I sign every two weeks on a Monday and even the sign in sheet says you're liable to detention, so you might not come back. What kind of life is that?

Similarly, **Catherine**'s experience of being sexually exploited by government officials in Albania has left her living in constant fear of being returned to Albania. She felt that if she were to be repatriated, she would quickly be found by those who exploited her and, as such, can think about little else other than receiving her asylum decision. **Catherine**'s caseworker discussed how distressing life is for her while she waits for her asylum decision to the point where everyday situations cause her severe anguish.

> To give you an example, I got an envelope out with something in one day to give her and she thought it was from the Home Office to deport her. That was how . . . anything that's in a brown envelope . . . so now I make sure that I keep it outside of the envelope before. But when the post comes to the door it's a real trigger for her.

This is a topic that has been dissected by Darling, whose research considers the ways that the UK government, by using letters, generates a unique bond between itself and asylum seekers. 'Letters are considered as things that hold the capacity to move individuals in affective and interpersonal ways' (Darling, 2014:486). They are documents which may be formal, but are often read in an informal space, thereby allowing the government to infiltrate a space in an asylum seeker's life that would not ordinarily be accessible to them.

When asked about how a negative asylum decision might affect **Catherine**, her caseworker voiced her concern.

> I think her risk would increase . . . massively. I think she might run away. I would also worry about her risk. I think she could be pushed to a state where she'd rather she died than went back to Albania.

Catherine's story highlights the sense of limbo created by the asylum process as people wait for their decisions and are unable to work or access education. Knowing that she cannot return safely to Albania but having to wait to find out if she will be supported to stay in the UK has caused her severe anguish as her life remains on hold. At the time of my interview with her caseworker, **Catherine** was is in her sixth year of waiting for a decision, meaning that she has been unable to settle or integrate for a significant length of time and, as her status is her priority, has been unable to deal with any of the traumatic effects caused by her experiences.

> I mean she has constant nightmares. She couldn't sleep at all when I saw her . . . She's hyperactive . . . She's really thin, really suffering chronically with PTSD isn't she. Her stress is very high and she's very tearful every time I see her.

Catherine and **Fredrika**'s experiences of the asylum system had a hugely negative impact on their mental health. Both women fear being repatriated and expect that there would be severe repercussions if they were to return 'home', yet they have no influence over the outcome of their asylum decisions. Though the asylum system may not have made them immediately vulnerable to situations of modern slavery, their fear of repatriation means that, should they continue to be denied asylum, there is every chance they will attempt to stay in the UK, searching for illegitimate work to survive in the hope of avoiding being returned to their home countries. In attempting to remain undetected by authorities, any labour they find will be unregulated, therefore increasing the likelihood that it will be, or become, exploitative.

Fredrika mentioned how she tries to think about her future positively, but her feelings oscillate when she is faced with such uncertainty.

> I just hope for the best. I'm being optimistic, but there's a thin line in between being optimistic and then going down rapidly . . . Yeah, like today, I'll be feeling very optimistic. Tomorrow I'll be something different. Completely something different.

This sense of despair was highlighted by **Gamba** when he was asked to think about his hopes for the future. He has been in the asylum system for six years and fears being repatriated as he knows several people from his political group have been killed for their activism. Although he wants to complete his university degree and be able to lead a 'normal' life, **Gamba** struggles to allow himself to think about the future because of the complexities caused by hoping.

> Hope is a very good thing for people to have, but when you hope, especially in my situation, if things don't happen you just get depressed. So most of the time you take it a day at a time and try not to dream. Just accept it.

The uncertainty makes it difficult for anyone to remain positive and some respondents simply did not want to talk about their futures because they found the topic so unsettling. This was particularly true of **Isaac** who has had an asylum claim rejected after it was discovered that he lied in his interview. He has a son who was born in the UK, his sister is in the UK, his mother has died, and he has no information on the location of his father or whether he is even still alive. He is originally from the Democratic Republic of the Congo, but has very few memories of living there and has no contact with anyone there. **Isaac** fears being repatriated to a country he does not know and having to leave his son and young sister in the UK. For these reasons, he prefers not to think about the future and takes each day at a time.

INTERVIEWER: So what do you hope for your future?
ISAAC: Do I have to say?
INTERVIEWER: You don't have to say anything you don't want to say, it's fine and we can move on if you don't want to talk about that.
ISAAC: Maybe move on.

At the time of our interviews, **Fredrika**, **Gamba**, and **Isaac** were all still waiting for the outcomes of their asylum claims. For them, the asylum system has constituted a removal of agency whereby they have no control over their futures. They must wait for the government to make the decision as to whether they will be granted asylum, and their only alternative options would be to voluntarily return home or try to find a way to survive in the UK by illegally seeking work without being identified by the authorities, a risk that would increase any vulnerabilities towards experiencing modern slavery. This has left these respondents in a state of uncertainty while they wait to receive the results of their asylum decision. During this time, they are unable to make any plans for their futures, not knowing how long they will have to wait, or where they will live once they get the results. This prevents asylum seekers from being able to deal with any mental health issues they are already facing, as demonstrated by **Catherine**, yet it also serves to further impact on applicants' mental health. It prevents asylum seekers from wanting to, or even being able to, integrate into their current society, therefore running the risk of creating societal divides. However, this distress regarding thoughts of the future is not limited to those who are still in the asylum process; some respondents who have been granted asylum still feel this way when thinking about their futures.

Hasim fled Uganda for political reasons and had been in the UK for seven years at the point of our interview. He was granted asylum in the UK, but his family are still in Uganda and, although they are safe now, he never knows how long that will last. Worrying about his family was an added stress on top of the difficulties associated with claiming asylum in the UK. 'The asylum system is hard. Finding opportunities, jobs is hard. It's a struggle. Life is challenging. It's not easy.'

Despite the fact that **Hasim** has been granted asylum and had been in the UK for seven years at the time of my interview with him, he still finds it difficult to contemplate his future.

> I use religion as a way of building hope [however] . . . I don't want to be really ambitious and hopeful. It's hard, you cannot hope for your future in a different world. I would easily answer that question in my own country but how do you answer when you're not in your own country? It becomes hard to see yourself where you want to see yourself with that future. . . . To ask what you hope for your future is a hard question.

The future **Hasim** has now is not one he had ever considered before he had to flee Uganda. He still sees Uganda as his home and he would love to return there, but knows he is unable to because he would be at risk. This makes it difficult for him to think about his future, because the future he wants for himself is not available to him.

This example of a refugee in the UK who has been granted asylum, lives in safety, and has a successful job that he enjoys, yet who continues to feel distress about his future and when thinking of his family reinforces the fact that not all asylum seekers are economic migrants who see the UK as 'paved with gold' as the media often seems to claim (May and Cazeneuve, 2015). **Hasim**'s experience emphasises how unsettled life can feel even after being granted leave to remain and that a lucrative life in the UK is still, for many, less desirable than their previous lives in their home countries.

Surviving the asylum system

As discussed in the previous sections, there are many reasons why those seeking asylum may turn to strangers for support or look for illegitimate labour when they have a distrust of authorities, are afraid of repatriation, or are unsure of how to navigate the system. However, a prominent finding from a two-year research project exploring the experiences of thirty asylum seekers in England discovered that forms of extremely exploitative and forced labour were commonly simply unavoidable for refugees and asylum seekers because government provisions (currently £40.85 per week) were simply not enough to meet their basic needs (Lewis et al., 2013; Dwyer et al., 2016). Even in situations where people entered into and managed to escape such labour exploitation, they found that their restricted legal positions as refugees or asylum seekers would leave them little option but to return to such dubious labour. This research concluded that:

> [t]ackling forced labour among refugees and asylum seekers requires a major overhaul of government policy to restore asylum seekers' right to work and to ensure universal access to basic employment rights irrespective of immigration status. (Lewis et al., 2013)

As such, a hostile environment towards migrants cannot work to decrease the vulnerability of asylum seekers and refugees to forced labour. This means that the government cannot simultaneously claim to prioritise tackling modern slavery *and* continue its hostile environment towards immigrants. If it is to continue the hostile environment, then it must accept accountability for encouraging the conditions necessary for modern slavery to thrive.

Highlighting the struggle to meet basic needs identified by Lewis et al.'s report (2013), **Gamba**, **Isaac**, **Fredrika**, and **Hasim** all emphasised in their interviews how they relied wholeheartedly on the support of charities and drop-in centres to be able to survive as they waited for the outcome of their asylum decisions, and some even lived with volunteers that they had met via the drop-in centres. Although she has reapplied for asylum, **Fredrika**'s initial claim was denied and she then experienced the forced destitution suffered by so many rejected by the asylum system. Because she strongly believes her life is at risk should she return to Uganda, **Fredrika** has 'chosen' to remain destitute in the UK while she reapplies for asylum. This reflects De Genova's (2002) work on the 'deportability' of asylum seekers whereby the asylum system generates a palpable notion that asylum seekers could be sent 'home' at any time. When being returned to your home country equates to a potential death sentence, this threat understandably generates a constant sense of extreme fear.

Literature indicates that this is a common story, and that by forcing refused asylum seekers into destitution, the UK government fails to accept any degree of accountability for these people, completely overlooking the particular vulnerabilities faced by those, such as **Fredrika** who are unable or unwilling to leave the UK (Lewis et al., 2013; Lewis and Waite, 2015; Dwyer et al., 2016). In such a position where the option of returning 'home' is not a possibility, and the right to work in the UK has been denied, research shows that refused asylum seekers are at real risk of exploitation.

> Destitution, resulting from lacking the right to work or access to any government support or benefits, was the primary driver into exploitative

> work for irregular migrants and refused asylum seekers in our study (Lewis and Waite, 2015:58).

The study referred to involved research with thirty participants, seventeen of whom were asylum seekers on arrival to the UK. Of those seventeen, fourteen entered the labour market after being refused asylum left them with no support and no right to work (ibid.). When left in such a precarious situation, these people become particularly vulnerable to exploitative labour. They have no government-supported housing or stipend and, if they are to remain in the UK, must find a way to survive. This will often mean there is little choice other than to enter the labour market. However, with no legal right to work, they are restricted to approaching employers who are willing to illegally employ a refused asylum seeker. Such employers have the opportunity to take advantage of this extreme misbalance in power; knowing that the worker has no legal access to the labour market, they have the possibility to enforce poor working conditions, long hours, and low pay in the knowledge that the worker has little choice but to accept (Dwyer et al., 2016). Workers that challenge such conditions are simply reminded that they have no other option but to accept the situation (Waite, 2017) and that there will always be someone else willing to take their place (Dwyer et al., 2016). To report their working conditions to the authorities will simply result in their own penalisation for working with no legal right to do so (Lewis et al., 2013; Dwyer et al., 2016).

This lack of statutory support and its resulting impact on mental health was an issue raised in several of my interviews with asylum seekers. Similarly to the impact of conflict discussed in chapter four, the asylum system reduces the options available to its applicants, prohibiting the majority from accessing employment or education, and stipulating the location in which they must live. This lack of freedom, coupled with the uncertainty of knowing when a decision will be made or whether it will be positive, can lead to feelings of hopelessness and despair. This is especially true for those who fear for their lives should they be repatriated; for them, a negative outcome of an asylum decision could equate to a death sentence. The uncertainty caused by the asylum system also prevents asylum seekers from trying to integrate; they have no money to socialise and are reluctant to form relationships or to try to settle in an area when they are unsure of how long they will be permitted to stay. This can generate feelings of isolation, and some respondents discussed experiencing suicidal feelings as a result. This negative impact on mental health as a result of the asylum system, and particularly for those denied their claim, is highlighted in the literature (Dwyer et al., 2016). It is evident then that a lack of communication only increases what is already a highly stressful situation.

These examples emphasise how a lack of appropriate support may encourage asylum seekers to pursue other methods of survival, such as looking for work, which would breach the rules of the asylum system for most asylum seekers and which would leave them with no protection should this work be, or become, exploitative (Dwyer et al., 2016; Waite, 2017). Such lack of support may also actually serve to discourage people from engaging with the system. As such, the hostile environment is likely to push people away from engaging with the authorities and into more long-term, illegal, and precarious situations. Further, the length of time that people must wait for an asylum decision essentially means that their lives must be put on hold; they cannot access education or find employment. For **Catherine**, this meant that she felt unable to address her PTSD because her entire focus was on waiting for the outcome of the asylum decision. Although the government suggests that decisions should be reached within six months, this is not always the case, and the longer the wait, the longer asylum seekers live in the UK unable to contribute financially and unable to actively integrate into society (d'Albis et al., 2018).

Hasim described in his interview how, as an asylum seeker, he believed that all his problems would be solved as soon as an asylum decision was reached. Yet, upon being granted asylum, he remained in a vulnerable position because he was unaware of how to apply for housing or employment. His experience was similar to **Oscar**, who received a positive decision and then was told to take his papers and go. He was given no information on where to go or of organisations that may be able to offer assistance. As a result, **Oscar** became homeless, despite having been granted the right to live and work in the UK. **Oscar's** story of vulnerability after being granted asylum is one that is reflected in the literature, where those who are granted leave to remain have permission to work, but experience some of the highest unemployment rates in the UK (Dwyer et al., 2016). Hynes and Sales (2010) discuss how the dispersal of refugees could be one of the reasons for high unemployment rates. Refugees are dispersed out of London and the south-east to other areas in the UK. This often means they are separated from their own family members and support networks (reflecting again some of the vulnerabilities generated by conflict as outlined in chapter four) and therefore must start the process of making connections all over again. However, perhaps more significantly, the areas that refugees are dispersed to are determined by the availability of temporary housing. In many cases, temporary housing is concentrated around areas of economic deprivation, therefore adding further barriers to accessing work.

A report commissioned by The Refugee Council (Basedow and Doyle, 2016) found that there are also severe delays in refugees receiving key documents which give them the opportunity to find legal work. Basedow and Doyle (2016) undertook qualitative research with eleven individuals who had been granted asylum, and found that delays in receiving vital documents were common. Of the eleven interviewees, six had received their national insurance number before their government assistance had ended, while the other five had not. Without a national insurance number, these refugees were unable to access legal employment. This leaves them in a situation in which they have been granted refugee status, but their government support has ended and they are unable to legally find work. In these circumstances, refugees become destitute and are left with limited options. In such situations they are extremely susceptible to offers of illegitimate labour by employers who are willing to illegally take on workers without their national insurance numbers. Such employers know that the workers have no authority to call for fair working conditions or rates of pay and therefore have the power to stipulate long hours for little pay in the knowledge that the worker has little other choice. The government must recognise its failings in providing these documents in time to those to whom it grants asylum and it must accept accountability for the vulnerabilities it causes for those who fall through the gaps. Asylum seekers and refugees are entirely reliant on the government. As **Gamba** states, 'Asylum seekers are not allowed to work . . . we can't fend for ourselves.'

The fact that such a high proportion of victims of modern slavery identified in the UK only experience the slavery within the UK (58 per cent in 2021) is unsurprising when considering the lack of support or information offered to those both seeking and granted asylum. Without effective communication, information, or support during this time of extreme instability, it can only be expected that offers of support or work from strangers would prove to be tempting. It must be acknowledged that some, like **Hattie**, do not know which country they are travelling to. They are so desperate to leave their situation that the end destination is irrelevant. **Barak** evidenced this in his exclamation that 'I want to go wherever! Even Somalia!' In such situations, it is simply not possible to research the legal requirements of the asylum system when they are unaware of where their destination country will be. The same can be said of those who may know where they intend to travel to but, like **Edan**, the situation dictates that they leave immediately, without allowing them time to research the situation that awaits them upon arrival. As such, the government has a duty to try and reach as many immigrants as possible if it intends to be accountable to its claim of prioritising tackling modern slavery.

Although some of the interview respondents for this title had their asylum claims rejected, they all appealed these decisions and continued to wait for the next outcome. This means that the interviews did not provide examples of those who received negative decisions and were awaiting repatriation. However, to acknowledge those who have fled to the UK in order to escape situations—or potential situations—of modern slavery, it must be accepted that the UK government, in some instances, is returning people to situations of slavery, to situations in which they are likely to become victims of slavery, or to their deaths (Bulman, 2018b).

These issues all point towards the need for increased knowledge among both asylum seekers and statutory agencies. Asylum seekers need to know what the system is, how to navigate it, and what they should expect, which would have benefitted respondents such as **Oscar** and perhaps prevented him from becoming homeless after being granted asylum. Statutory agencies need to know how they could decrease the vulnerabilities of asylum seekers towards becoming victims of modern slavery and the importance of providing accurate information and clear communication.

6.2.3 Tied visas

Reflecting the vulnerabilities generated by the asylum system in terms of restricting the options available to migrants, another key way in which the UK government is allowing the perpetuation of systems of slavery is through its tied visa system for overseas domestic workers. In 2012, the UK government introduced the tied visa, which means that overseas domestic workers are tied to their employers once they come to the UK. This means that should the worker leave the employer for any reason, including to escape unfair or exploitative labour conditions, the worker will have breached their visa and is then liable for repatriation. As a result, for those in exploitative domestic work situations, the options available to the workers are reduced, an issue which, as discussed throughout this title, is one that can increase the likelihood of a person experiencing modern slavery. In the situation of a tied visa, the workers' legal choices are to stay in the exploitative situations or to be returned to their home countries (Sloan, 2015). An amendment was made in 2016 which allows domestic workers to change employers, but only if their original six-month visa is still valid, which is an incredibly short timescale for reporting the abuse, raising, and concluding legal action. For those who have chosen the option of moving to the UK in order to escape a dangerous situation in their home countries, should their employment situation become exploitative, they may be reluctant to leave because they are so desperate not to be returned to their home country, thereby resigning themselves to a life of exploitation which the UK government will not allow them to challenge. However, should they choose to leave because of exploitation but want to avoid repatriation, the situation may become such that they choose to stay in the UK illegally, seeking support from agencies, acquaintances, or strangers in order to avoid the restrictive legal policies. Although this may lead to situations which still remain preferable to being returned home, there is also the potential for such situations to lead to modern slavery. As Moss describes (2011:no pagination), the choice of the UK government to disallow overseas domestic migrants the option to change employers:

> betray[s] the fact that the Government is less concerned with policies that have been hailed by parliamentarians to be effective in preventing trafficking, such as the domestic worker visa protections, and more concerned with being seen to be tough on so called immigration crime.

6.3 Conclusion

This chapter has focused on two main areas: intersectionality and structural dynamics, and ways in which UK government systems encourage modern slavery. Focusing on these topics has addressed the impact of some key structural issues on generating situations of modern slavery.

The chapter has determined that the use of intersectionality alone in understanding people's identity is not enough to identify who may become vulnerable to modern slavery. People's age, gender, or ethnicity alone are not significant enough factors to put them at risk. Instead, their intersecting identities should be understood in tandem with the context and structural dynamics that they face. This means that it will be difficult to make any direct comparisons between people's experiences, because it will be rare that people will have the same intersecting identities *and* experience the same context and structural dynamics. However, this research has indicated that the context and structural dynamics are more pertinent in identifying whether or not someone will be at risk of modern slavery than a person's identity intersections. The respondents who contributed to this research had extremely varied identities with differences in age, gender, ethnicity, nationality, and religion, yet they all lived through a similar context: conflict. Although the conflict varied for each respondent—for some it was war, for others it was familial conflict, employment conflict, or marital breakdown—a commonality between all the conflicts was the context that the conflict increased their vulnerability to modern slavery in two ways: by reducing the options available to those living through it, and leading to a breakdown in their support networks. It was this reduction in choice that forced the respondents into making decisions where every outcome held some element of risk, and the breakdown in support networks meant that they weren't able to turn to people they knew and trusted for help. As such, it was the context more than their identities that held inherent risk.

As outlined in chapter four, conflict generates two specific vulnerabilities which increase the likelihood of a person experiencing modern slavery: reducing the options available to a person, and breaking down their support network. This chapter demonstrates that these vulnerabilities aren't exclusively generated by conflicts and, in fact, there are policies in the UK that generate the same vulnerabilities and are responsible for increasing the risk that a person might become a victim of modern slavery.

In relation to the ways in which UK government systems encourage situations of modern slavery, there is drastic need for change. When she was prime minister of the UK, Theresa May claimed that her government would 'lead the way in defeating modern slavery' (May, 2016) and the UK government continues to state that tackling modern slavery is a priority. This is a non-controversial cause which serves to capture enthusiasm from all ends of the political spectrum, making it easy for the government to champion (McGrath, 2014; Kotiswaran and Okyere, 2015; O'Connell Davidson, 2016). Despite claims of 'leading the way', the government continues to focus on problems in source countries, despite the fact that the majority of victims in the UK only experience slavery after arriving in the UK.

The UK response to modern slavery conflates it with immigration crime which fails to reflect the genuine picture where UK nationals are the most commonly identified victims, and where the majority of victims have only experienced their exploitation within the UK. The NRM has been shown to be prejudiced against those potential victims who are not from the EU

(Cooper et al., 2017; Robinson, 2017), and conviction rates of perpetrators remain insignificant. There were 344 modern slavery cases heard in court between 2015 and 2019, and seventy-four (21.5 per cent) resulted in a conviction, with only sixty-two receiving an immediate prison sentence (Clugston, 2021). Further, the long waiting times to receive a Conclusive Grounds decision serve to exacerbate trauma and could encourage some to circumnavigate the system in order to begin to move on without having to wait such a long time to hear whether the Home Office believes their story.

The asylum system repeats the vulnerabilities generated by conflict as outlined in chapter four. It impacts agency and choice by leaving asylum seekers with limited support or options. It operates with a lack of clarity or communication, leaving many without knowledge of what is required of them or why certain information is needed. When this also exists within a hostile environment towards immigrants, it can lead to misunderstanding and distrust, where some may feel uncomfortable disclosing their traumatic experiences to those they believe have a vested interest in repatriating them to a country in which they feel unsafe.

The limiting of agency and resulting uncertainty about the future has a significantly detrimental impact on mental health for asylum seekers, and for some the outcome of the decision equates to a potential death sentence should they be repatriated. For many, this can cause a sense of hopelessness and despair, where thinking about the future becomes futile. For some this could encourage an avoidance of the system, leading to a life hiding from authorities and seeking to remain in the UK illegally, finding illegitimate work which holds the inherent risk of being exploitative because of its lack of regulation.

Those who are in the asylum system are commonly prohibited from working. This restricts their choices to: voluntarily returning to their home country, embracing the asylum system and accepting that they have no control on the timings or the outcome of the decision, or trying to make a life in the UK illegally and remaining hidden from authority. Again, this final option places them at risk when the only people willing to employ them will be those who are happy to do so illegally, and therefore the employee has no control over the terms of their employment.

Some of these issues are further reflected in the tied visa system which reduces the options available to overseas domestic workers. The visas tie the worker to their employer, meaning that if their situation becomes exploitative, in most cases they are left only with the options of either returning to their home country, which many of them have worked hard to leave, or accepting the exploitation. This system places all the power in the hands of the employer and makes it almost impossible for someone on a tied visa to be able to raise a claim against their employer should they become exploited.

Defeating modern slavery simply does not fit into the environments that have been outlined in this chapter. The UK government cannot be praised for championing modern slavery while it continues to stall on central issues, ignore its own flaws, and perpetuate systems that are biased against migrants.

Chapter seven
From victim blaming to victim agency

Chapter six considered the role of structure in causing situations of modern slavery by considering how restrictive UK policies may serve to put people at risk. This chapter continues to give meaning to the findings developed through the research, but moves away from the role of structure and towards the role of agency in generating situations of modern slavery. It debates the usefulness of victim terminology and the impact its use has on generating unrealistic depictions of those who suffer modern slavery, which therefore risks encouraging misunderstandings among the public, practitioners (such as police, social workers, medical professionals, and lawyers), and victims themselves. The chapter then challenges the notion that victimhood and agency must be mutually exclusive by demonstrating the prevalence of agency in the lead up to situations of modern slavery. Finally, it considers the interplay between structure and agency in generating and perpetuating situations of modern slavery. These are all fundamental aspects in understanding who is vulnerable to becoming a victim of modern slavery, why they are at risk, and the conditions that might exacerbate the likelihood of becoming a victim.

7.1 Victim terminology

First, although discussed in chapter two, it is important to highlight again that the term 'victim' is used throughout this title with acknowledgement of the flaws and controversies surrounding its use. Increasing numbers of victims are resenting being identified with the term because of its negative connotations and its capacity to deny their independence and strength (Van Dijk, 2009). American feminists have advocated for the use of the term 'survivor' to replace that of 'victim' in order to acknowledge the agency

From Conflict to Modern Slavery. Alicia Heys, Oxford University Press. © Alicia Heys 2023.
DOI: 10.1093/oso/9780192846549.003.0007

that individuals have in situations where they are not necessarily passive and weak. While there are clear benefits to the use of the term 'survivor' and flaws with the term 'victim', I favour the latter for this title as, unlike its counterpart, it is applicable to situations not only in which the person in question has managed to escape their exploitative situation, but also to those who continue to suffer in modern slavery. Although the term 'victim' holds certain connotations, I do not equate the term with a person who is powerless and passive. However, the impact of this choice of terminology will now become the focus.

7.1.1 The removal of agency

The idea of someone consenting to a situation of modern slavery is so counter-intuitive that those who suffer this crime tend to be understood as having no agency or choice in the situation. From the outside, experiences of modern slavery are often understood as constituting a complete removal of agency whereby the victim played no part and had no choice (De Angelis, 2016). This lack of agency is fundamental in Christie's discussion of the 'ideal victim' which suggests that people are more likely to be recognised as victims if they are blameless and weak and who, at the time of victimisation, were undertaking 'respectable' activities (1986). This then causes problems in identifying as victims those who appear not to be weak, or those who had some agency, be it in the lead up to the exploitation, or within the situation itself. It also poses problems for those whose activities are not considered respectable. This could cover a range of issues from people having been in prison to committing criminal activities to provide for themselves.

In the literature on modern slavery, there is one key topic that receives the focus of attention when questioning the authenticity of a person's victimhood because of their non-respectable activities. This topic concentrates on women who have previously been sex workers and have become victims of modern slavery, or those who have agreed to undertake sex work but have found themselves in situations whereby the conditions they agreed to have not been upheld (Doezema, 1998; Blume, 2015). Because sex work is often not considered respectable, for those who had some degree of agency in choosing this 'non-respectable' occupation, there is scepticism around the possibility that they constitute victims (Wilson and O'Brien, 2016) and a tendency to assume that they are accountable for their own suffering. To fit the profile of an 'ideal victim' and not be treated with scepticism, victims of modern slavery for sexual exploitation are expected to have been deceived into their exploitation, having had no choice in undertaking sex work.

Wilson and O'Brien (2016) highlight how this lack of acknowledgement of victimhood in relation to those who have had some degree of agency in taking part in sex work is reflected in the US government's Trafficking in Persons reports. Their research showed that of the 361 victim narratives of sexual slavery they looked at, only one victim was understood to have voluntarily entered sex work; the remaining 360 had encountered sexual exploitation but were not perceived to have undertaken sex work voluntarily. This emphasises the huge impact that agency can have on understandings of victims; it is extremely unlikely that these numbers accurately reflect the proportion of women who voluntarily and involuntarily undertook sex work and experienced modern slavery. As this example demonstrates, those with agency related to sex work were extremely unlikely to be recognised as victims as they did not fit the criteria of the 'ideal victim' who is weak, blameless, and respectable.

In relation to modern slavery for sexual exploitation, Weitzer (2007) highlights how this 'ideal victim' narrative is wholly inappropriate, considering how the relationship between migration, sex work, and agency commonly means that women are aware that they will be working in sex work; however, this agency does not negate their experiences as victims. Notions of the 'ideal victim' within modern slavery discourse therefore serve to confuse victimhood and agency. On the one hand, as Srikantiah (2007) posits, the agency of those who choose to engage in sex work is denied. Those advocating for the criminalisation of sex work simply do not believe that a woman could choose such work, but that these women must have had no agency in order to find themselves in it (Butler-Sloss, 2011; Skrivankova, 2011). And yet, on the other hand, rather than labelling all these women as victims because they have engaged in sex work which it is believed they cannot have consented to, those who do claim to have consented to the work are labelled as complicit in their exploitation. This demonstrates how agency is therefore removed from victims of sexual exploitation regardless of their choices concerning sex work; their ideas of their own agency regarding their choices are entirely disregarded.

Attributes relating to the 'ideal victim' are inconsistent with the actual lived experiences of victims of modern slavery whose agency often plays some role in their situation unless they are one of the few victims who suffer kidnapping and have no degree of choice leading up to their exploitation (Doezema, 2001; O'Connell Davidson, 2006). While there may be inappropriate notions of who constitutes an 'ideal victim' based on weakness, blamelessness, and respectability, an individual does not need to be an 'ideal victim' in order to be a victim. To reassert the definition of the Bellagio-Harvard guidelines, a victim of slavery is someone who has been controlled for the purpose of exploitation; the extent of their agency or involvement is therefore irrelevant in defining someone as a victim of modern slavery.

7.1.2 Gendering of the 'ideal victim'

The focus on victims, victimisation, and agency in relation to modern slavery is almost exclusively on women's experiences (Blume, 2015). This highlights an important point that the experiences of men as victims risk being disregarded if they are deemed not to fit that ideal of being physically weak and passive. 'In addition to physical strength, men are understood to have a better capacity to defend and care for themselves; men are perceived to have more control over their labour than women' (Blume, 2015:8).

Focusing on the victimhood of women who fit this ideal is to separate those who experience modern slavery into female victims where the focus is mainly on non-consenting sex work, and male agents where the focus is mainly on labour exploitation which does not hold the same controversy around consent as sex work. While agency has received significant attention in the literature in relation to the exploitation of women working in commercial sex, such attention has not been offered in equal measure to other forms of exploitation or to the exploitation of men (Choi-Fitzpatrick, 2012). 'Migrant men are seen as the norm—and are thus visible—but their gendered experiences are never highlighted and never questioned' (Blume, 2015:5).

De Angelis's work focuses on the trafficking of women (2016), and she advocates for discussions about trafficking to recognise that victimhood and agency can exist together rather than as opposites. Sen's framework provides a grounding for this (1985, 1999). Sen discusses how women's agency is limited in a way that men's agency is not, both in terms of their 'well-being freedom'—that is larger-scale aspects such as their economic security—as well as their 'agency-freedom', or the control they have over their immediate situation. Both aspects of freedom are constrained for women more so than men, which could explain why there is a tendency to avoid referring to men as victims. Men have more freedom over their agency, and the more agency a person has, the less likely it is that they will be identified as a victim, as illustrated by the US government's Trafficking in Persons reports discussed in section 7.1.1.

Focusing on female victims to the extent that men become sidelined from conversations about victims of modern slavery only serves to further embed the concept of an 'ideal victim' and reinforce the idea that it is women rather than men who become victims. However, the impact of the inappropriate focus on women as victims does not end with men being overlooked, and can actually influence policy responses (Quirk and O'Connell Davidson, 2015; Wilson and O'Brien, 2016). This is something discussed in the extant literature, particularly in reference to the ways in which the conflation between women, sex work, and modern slavery has been used to push and justify political agendas relating to sex work (Weitzer, 2014; Blume, 2015). The focus on women as victims has further impact, in that by highlighting the 'women as victims' agenda, front-line responses have, historically, been largely focused on women. This is noticeable throughout the development of legislation as discussed in chapter one, where focus was often placed on protecting women and children. This overlooks any similarities between the experiences of genders and leads to overgeneralised and misconceived understandings of the victim experience and levels of agency. Fundamentally, it also means that male victims have likely been left without acknowledgement or support. The main flaw of such a victim typology is that it serves to prioritise those victims who fit the criteria and dismiss those who do not. However, as identified above, the 'ideal victim' does not necessarily reflect the 'real victim'.

It is only in the past few years that the number of males being identified as potential victims of modern slavery in the UK has started to draw anywhere near close to the numbers of females identified. Now these recognitions have been made, a significant difference in statistics is noticeable and the balance has switched with more males than females now referred into the NRM. Table 7.1 below shows a comparison between the percentage of males and females referred into the NRM between 2013 and 2021 (National Crime Agency, 2014, 2015, 2016, 2017, 2018, 2019; Home Office, 2020, 2021, 2022a). The discrepancy in percentages reflects the rounding of decimals and transgender individuals referred into the NRM.

The table shows a clear and constant change over time in the ratio between males and females identified as potential victims of modern slavery in the UK, where in 2013 females represented almost two-thirds of all potential victims, but in 2021 over three-quarters of referrals were for males.

Table 7.1 Males and females referred into the National Referral Mechanism

Year	Males	Females
2013	36%	64%
2014	39%	61%
2015	46%	53%
2016	49%	50%
2017	52%	47%
2018	61%	39%
2019	68%	32%
2020	74%	26%
2021	77%	23%

This indicates a change in understandings of who constitutes a victim, and is reassuring in the sense that it appears the victimhood of males is no longer being overlooked.

Reflected in the fact the Home Office developed a modern slavery strategy in 2014 shortly preceding the Modern Slavery Act of 2015, modern slavery as a form of exploitation became widely publicised. Awareness campaigns were developed, and significant training was delivered to front-line staff from police to local authorities, and from non-governmental organisations to the health sector. As time passed and these practitioners gathered first-hand understandings of how modern slavery might present, training was updated and recognitions of modern slavery expanded. This growing understanding of the experiences that might fit under the rubric of modern slavery could go a significant way to explaining the changes highlighted in Table 7.1 above, as labour exploitation came to be more widely recognised as a form of modern slavery, and understandings of victims were less closely concerned with females. Further, labour exploitation tends to be less hidden than sexual exploitation, and with campaigns encouraging members of the public to report their concerns, it is perhaps logical that the numbers of males referred into the NRM began to rise, not necessarily because more males were being exploited, but because practitioners (such as police, social workers, and NGOs) were learning to recognise men's and boys' experiences as modern slavery. Similarly, over the past few years, the recognition of so called 'county lines' cases as fitting the rubric of modern slavery has driven an increase in referrals, where a high proportion of these victims are young males.

To elucidate further on these changes in understandings of how modern slavery might present, in 2013, 44.4 per cent of cases referred into the NRM related to sexual exploitation (National Crime Agency, 2014). In 2019, the way that referrals were reported changed slightly to account for individuals who had suffered multiple forms of exploitation and included criminal exploitation as a category in its own right where it had previously been grouped under labour exploitation. This makes it somewhat difficult to make a direct numerical comparison; however, in 2021 sexual exploitation as the sole form of exploitation accounted for only 10 per cent of referrals into the NRM. Cases which involved sexual exploitation in addition to other forms of exploitation accounted for an additional 7 per cent of referrals (Home Office, 2022a). As such, regardless of whether we look at sexual exploitation singularly or as one form of exploitation in many, it is clear that it is no longer making up the majority of referrals into the NRM. Again, this signifies that front-line staff are gaining a better understanding of the fact that modern slavery constitutes more than just sexual exploitation and that victims are not always female; it also reflects the increase in referrals for 'county lines' cases noted above.

Although it might be assumed that including men in discussions of victimhood would alter understandings from the feminised 'weak and passive' victim to a more inclusive understanding that accepts that victims may have agency and are not always weak, this is not necessarily the case. As Blume (2015) discusses, widening the typology of victims to include men might not raise the standards of what is meant by the term 'victim', but may in fact lower them. This means that rather than female victims being understood on a level comparable with men, where their agency is recognised and their power and independence is acknowledged, there is a possibility that it could simply serve to mean that male victims are understood on a par with female victims: that they are weak, passive, and have no control over their situations.

7.1.3 The impact of victim terminology on agency

In succumbing to this 'ideal victim' narrative, a tendency has developed among activists, suggesting that:

> [s]laves are victims who need to be rescued—helpless, dependent, a little pathetic, and, we expect, grateful for a chance at freedom. What this view misses is the resilience and strength of people caught in slavery, their endurance, intelligence, and compassion. (Bales, 2007:62)

Bales highlights here one of the most fundamental problems with victim terminology, that to assign the term 'victim' to an individual is to remove their agency and suggest they are nothing more than a passive person caught in a situation over which they have no control or power. The importance of language is clear in relation to victimhood and modern slavery, where the assignation of the victim label can change the way that the victim is perceived both by themselves and by outsiders (Foucault, 1977; Green, 2015). As Giddens acknowledges, language can have a huge impact on a person's daily life as they are expected to live up to their label and some may find their activities changing in a nod towards what is expected of them (1986). This was reflected in **Fredrika**'s story where she had a legitimate reason for claiming asylum. As a reminder of her story, **Fredrika** is homosexual and certain she would be killed if she were to be returned to Uganda; however, after receiving negative and hateful responses from her family after she disclosed her sexuality to them, she was too afraid to talk about her sexuality in her asylum interview because of how she might be perceived. Because of this fear, **Fredrika** lied in her asylum interview, trying to present herself in—what she deemed to be—the best possible light in order to increase her chances of receiving a positive decision.

Applying victimhood to someone also goes against notions of intersectionality: it suggests that the victim aspect of a person's identity is the prominent and most relevant feature, and it fails to acknowledge the ways in which their victimhood might intersect with other aspects of their identity which, for them, may be much more important. Implying that all victims are weak and powerless also disregards the vast complexities of situations of slavery and fails to acknowledge the role that the individual's agency and choices may have played in their situations, an issue addressed further in section 7.2.

While this discussion so far has focused on the ways in which the 'ideal victim' is believed to have no agency, there is also much academic discussion about how terming someone as a victim can actually lead to a removal of agency, thereby reinforcing the notion of victimhood simply through the use of the label. The label of being a victim ascribes a role of passivity that many may find constricting.

Those victims of modern slavery who want to access support through the NRM must demonstrate that they are victims. However, because of the limitations of the 'ideal victim' and the tendency that those who fit this ideal will receive better treatment than those who do not (Williams, 2004; Davies, 2007), encouraging someone to identify themselves as a victim may be one way in which their agency is actually removed. This person might not deem themselves to be a victim (De Angelis, 2016; Heys et al., 2022), or may be reluctant to use the term. However, because of the pressure of needing to be identified as a 'genuine victim', some, such as **Fredrika**, may fear disclosing their true experience as they are so anxious about the impression they must make to the agencies assisting or making decisions on their situation. They believe that they will only be supported if they fit the criteria of the 'ideal victim' as presented to them through narratives, media, and anti-slavery campaigns. These suggest they should be weak, blameless, and respectable, but also that they should display signs of physical suffering (Aradau, 2004) meaning that in order to increase the likelihood of receiving support, they may be encouraged to take on a persona that does not accurately reflect their experience, despite them genuinely being a victim. Scenarios such as this only serve to reinforce the 'ideal victim' narrative.

Modern anti-slavery campaigns have received much criticism in relation to reinforcing this stereotypical 'ideal victim' who is passive, voiceless, and in need of rescue. Quirk and Richter (2015) discuss this predisposition of modern anti-slavery campaigns using sensationalist images, and Quirk and O'Connell Davidson (2015:no pagination) refer to them as 'simplistic and misleading images'. They often depict women in chains, handcuffs, ropes, or blindfolds, or with barcodes printed on their bare skin. While such images may garner the attention of the sympathetic public who deem those depicted in the images to be deserving of their pity and compassion (De Angelis, 2016), these images reflect the 'ideal victim', rather than the 'real victim'. As mentioned above, this can encourage 'genuine victims' to alter their persona in order to fit the ideal narrative in the hope of receiving a more favourable outcome. However, the use of such images can also misinform the public of the experiences of victims of modern slavery. By using these images that depict desperate and helpless, usually female, individuals, the public are offered a reinforced view of the 'ideal victim', leading them to disregard or wrongly interpret situations of modern slavery in which the victim is male, or where the victim displays some level of agency.

These campaigns could also impact policy and governmental responses to such situations (Quirk and O'Connell Davidson, 2015). While the 'ideal victim' continues to be portrayed as a weak, passive individual lacking agency, those that have had any choice or any knowledge about their situation are less likely to receive sympathy and support, and are more likely to receive criminal justice or immigration sanctions (De Angelis, 2016). As a result, 'popular representations of trafficking and slavery have too often hurt—rather than helped—efforts to both understand and combat global exploitation, discrimination and vulnerability' (Quirk and O'Connell Davidson, 2015:no pagination).

To treat victims as having no agency is also to make assumptions on their behalf, which serves to further enforce any lack of agency. Morris (1997:29) explains how detrimental it can be to deny victims the opportunity to tell their story. 'Silence and the loss of voice may eventually constitute or represent for some who suffer a complete shattering of the self.' As such, to assume that a victim would not want to share their story and to deny them the chance to do so is to remove their choice in the situation. This reiterates some of the problems involved with using gatekeepers to access respondents from 'vulnerable' populations. As outlined in chapter one, sometimes gatekeepers can be particularly protective over their clients when approached about research opportunities. They may feel they have a responsibility to protect their client from any potentially triggering experiences by denying a researcher access. However, this further denies these individuals the agency of deciding for themselves whether or not they would like to contribute to the research.

Denying a victim the opportunity to voice their experience denies not only their agency in choosing whether or not to share their story, but who they are as a person, having been shaped by their experience of being a victim. This is reinforced by De Angelis (2016) who asserts that placing all victims of slavery into one homogenous group serves to deny their unique and individual experiences, but also removes a sense of who these people are outside of their slavery experiences, considering them only as victims. Van Dijk (2009) adds to this with the claim that assigning a victim label can generate a discrepancy between the understandings that others have of the victim and their own self-image, meaning that outsiders consider them only by their victim label as opposed to viewing them as a unique person behind the label. Again, this relates back to intersectionality and rejects all the other intersecting aspects of a person's identity by viewing their victimhood as the most pertinent factor. Significantly, this also overlooks any aspect of a person's life after the slavery situation. 'Women rebuild and refashion their lives post-trafficking in a variety of imaginative ways. Principally, women celebrate survival as the exemplar in achieving agency' (De Angelis, 2016:15). This quote from De Angelis emphasises how a person's overcoming of a situation of slavery could be the very aspect of their situation that provides them with a sense of agency. Therefore, to understand a person only as a victim is to deny their post-slavery identity and the agency they have discovered.

7.1.4 The notion of rescue

The denial of agency relating to situations of modern slavery is underlined with the terminology of 'rescue' where agencies emphasise the importance of 'rescuing victims' from slavery. Such choice of vocabulary emphasises the tendency of outsiders to consider those in situations of slavery to be passive and powerless, requiring the assistance of such outsiders to escape their exploitation. Although in some situations this may be true, it is not universal, and not all those who suffer modern slavery are the passive victims that this choice of terminology implies.

The use of the word 'rescue' may be fundamentally hypocritical in several ways. Some may enter a situation of modern slavery with a degree of choice, perhaps regarding the nature of the work but not the conditions, or vice versa. There is the potential that this situation could be preferable to the one they left, for example, if the slavery situation provided safe accommodation (even if it offered no pay), after the individual had fled a situation in which they had no housing or employment. In such circumstances, those organisations who 'rescue' these victims without first discussing with them their options and the likely outcomes of such a 'rescue', may cause the victim to leave the slavery situation only to end up in worse conditions. For example, if the person does not have the right to live in the UK, and that right is not granted after being 'rescued', then such 'rescues' offer false promises of security, especially if the victim is fearful of repatriation.

A positive recent change in policy is the Modern Slavery Victim Care and Coordination Contract (MSVCC) mentioned in chapter six. This introduced a new Recovery Needs Assessment which means that once an individual receives a positive Conclusive Grounds decision through the NRM, their needs are reviewed and follow-on care put in place to prevent what had been previously been identified as a cliff-edge drop-off in support. Prior to this, individuals leaving the NRM were faced with no housing, no employment, and no recourse to public funds, meaning some might have rightly identified that their situation of slavery was actually favourable, not only to life before the situation of slavery (as discussed by O'Connell Davidson in Martins, 2016), but to life after the 'rescue'. By failing to offer guaranteed support to victims of modern slavery after leaving the NRM, the UK government was accountable for generating an environment where, for some, an experience of slavery offered more safety and security than that offered by the government. The changes introduced through the Recovery Needs Assessment in the MSVCC is changing the system in this respect; however, there have already been issues identified regarding discrepancy in care through the new MSVCC, with British nationals seemingly less likely to access the provisions offered (Heys et al., 2022). Further, the new system does not overcome the wider environment of hostility that may prevent victims from coming forward. For example, those seeking asylum who have no choice but to find illegitimate labour in order to meet their basic needs have no recourse to support should this labour become exploitative, because they will be detained or deported for breaking the rules of their asylum application.

There is also a false assumption that victims can come out of the support system and return to life with security and viable options available to them. This is simply not reflective of reality. As Choi-Fitzpatrick explains:

> current policies are rooted in a neoliberal assumption that coerced victims can simply be returned to the market where they will be able to pursue other viable choices and to supportive families and societies. These assumptions are both simplistic and false. (2012:21)

This reflects the notion of hyper-precarity discussed by Lewis et al. (2013, 2014) whereby the labour exploitation of those in the asylum system as well as those both granted and refused asylum should be understood not by the precarious labour, but by the precarious lives of those experiencing the labour. The socio-legal status of asylum seekers and refugees, coupled with migration contexts and gender relations means that, as Choi-Fitzpatrick stipulates (2012), it is not the working situation that is precarious, but the entire underpinning of these people's lives in the UK. As Lewis and Waite point out:

> [u]nless one or more persistent insecurity is altered or resolved, racialised and gendered migration, work and welfare regimes and neoliberalism combine to create an ongoing 'precarity trap' for migrant

> forced labourers. For these reasons, a singular focus on 'rescue' from any one particular forced labour situation is unlikely to offer a durable solution unless other insecurities contributing to the 'precarity trap' are addressed. (2015:65)

The role of a 'rescuer' is also imbued with notions of power, superiority, and control. The role is socially valued and is inherently superior to that of the victim. Rejection of the 'rescue' is therefore seen by these 'rescuers' as deviant and evidence that the victim is too traumatised to make decisions in their own best interests. Although the organisations undertaking the 'rescues' may believe that no person would choose to be exploited, unless they explain the likely outcomes to the victim and allow them to make an informed decision, then by undertaking a 'rescue' they are withdrawing agency and choice from that individual by removing them from a situation which may be preferable to the long-term options that are available to them. Unless the organisation continues to support the victim through the NRM and after exiting, into accommodation, employment, and integration into society, then such 'rescues' are nothing more than a short-term relief from exploitation.

7.2 The victim/agent binary

While the terminology of victimhood can serve to remove an individual's agency as described in section 7.1, slavery itself is understood as a situation in which a person's agency is removed. As Landman describes:

> [f]irst, fundamentally, slavery involves the question of human dignity and the value of a human being which under conditions of slavery is reduced to property, possession, or a subject of control by another that fundamentally denies that person true social and political agency. (2018:144–5)

As this quote implies, notions of slavery always return to ideas of possession, and with that possession must come some degree of a lack of agency for the victim to be controlled. The whole concept of slavery involves a victim who no longer has full self-determination to be able to make their own choices, meaning that the victim can be understood as having had the powers attaching to the right of ownership removed from their own control and given to the perpetrator controlling them, hence they then become understood as property (Allain et al., 2012). As described in section 7.1, many understandings of victims are based around a notion of the 'ideal victim' which suggest that, in order to be defined as a victim of modern slavery, all agency must have been removed from the victim and their choices leading up to the slavery must have played no part in the outcome. However, while definitions of slavery indicate that the powers attaching to the right of ownership must be held by a perpetrator to the extent that they have control over the victim, this does not necessarily equate to a complete removal of agency.

There are significant flaws associated with the tendency to understand victims of modern slavery on a forced/voluntary or victim/agent binary, where only those with no agency and no level of choice leading to the situation (thereby fitting the criteria for the 'ideal victim') are considered victims. As described in section 7.1, the notion of an 'ideal victim' who has no agency is not reflective of a 'real victim'. While, of course, there will be examples of people who experience modern slavery as a result of a complete removal of agency, many victims have some level of agency and choice leading to their exploitation. However, in such a scenario, forced and voluntary exist on a scale rather than a binary; there is no black and white distinction as a person's level of choice will depend on their situation. This reflects Skrivankova's work which emphasises that 'there is a continuum of experiences ranging from decent work through minor and major labour law violations, to extreme exploitation in the form of forced labour' (2010:4). While it is likely that there will always be some level of force in situations of modern slavery, as it is improbable that any person would volunteer to experience exploitation, violence, and being held hostage should their agency be free and uncontrolled (O'Connell Davidson, 2013b), there may very well also be a degree of agency and choice on the victim's part that has led towards the situation.

As stated, this 'choice' will likely sit on a spectrum where a person with complete agency is least likely to enter a situation of modern slavery, and a person with no agency is the most likely. Of all the respondents from this research project, there was one who particularly highlighted a complete removal of agency. **Beth** experienced modern slavery on two occasions, once in Uganda and once in the UK. Although her experience in the UK was one in which she had some level of agency, this agency was entirely removed during her experience in Uganda. As a child, **Beth** was kidnapped by the Lord's Resistance Army and held against her will as a 'wife' of one of the commanders where she was kept for four years and sexually exploited. Her complete lack of choice and agency in this situation puts her in the category of an 'ideal victim'. While the removal of agency cannot be denied in **Beth**'s case, it is not reflective of the lived experience for the majority of victims, and the rest of the respondents interviewed who experienced modern slavery did have a degree of agency leading towards their exploitation.

Usually, individuals will have some input, agency, and a degree of choice in situations that lead to their exploitation; however, such choices have usually been limited and are not reflective of those available to a person who has complete agency. From the interviews, this can be illustrated by **Hattie** who 'chose' to engage the services of a smuggler to help her illegally leave the country. **Hattie** needed to flee the country out of fear of unfair arrest, and this threat limited her options and restricted her agency. While she would never have previously considered trying to leave the country illegally, the threat of arrest left her with the limited choices of either finding a way out of the country or accepting arrest for something she did not deem a crime. With these being the only options available to her, **Hattie** 'chose' to covertly leave the country and 'chose' to make a deal with a smuggler to pay off her debt on arrival at the destination (which transpired to be a situation of debt bondage and sexual exploitation). While these were technically choices that **Hattie** made, she would not have made those choices if not for the conflict situation with her employers limiting her agency and the possibilities available to her.

This example highlights how notions of choice and agency are not as easily defined as a person simply having a choice or not having a choice. O'Connell Davidson (2013b) defines this confusing notion as the difference between an active and a voluntary (or autonomous) choice. Here, an 'active' choice is simply the act of making a choice, while an 'autonomous' or 'voluntary' choice is one that is made without the influence of any external forces. **Hattie** made an active choice to enter a deal with a smuggler, but it was not a voluntary choice. Her situation forced her into making this decision; if she had not feared being arrested and never released, it is unlikely that she would have made such a choice. Regardless of whether decisions constitute an autonomous choice or merely an active one, in the majority of cases it would be misguided to suggest that victims of modern slavery (both leading up to and within their exploitative situations) have no agency whatsoever.

This dilemma is emphasised in the International Organization for Migration's (IOM) world migration report which states that 'less than 1 per cent of IOM-assisted victims were kidnapped at the point of trafficking and, conversely, over fifty per cent were recruited through a personal contact' (International Organization for Migration, 2011:133). This shows that in a firm majority of cases, victims of modern slavery do hold some degree of agency where they enter into agreements with acquaintances and are more than just passive individuals.

These examples demonstrate how migrants who find themselves in situations of modern slavery cannot be easily divided into:

> [t]hose who were driven to move by forces beyond their control or who were forcibly moved for purposes of exploitation by 'traffickers'; and on the other hand, those who exercised agency, choice, and control over their own migration, including those who entered into a partnership with 'smugglers' to make an unauthorized border crossing. (O'Connell Davidson, 2013b:177)

The line between being forcibly moved and exercising agency is not distinct, as again illustrated by **Hattie** who straddles this divide having been driven to move by forces beyond her control and yet also choosing to enter a partnership with a smuggler. This is further emphasised by Brysk and Choi-Fitzpatrick who state that 'trafficked individuals are neither helpless victims (as in the moral crusader narrative) nor rights-bearing individuals (as in the human rights framework)' (2012:5). Instead, they most likely sit somewhere between these two extremes.

This discussion highlights how it is inaccurate to suggest that freedom and slavery are direct opposites or mutually exclusive (Schneider, 1993; De Angelis, 2016). To do so would be to overlook any extent of freedom that those experiencing slavery have, and would also ignore any lack of freedom experienced by those that are not victims of slavery. Such concepts consider that the only available scenarios are that a person has agency and free choice or that they do not, when agency and coercion should rather be understood as on a scale. In reality, those who experience modern slavery rarely suffer a complete denial of agency but will have had some degree of choice in the situations that led to their exploitation. However, these apparent choices are forced rather than voluntary. 'Choosing' from a set of very limited or bad options is an act of agency but, due to the constraints or conditions under which the choice is made, does not negate their status as a victim of modern slavery. However, it is also important to emphasise that, as the Bellagio-Harvard Guidelines advocate, the removal or limitation of agency alone is not enough to define a person as a victim of modern slavery; there must also be the intent of exploitation (Allain et al., 2012).

7.3 Macro- and micro-level impacts on agency

These ideas of agency and victimhood existing on a spectrum rather than being binary opposites are unpacked by Landman.

> At the individual or micro level, a person will have varying degrees of personal agency (i.e. negative liberty) and the ability to freely exchange their labour within a rights protective labour market. At the societal or macro level, a person will be embedded in economic, legal, political, and social structures that also affect their relative degree of agency. (2018:147).

This highlights how notions of agency are not as simple as denoting whether or not an individual has control over their own choices, and links back to Sen's argument that the macro-level environment is more restrictive on women than on men (1985, 1999). Fundamentally, agency should be understood in two significant ways: agency at the micro level and agency at the macro level, where micro refers to relationships between individuals and macro to relationships between an individual and larger societal structures and systems.

It is generally accepted that agency can be removed at both the micro and macro level, but a person will only be understood as a victim of modern slavery if their agency is removed at the micro level—that is of one person by another—rather than by a restrictive system. However, it is important to acknowledge the complex interactions between the macro and micro level. The concept of an individual's ability to exercise agency being constrained by environmental and social structures (the macro level) is one that receives significant attention in the literature (Sen, 1985, 1999; Archer, 1995; Lister, 2004; De Angelis, 2016) and for many, the removal of agency at the micro level is only possible because of the constraints imposed by these macro-level structures. Indeed, while the Bellagio-Harvard Guidelines explain that 'In cases of slavery, the exercise of "the powers attaching to the right of ownership" should be understood as constituting control over a person in such a way as to significantly deprive that person of his or her individual liberty', there is no explicit commentary as to whether this control has to be by an individual or if it could be by a larger, macro-level enterprise, just that there has to be the intent of exploitation (Allain et al., 2012).

At the macro level, the state structurally removes agency from some more than others and, in doing so, makes it possible for agency to be removed at the micro level. For example, in the eighteenth and nineteenth centuries, the legal justification of slavery at the macro level meant that the removal of agency at the micro level was acceptable, and even expected. This indicates that slavery existed because the macro level permitted, and even encouraged, the removal of agency at the micro level. Although slavery is no longer legal, the macro and micro systems continue to interact in a similar way in relation to slavery.

To return to the example of **Hattie**, the impact of the removal of agency at the macro and micro levels becomes apparent. As a brief reminder, her employers at the factory where **Hattie** worked in Vietnam fired her for standing up for workers' rights and she and her friends were subsequently reported to the police. They had to sign in at the police station once a week, but after the third week some of her friends did not return from the police station, leading her to flee and a warrant being issued for her arrest. For Hattie, this meant that there was a macro-level system that removed her agency; she was not able to live a free life with autonomous choice because the factory had reported her to the police and the police had issued a warrant for her arrest because she had fought for fair wages. This removal of agency at the macro level meant that **Hattie**'s choices were limited. She could make an active choice, but not an autonomous one: she could either remain in Vietnam and face arrest for standing up for workers' rights, or she could try to leave the country. The only way to leave the country without drawing the attention of the police would be to do so illegally, which required a smuggler. This means that the macro level removal of agency led **Hattie** into making this deal with a smuggler. Because of a lack of options, **Hattie** agreed with this smuggler that he would get her out of the country and, as she did not have the funds to pay him up front, that she would work for him on arrival at her destination country to pay off the debt. However, **Hattie**'s agency was then removed at the micro level once she was out of Vietnam. She had no one to turn to for help, she did not know what country she was in, and even if she had known, she knew that she was illegally in that country and therefore at risk of repatriation if her presence were to be discovered. As such, the removal of agency at the macro level meant that **Hattie**'s smuggler was easily able to deny her agency at the micro level, leading her into a situation of modern slavery. Even once in a new country, her lack of agency at the macro level continued because of her fear of being repatriated. For her, the situation of modern slavery occurred because of a removal of agency at the micro level, but this would not have been possible without the vulnerabilities she experienced at the macro level.

Although macro-level systems may no longer encourage slavery as a practice in and of itself as they did when slavery was legal, some of the systems act in such a way as to permit the existence of slavery today. For example, both the UK tied visa system and the UK asylum system are macro-level structures which permit the removal of agency of those within their systems to some extent, as discussed in chapter six. For those with a tied visa, their agency is removed by the limitation of the changing of employers regardless of the working conditions they enforce; domestic worker migrants must remain with the employer to whom their visa is tied, or they must return to their home country. For those in the asylum system, agency is removed by the proscription of obtaining employment or an education; the allocation of a location in which they must live; and through threats of, and actual, detention and repatriation.

By removing agency in these ways at the macro level, the government is increasing the likelihood that these people will also have their agency removed at the micro level (see, for example, Sloan, 2015). In the tied visa system, the macro-level removal of agency means that the employers can remove agency at the micro level, as the domestic workers who are working for them under the tied visa have little option other than to accept the conditions that the employer sets, or to return 'home'. This is exemplified by **Ofira** whose description of her situation indicated that she was on a tied visa. Unlike those on other working visas who have the option to change employers and remain in employment in the UK, the tied visa system reduces the agency of those confined by it by preventing the changing of employers. Instead, should they feel they have a valid reason to stay in the UK, they are required to apply for asylum after leaving the domestic labour situation, leaving them without access to employment for the duration of the decision-making process. This reflects the vulnerabilities generated by conflict as discussed in chapter four, which showed that the limiting of available options coupled with a reduction in support networks works to increase the likelihood that a person will experience modern slavery. In the case of tied visas, workers have their options limited by having the choice of either staying with their employers even if their situation becomes exploitative, or accepting repatriation. Their support network is also reduced as they move abroad with their employer and thus have reduced contact with family and friends who remain in the home country.

In the asylum system, the lack of legal routes into employment, the low stipend, and the assigned locations for housing are examples of the removal of agency at the macro level. These macro-level restrictions may lead to the removal of agency at the micro level should an asylum seeker choose to supplement their stipend with illegal work, which is unavoidable for many, as discussed by Lewis et al. (2013). During his interview, **Isaac** discussed how his agency was impacted by macro-level systems when he was going through the asylum system. He had been offered various jobs while part of the asylum process and had felt unable to accept them because of his fear of being detained or repatriated, and yet he could have desperately benefitted from the extra money to help support his baby and his young sister. Having been detained previously with no explanation as to the reasons for this detention, **Isaac** indicated that he may have had more freedom and choice and lived in less fear had he not had to submit to the constraints on his agency that had been imposed by the asylum system. There are cases where people in **Isaac**'s position have chosen to accept work despite the legal constraints imposed by the asylum system (Lewis et al., 2013). The removal of agency forced by the asylum system in such situations means that there are severe restrictions on the employment opportunities available, as the individuals must remain hidden in order not to be detected by the authorities. This means that employers offering employment to people who do not have the legal right to accept it hold all the power over those in desperate need of work. It means the employers can set the rates of pay, the hours of work, and the conditions of labour, and leave the employee with no option but to accept.

In such situations, the asylum system is accountable for the macro-level removal of agency in prohibiting access to labour that would, in turn, permit the removal of agency at the micro level, as any asylum seeker accepting work illegally would not have a route to report an employer should their working conditions become exploitative; nor would they be able to ask for help should they find themselves unable to leave this labour situation, as to do so would be to risk detention for working illegally. This allows those individuals who provide labour to asylum seekers to be able to remove agency at the micro level in a way that would not be possible if the macro-level systems were structured differently.

In these scenarios the government, by imposing such strict rules against asylum seekers gaining employment, is denying accountability and may try to absolve itself of any wrongdoing by arguing that these restrictive policies are a way of preventing exploitation because if asylum seekers did not seek employment then they would not find themselves in exploitative labour. However, such claims would overlook the huge role that the government's own restrictive policies play in exacerbating vulnerabilities towards exploitation; if asylum seekers were provided with a stipend that they could survive on without needing to find extra money, they would not need to seek precarious labour. Equally, if they were not prohibited from finding employment then they would have access to legitimate sources of labour rather than only the illicit labour that is available to them currently. This is a reflection of the discussion in chapter six regarding the government's reaction to smuggling and ideas that their strict immigration rules are a method of deterring traffickers (Stepnitz, 2012; O'Connell Davidson and Howard, 2015; Wilson and O'Brien, 2016). This method of the UK government attempting to absolve itself of responsibility to asylum seekers is particularly evident in relation to the privatisation of asylum housing and detention. As a result of this privatisation, the government is offsetting its own responsibility, placing it instead on private actors. This has led to the production of a new economy in an 'asylum market', and therefore to new authorities, policies, and governance in this field (Darling, 2016; Glorius et al., 2016).

Regardless of the government trying to distance itself from its responsibilities, as Jessop (1999) states, the nation state holds the political power, meaning that the welfare provided to migrants is dependent on the state that they are entering. With neoliberalism in the stage of roll-out mobilisation, states are no longer primarily concerned with market expansion and instead, neoliberalism is more commonly linked with prioritising new social and penal policies which are 'concerned specifically with the aggressive reregulation, disciplining, and containment of those marginalised or dispossessed by the neoliberalization of the 1980s' (Peck and Tickell, 2002:389). In this era of welfare retrenchment and ideas of the undeserving migrant (Sales, 2002), it is evident that the welfare provided to asylum seekers in the UK is not at all reflective of that received by UK citizens (although their welfare support also continues to decline). Rather, there is a combined effort of attempting to prevent asylum seekers entering the country, and simultaneously reducing the support offered to them (Bloch and Schuster, 2002). This indicates that considerations of need are now coming second to considerations of contribution, which further amplifies the hostile environment and emphasises asylum seekers as a separate class of (non-) citizen.

> In many instances, the nation state's responsibility for the welfare of forced migrants is effectively being devolved downwards to a complex network of regional and local actors that includes local authorities, private companies and voluntary and charitable agencies. In addition Member States are keen to reflect the problem of forced migration sideways onto other states. (Dwyer, 2005:9)

As a result of the declining welfare support offered to asylum seekers in the UK, these individuals are having to turn to illegal work or NGOs in order to meet their basic human needs: provisions which would have previously been covered by the government (Kjaerum, 2002; Dwyer and Brown, 2004). As the state limits the claims that forced migrants have to public welfare, 'the third sector is playing a significant role in supporting those who have been failed by a state which has a duty to provide for all of their essential living needs' (Mayblin and James, 2019, no pagination).

However, many of the NGOs that offer support in such instances are reliant on government funding and therefore their independence is immediately compromised (Cohen, 2002), or they are comprised of under-funded groups of unpaid forced migrants who have established organisations in the hope of being able to offer advice to fellow forced migrants who are facing some of the difficulties they have overcome (Dwyer, 2005). Without funding or robust levels of volunteers, such precarious organisations are not sustainable in the long term.

Instead of developing a maintainable collaboration with these NGOs, the government is leaving them to fill a gap that they should not have allowed to exist. In fact, refugee third-sector organisations in the UK are spending over £33.4 million per year on poverty alleviation, which shows that levels of government support for refugees and asylum seekers are simply inadequate (Mayblin and James, 2019).

This discussion expands on Bollas's construction of violent innocence (1993), which relates to a denial of the reality regarding situations in which a person or organisation deems themselves innocent of the violence inherently bound to them. Such violent innocence is evidently displayed by the UK government as it continues to show outrage at the perpetrators of modern slavery, while simultaneously absolving itself of the ways in which it encourages such slavery to exist. As Gadd and Broad identify: 'the politics of modern slavery render it difficult to imagine offenders as anything other than the "evil" nemesis of "innocent" victims' (Gadd and Broad, 2018:1440). However, to demarcate victims and perpetrators in this way is to overlook the complex relationships between the two, where the situation of slavery generated by a perpetrator may actually be preferable to the victim than their alternative, or where the victim exploits other victims in order to improve their own conditions. Equally, to set victims and perpetrators as binary opposites is to omit the impact that macro-level structures have on micro-level relationships.

If it is true that modern slavery can only exist in situations where agency is removed at the micro level, then these discussions show how situations of modern slavery in the UK are sometimes only possible because of the macro-level vulnerabilities generated by government policies. In these cases, to suggest that situations of modern slavery can only be defined as such if the agency has been removed at the micro level is to imply that it is only the micro level at which the slavery exists. However, as the above discussions have outlined, there are numerous situations in which the micro-level removal of agency would not be so widespread—if possible at all—if it were not for the impact of the macro level. This further emphasises the hypocrisy of a government that claims to prioritise tackling modern slavery and yet imposes policies that promote the removal of agency at the macro level which, in turn, allow for and endorse the removal of agency, and thus the existence of modern slavery, at the micro level.

7.3.1 Structure and agency

Without attempting to discuss in detail the wealth of academic literature that addresses agency and structure, it is nonetheless important to acknowledge the two in reference to their impact on situations of modern slavery. Historically, sociology has tended to identify structure and agency as two unique and separate entities (Giddens, 1986; Green, 2015), with the key theories separating them being structuralism and individualisation. Structuralism is a theory often related back to scholars such as Levi-Strauss and Saussure. It rests on the idea that it is structures that influence social life, and argues that meaning can only be inferred with reference to the overarching structures that impact individuals' decisions. To relate this to modern slavery, structuralism would argue that situations of slavery arise only as a result of the overarching structures such as conflict or the asylum system; that is, structures influence people to such an extent that without their impact, people may not become vulnerable to modern slavery. While, undeniably, some structures may cause people to become vulnerable to modern slavery as discussed in chapter four, it would be misguided to suggest that it is these structures alone that cause the vulnerabilities; to do so would imply that everyone living under the same structure, the same conflict for example, would likely experience the same end result. This focus on generalisations is a key flaw of structural sociology (Giddens, 1986).

Most social theory regarding the structure and agency debate concentrates on the importance and power of agency (Giddens, 1986). These schools of thought advocate the belief that human behaviour is not solely influenced by the structures of the societies in which people live, but that individuals have agency over their own lives and decisions. Individualisation is one such theory, associated with theorists such as Ulrich Beck, Elisabeth Beck-Gernsheim, and Zygmunt Bauman (see specifically Beck and Beck-Gernsheim, 2001). The theory of individualisation argues that individuals have control over their situations and experiences, opposing the structuralist idea that individuals and human behaviour are led and limited by collective structures.

> To put it in a nutshell, 'individualization' consists in transforming human 'identity' from a 'given' into a 'task'— and charging the actors with the responsibility for performing that task and for the consequences (also the side-effects) of their performance. (Bauman, 2001:xv)

Giddens' work (1986) focuses on creating a bridge between the theories that focus only on structure and those that focus only on agency. He advocates for an understanding whereby the two concepts sit alongside each other as opposed to independently. Giddens argues that the individual cannot exist outside of the structures to which they are tied, but equally that the structures would not exist without the input of the individual. This is his theory of structuration, a concept that highlights how agency and structure both exist in a cycle of continual mutual influence, whereby the two cannot exist independently of each other.

> The basic domain of study of the social sciences, according to the theory of structuration, is neither the experience of the individual actor, nor the existence of any form of societal totality, but social practices ordered across space and time. Human social activities, like some self-reproducing items in nature, are recursive. That is to say, they are not brought into being by social actors but continually recreated by them via the very means whereby they express themselves as actors. In and

> through their activities agents reproduce the conditions that make these activities possible. (Giddens, 1986:2)

This notion of structure and agency working in tandem is particularly relevant to modern slavery and is where discussions of the macro- and micro-level removal of agency should be situated as, for many situations of slavery, the removal of agency at the micro level would not be possible without the vulnerabilities generated at the macro level. Where micro constitutes the impact of agents and macro constitutes the impact of structure, agency, and structure are thus intertwined and inseparable in understanding the vulnerabilities that lead to situations of modern slavery.

To introduce conflict to structuration theory is to understand the conflict as representative of structure, be that in relation to state-level conflict, marital expectations, familial norms, or any of the other many forms of conflict as broadly defined in chapter two. The conflict then influences people's agency by leaving them limited choices which they must choose between; they still have some degree of agency to make choices, but their options have been defined by the structure of the conflict. Take **Ifra** for example. She was living and working in Bangladesh as a politician when an opposing political party threatened to kill her. This conflict with her political opponents meant that the realistic options available to her were reduced. She had the 'choice' to stay and continue working, but to do so would be to live in constant threat. As a result, she 'chose' to leave the country, but this would never have been her choice if not for the conflict she faced.

The work of feminist geopolitics must be introduced here as it reflects some of the integral parts of structuration theory. Feminist geopolitics is an analytic approach connecting seemingly dissimilar people, places, events, and issues, and it highlights connections through the ways that power, inequality, and exploitation are produced (Massaro and Williams, 2013). As Dowler and Sharp (2001) identify, there is a considerable amount of literature on political violence, but the majority of this centres on the workings of war. Such focus looks predominantly at men as the initiators and the soldiers of these conflicts, and therefore overlooks the role that women play. To reframe understandings of war by introducing the actions of women would be to link the public and private spheres which would then highlight how in such conflict, the two are inseparable and mutually constitutive: the violence experienced in the home is a product of, and a causation for, violence in war and vice versa.

Brickell and Cuomo (2019) emphasise the importance of understanding the ways in which geolegal spaces exist and operate in order to better comprehend notions of conflict and violence that occur outside notions of war. Such feminist geopolitics highlight the way in which binaries such as that between the intimate and the global can be pulled apart to show that there is no true separation between conflict in the home and conflict on the battlefield (Hyndman, 2004; Mountz and Hyndman, 2006; Pratt and Rosner, 2006; Pain and Staeheli, 2014). To understand violence against the global and the intimate in this way is to see the two as mutually constituted entities that, like the micro and macro discussions of slavery, cannot exist in isolation; instead, they should be understood as part of a single phenomenon. This highlights the inseparability of structure and agency in generating vulnerabilities towards modern slavery.

However, relating to situations of conflict and experiences of modern slavery in the UK, it is not just the conflict that should be understood as a contributing structure, but the policies created by the UK government. On arrival to the UK, structure influences individuals' agency; if the individual is required to apply for asylum, then the system limits them to three options. The first option is to apply for asylum and respect the legal restrictions preventing them from seeking employment or education while they wait for a decision; the second option is that they apply for asylum and illegally seek employment as many do (Lewis et al., 2013); the third option is to try and avoid being identified entirely and attempt to establish a life, accommodation, and employment without being acknowledged by any authority. These options highlight the impact that structures have on limiting autonomous choices to active-but-restricted choices. The impact of structure is clear here, but it does not negate the impact of agency. While the structures may limit agency and leave people the opportunity to make only constrained choices, there is still a level of agency allowing them to make some degree of choice.

From the interviews, **Nadim**'s story exemplifies such a situation where agency and structure interacted to lead to a situation of exploitation. **Nadim** chose to flee Syria because of the war and, while he made this choice to flee, it is unlikely he would have done so if the war had not placed him in such a vulnerable position. He escaped to neighbouring Lebanon, but there was such a huge influx of Syrians into the country that there was vast competition for a small number of jobs. This meant that the structure of the war afforded employers the freedom to lower wages and offer jobs with poor working conditions such as long hours and no breaks, because there would always be someone desperate enough to do the work. This structure of employment then therefore limited the options available to **Nadim**: he could either not work and thereby not have the means to provide food and shelter for his family, or accept poor working conditions in return for low pay. Such choice is really no choice at all, and of course **Nadim** 'chose' the exploitative labour. Steinfeld defines this as labour compulsion, which relates to 'situations in which the compelled party is offered a choice between disagreeable alternatives and chooses the lesser evil' (2001:14).

While in Lebanon, **Nadim** moved between several similar jobs, each one exploitative. Although he always had the physical choice to leave these situations, he could not justify being out of work and was unable to find any non-exploitative working situations. As such, although he had the agency to be able to leave individual jobs, he did not have the choice to escape exploitation. For **Nadim** it was always a case of either working in exploitative conditions in order to provide for his family, or not working in exploitative conditions and not being able to provide for his family.

The sudden societal change resulting from the conflict in neighbouring Syria and the displacement of thousands of people caused a direct impact in Lebanon by generating a much larger pool of potential employees. In situations such as these, people desperate for work may themselves begin to offer to work for lower wages to undercut the competition and ensure they are able to find employment and provide for their families. This is highlighted in the literature by Lewis et al. (2013) who discuss how migrants in a vulnerable position will often choose not to collaborate to improve their working conditions because they are so desperate for the work that they are willing to accept the terrible conditions if it means that they will get the job over their competitors. Simultaneously, where the work is unskilled and the labour pool vast, unscrupulous employers offer lower wages and longer hours, knowing that there will always be someone who will accept the work.

It is in this context that it is possible to understand the impact of agency in situations of modern slavery. The individual may have to make decisions similar to those by **Nadim** who had to choose between staying in the conflict with no food, shelter, or income, and taking the risk to cross the border into Lebanon. It was this active decision that led him towards exploitative labour. Similarly, **Ifra** had the choice to stay in Bangladesh where she would be killed, or to take a risk with a stranger. Though this was a constrained choice influenced by the impact of the conflict she was experiencing, it was still a choice. Once in the UK, she faced further constrained choices including whether she should accept the offer of a job from a stranger or try to find support elsewhere in a country where she knew no one and did not know where she could access support. Again, this was a constrained choice, but it was still a choice. Ifra had agency that allowed her to make choices between limited options, but the outcomes of which led her into a situation of modern slavery where she was kept for domestic servitude and forced labour for three years.

However, what these stories highlight is that neither agency nor structure is entirely responsible for situations of modern slavery: it is the relationship and interaction between the two that causes agentic decisions to exacerbate the pre-existing vulnerabilities caused by structures. For this reason, any generalisations that are based on the impact of structure or agency alone can only go part way to understanding what it is that puts people at risk of modern slavery.

Given the rarity that those suffering situations of modern slavery have completely no agency or choice in the lead up to their exploitation, it must be considered why people with agency put themselves at risk of modern slavery. Structural factors are key in answering this question and, as this research has shown, conflict is a significant structural factor that can cause people to make active but not autonomous choices that may lead them towards situations of slavery. For many, it is the desperation of needing to leave their current situation of conflict that reduces the voluntariness of their decisions and leaves them with limited choices. For those whose choices are to stay in the conflict where their lives might be in danger, or to take a risk on trying to escape, there is little freedom in their choice and they are likely to choose the latter option in order to increase their chances of safety. Prior to conflict they may not have tried to leave their current situations, but the conflict has led to a removal of autonomous or voluntary choices, leaving them with little option or alternative. While they may still have a *choice*, it is not a free choice as it might have been if their lives were safe and they were not suffering through conflict. Unfortunately for some, the result of these choices is not always safety, and may well lead them into scenarios worse than that of the conflict. As such, situations of modern slavery should never be generalised as resulting from the impact of large-scale structures alone. While these structures may play a large part in generating vulnerabilities towards modern slavery, it is the interplay between structure and agency that determines whether an individual becomes a victim.

7.4 Conclusion

This chapter considered the role of agency in generating situations of modern slavery. It addressed a number of issues including victim terminology, the flaws of understanding modern slavery through a victim/agent binary, and the relationship between structure and agency in leading people into situations of modern slavery. This chapter determined that victim terminology can have a detrimental impact on those who experience modern slavery but who do not fit the expectations of an 'ideal victim'. People are less likely to be recognised as victims or receive sympathy or support if they fail to appear weak and passive, or if they had any agency leading up to their experience of slavery. This is particularly evident in the lack of recognition of male victims, which has only begun to change in recent years, and the denial of the victimhood of women who choose to undertake sex work. Further, the simple assignation of the label 'victim' to a person can serve to remove agency and alter the way they are perceived, both by themselves and by others. However, notions of an 'ideal victim' are rarely reflective of the experiences of a 'real victim'.

This chapter also tackled the common approach of understanding victimhood and agency as binary opposites. Instead, I argue that the two concepts sit on a spectrum where those who experience modern slavery very rarely suffer a complete denial of agency, but have some level of choice in the decisions that have led to their situations of exploitation. Nevertheless, there is usually some limit on this agency and any choices tend to be active rather than autonomous. It is important to recognise that any extent of agency leading up to or during a situation of modern slavery does not negate a person's status as a victim.

This links to discussions of how a person's vulnerability is rarely a result of agency or structure alone, but it is a combination of the two that increases the likelihood that someone will become a victim of modern slavery. Claims that a situation can only be understood as modern slavery if agency is removed at the micro level fail to engage with the complex interactions between the macro and micro levels. The removal of agency at the micro level and a resulting experience of modern slavery may only be possible if the macro level allows or encourages it. Where the macro level reflects structural systems, this means that structure generates vulnerabilities that are then exacerbated by agentic choices at the micro level. This indicates an inseparability between agency and structure in generating the conditions for modern slavery to occur.

Chapter eight
Conclusion

With this work, I set out to discover what direct link, if any, exists between conflict and modern slavery. From initial engagement with respondents who self-identified having lived through a range of conflicts, I generated a broad definition of the term 'conflict' which incorporated the following types of definitions: legal, practical, lived experience, and dictionary. This led to the development of a definition of conflict which identifies it as a set of conditions whereby parties identify and act on mutually incompatible goals. While this act may be violent, the presence of violence is not necessary in order for the situation to be defined as conflict. It is possible to be affected by a conflict without being an active participant.

The fundamental finding from this research is that conflict generates two specific vulnerabilities that increase the risk that someone will become a victim of modern slavery: a reduction in the options available and a breakdown in support networks. It is in this way that understandings of the link between conflict and modern slavery should be approached: not necessarily by a direct link to conflict, but by the transitional effects it causes. However, in investigating risk factors after individuals had fled conflict to the UK, it became clear that there are other structural conditions besides conflict which generate the same two vulnerabilities. This title considered how certain UK policies are serving to create the very same vulnerabilities caused by conflict: a reduction in options and a breakdown in support networks. As such, it is important to recognise that any contexts which generate these vulnerabilities, such as the hostile environment, the treatment of refused asylum seekers, and the tied visa system, are producing environments which are conducive to encouraging situations of modern slavery.

I also tackle the common approach of understanding victimhood and agency as binary opposites, where those with agency are less likely to be recognised as victims. I argue that these two concepts sit instead on a spectrum

From Conflict to Modern Slavery. Alicia Heys, Oxford University Press. © Alicia Heys 2023.
DOI: 10.1093/oso/9780192846549.003.0008

where those who experience modern slavery very rarely suffer a complete denial of agency, but have some level of choice in the decisions that lead to their exploitation. However, there is usually some limit on this agency and any choices tend to be active rather than autonomous, impacted by overarching structures, such as conflict. Overall, it is imperative to recognise that agency and structure are inseparable in generating the conditions for modern slavery to occur. Understandings of conflict-related modern slavery should therefore be located within a structuration approach which recognises the impact of both structure and agency in leading to situations of slavery. It is also important to recognise that any extent of agency leading up to or during a situation of modern slavery does not negate a person's status as a victim.

These findings have the potential to encourage better understandings of when and why people might become vulnerable to modern slavery. The research therefore has benefit for policy makers and practitioners alike who can implement effective prevention measures that respond to lived experience in order to pre-empt a reduction of, rather than an exacerbation of, conflict-related vulnerabilities. The remainder of this chapter summarises the findings of this research and concludes by outlining its practical implications.

8.1 Slavery triggered by conflict

The research discovered that intersectionality is not enough to determine whether a person is likely to become vulnerable to modern slavery. While intersectionality may be useful in highlighting some of the common identity traits of vulnerable individuals, it has limitations when considered in isolation. It fails to provide both scale and coherence, and it overlooks the impact of external factors. There is no single or intersecting identity trait that is always responsible for increasing the likelihood that one person will become more vulnerable to modern slavery than another. To suggest otherwise is to generate detrimental stereotypes of vulnerability which reinforce inaccurate typecasting. Instead, it is the context of the situation that should be prioritised in identifying risk. Contexts that limit people's choices and lead to a lack of support are those that are most likely to generate a risk of modern slavery; this is regardless of the identity of the person in question.

8.1.1 Lack of choice

The gathering of first-hand accounts from people who have fled conflict and experienced modern slavery identified a lack of viable choices as a key vulnerability that led them towards situations of modern slavery. Conflict had limited their agency by reducing the options available to them, leaving the respondents physically able to make choices but only between restricted options which all held inherent risk, thereby highlighting the difference between active and agentic choices. Even when the respondents were aware that their choices could lead to dangerous situations, desperation to escape the conflict meant that there was little alternative and they took the option that appeared to be the 'lesser evil' in the hope that their choice would lead them to a safer situation. While some respondents were lucky to achieve this outcome, many found themselves fleeing conflict only to experience modern slavery.

8.1.2 Lack of support

The other key factor identified through this work as leading people towards situations of modern slavery was a lack of support. Some respondents experienced this lack of support during conflict, such as those whose family members were killed. For others, the lack of support occurred after their arrival in the UK. In some instances, it followed rejection from the respondent's family, preventing them from turning to them for help when they needed it. For others, the lack of support was experienced by respondents who were failed by UK statutory agencies which could have reasonably been expected to provide assistance that would have limited the likelihood that they would have become victims of modern slavery. Whatever the cause of the lack of support, it reinforces the lack of viable options already facing these individuals in limiting their options further by removing the possibility of turning to their support network for safety, advice, or assistance.

Discovering the direct link between a lack of viable options, a lack of support, and modern slavery is a fundamental step forward in identifying the vulnerabilities that put people at risk of modern slavery. These findings go beyond the tendency of claiming that people become victims due to 'some form of vulnerability'. This research identifies that a reduction in options, coupled with a breakdown of support networks are the key vulnerabilities that will increase the likelihood that a person will become a victim of modern slavery. Such findings are crucial if any prevention or intervention effort is ever to target the relevant issues and successfully work to combat the root causes of modern slavery.

8.2 A scale of victimhood and agency

I argue that victimhood and agency should be understood as sitting on a spectrum as opposed to as binary opposites. Data gathered from interviews with individuals who have experienced modern slavery shows that those who become victims very rarely suffer a complete denial of agency but have some level of choice in the decisions that lead to their situations of exploitation. This goes against the often-cited image of the 'ideal victim' who is passive, weak, and who has no control over their fate. The stereotypes created by such discourse are damaging as they fail to reflect the experiences of a 'real victim' and perpetuate the false stereotypes of slavery only affecting those without agency. Understanding victimhood as existing on a scale reflects the true experiences of victims who would not have freely chosen a situation of exploitation, but whose lack of agentic choice instigated an active, but not autonomous, decision that led towards slavery. I emphasise that agency is extremely variable and highlight the importance of acknowledging that a person's status as a victim of modern slavery is not negated by the possession of agency—to any degree—leading up to or during their exploitation.

8.3 Risk generated by UK policy

A significant finding of this research was the contradictory nature of the UK government which claims on the one hand to prioritise tackling modern slavery and on the other perpetuates biased and restrictive policies that increase the likelihood of the occurrence of modern slavery. The UK government's choice of modern slavery as a cause to champion is an easy and non-controversial decision; tackling modern slavery is a cause that invokes no opposition from any political view. However, there is significant work to do if the government is to embody its claim of holding modern slavery as a priority issue.

The figures provided by the NRM—championed as the government's method of assisting and counting victims of modern slavery—are the ones most commonly cited in the UK in relation to modern slavery. However, the quoted statistics most often relate to the number of people that are referred into the system rather than the number of those who are positively identified as victims after the two-tier decision process. The yearly increases in such figures are lauded for reflecting better identification systems, and yet the rates of convictions and sentences for perpetrators of modern slavery remain negligible. Further, the extremely long waiting times for receiving a Conclusive Grounds decision serve to exacerbate trauma for those who have already been exploited. Putting these individuals through a two-tier decision-making process, in which it currently takes over a year and a half to receive a decision on whether that person really is to be believed to have been a victim is fundamentally different to the treatment of victims of any other form of crime.

Focus continues to be placed on source countries in trying to identify the reasons that people become vulnerable to modern slavery in the UK. On the surface this may appear logical because of the high rates of foreign nationals identified as potential victims in the UK, yet such tactics fail to engage properly with the statistics. Further investigation of the data indicates that, by nationality, the largest group of victims in the UK are actually UK nationals. Equally, when looking at where the exploitation occurred, the largest group experienced their exploitation in the UK. These factors signify that instead of focusing on other source countries, focus should be placed on how the UK causes such risk to modern slavery. Perhaps placing focus on the source countries is a tactic to remove accountability from the UK government and draw attention away from the issues in the UK that generate vulnerabilities to modern slavery. These issues are intertwined with the drive to create a hostile environment for undocumented migrants and have seen a confusing move to conflate modern slavery with immigration crime which does not reflect the evidence.

The systems facing migrants, particularly asylum seekers, who arrive in the UK are not conducive to reducing the risk of modern slavery. After applying for asylum, refugees receive little communication and insufficient means to live while being prohibited from seeking legal employment. When the stipend does not offer enough to survive, this leaves asylum seekers with little choice but to seek illegitimate employment and accept that, should it be exploitative, they will have no way out without facing detention or repatriation. The asylum system fails to provide adequate information or support to those who apply, to those who are denied, and even to those who receive a positive decision. The forced destitution of those denied asylum increases the likelihood that they will experience modern slavery, especially for those who are unable or unwilling to leave the UK. Equally, by granting asylum without explaining the resulting entitlements or signposting to organisations that could offer support, refugees are abandoned in a country they do not know. Unnecessary vulnerabilities are generated for those who have no support and are unaware of their entitlements, leaving them little option but to turn to strangers for support; strangers who may be looking to profit from their exploitation.

This research shows that UK policies, by reducing legitimate options, are actually directly responsible for generating and perpetuating the contexts that encourage situations of modern slavery to occur. Claims that the government will prioritise tackling modern slavery are unfounded while the same government continues to push the hostile environment as these two political agendas are contradictory.

8.4 The roles of structure and agency

This title has used the first-hand accounts of people who have fled conflict and experienced modern slavery to assess the influence that structure and agency have in generating the conditions required for modern slavery to occur. While slavery is generally understood as a removal of agency at the micro level—that is by one person of another—I argue that the relationship is much more complex than this. In reality, while the restriction of an individual's agency is necessary in order for a situation of slavery to occur, the power to be able to limit this agency is not always held at the micro level. In most of the instances identified through the interviews, the individuals' agency was impacted significantly by macro-level structures. These structures varied, indicating that it was not the impact of a particular structure that caused vulnerabilities, but the common thread of such structures leading to a restriction of agency and a limiting of choices. For some, these structures related directly to the conflict; for others, the impact of macro-level structures limiting their agency was only felt after arrival in the UK, predominantly in relation to the asylum system.

The restrictions that these macro-level structures placed on these individuals led to a limiting of the options available to them. With a lack of options, they had no choice but to make decisions that held some inherent risk. For some, these choices pushed them towards situations in which their agency would be further removed at the micro level: situations that are recognised as modern slavery.

The experience of modern slavery is not identified as such unless a person's agency has been severely limited at the micro level and they have simultaneously experienced exploitation. For many, this limiting of agency at the micro level would not have been possible if not for the impact of structures at the macro level. However, when an individual suffers exploitation equivalent to modern slavery, as it stands, it is not defined as such if it is perpetuated by a system rather than an individual, regardless of whether all other factors are the same.

While understanding the impact that structures have is important, placing focus on them alone generates inaccurate conclusions about the nature of modern slavery. As the discussion on intersectionality showed in section 6.1, suggesting that individuals who experience the same structure are all equally likely to experience modern slavery is unfounded and fails to acknowledge the agentic processes at play. Not only does a structural approach fail to recognise the important role of agency in generating vulnerabilities to modern slavery, it also disregards the vast differences in people's situations prior to their exploitation. I demonstrate this with the example of conflict. Conflict is just one of the many causes of vulnerabilities, and yet even under this rubric, the experience of conflict is different for each individual, from political fallout to employment disagreements. To generalise conflict as a cause of modern slavery is to disregard the breadth of the term and the vast differences experienced by people who suffer different forms of conflict. While such a generalisation is not inaccurate, it fails to engage with the more complex interconnection with agency. Instead of linking vulnerabilities to modern slavery directly back to conflict, the intermediary impacts should be acknowledged: those of a breakdown in support networks and a lack of legitimate options resulting from a reduction in agency caused by conflict. In recognising these vulnerabilities as key drivers towards situations of modern slavery, we can consider how there are many root causes beyond conflict which generate the same conditions and thus increase vulnerability. This title has shown how these precise vulnerabilities are generated not only by conflict, but also by restrictive and hostile policies within the UK.

Instead of claiming that modern slavery exists purely because of the impact of either structure or agency, I argue that the two are inseparable in generating the conditions for modern slavery to occur. However, while there is still a level of agency involved in individuals being able to make decisions that may lead them towards modern slavery, the available options are often dictated by the overarching structures at play. These issues highlight the hypocrisy of a government that claims to prioritise tackling modern slavery while simultaneously imposing policies that encourage the removal of agency and limiting of options at the macro level and which, in turn, promote the removal of agency, and the existence of modern slavery, at the micro level.

8.5 Practical applications and further research

The findings of this research extend past academic interest to offer a new understanding of the vulnerabilities caused by conflict that increase the risk of modern slavery, going beyond the current tendency of suggesting that people become victims of slavery because of 'some pre-existing vulnerability'. By identifying what these vulnerabilities are: a reduction in the options available to people and a breakdown in support networks, this research provides new information to enable the development of effective interventions to specifically target those most at risk. The practical suggestions offered below begin with small-scale, easy-to-implement changes, followed by suggestions that tackle the more overarching issues. Some of the practical suggestions give rise to ideas for further research; the most relevant of these are included below in reference to their corresponding practical applications.

First, there should be a method for employees to anonymously report exploitative labour. Offering a reporting mechanism in all workplaces would allow those working in exploitative conditions—whether they are doing so legally or otherwise—to inform an authority of their situation. The current framework leads to punishment for any asylum seeker found to be working, meaning that should they face exploitative conditions, there is little they can do but accept these conditions, or look for other labour which is equally likely to offer only poor conditions. Such a mechanism should instead encourage punitive measures for employers forcing their employees into exploitative conditions rather than for the workers who have little choice other than to accept them.

Training of staff in statutory organisations is also an immediate requirement that has been identified in this research. This is pertinent for those making asylum decisions who should receive training specifically on the reasons why asylum seekers may not offer the truth in their interviews. Should it be discovered that an asylum seeker has been deceitful in their claim, this will currently count against them, reducing the likelihood that they will receive a positive decision. However, to understand the reasons behind this deception would encourage a greater understanding of the desperation of those claiming asylum. Additionally, better explanation should be provided to asylum seekers prior to their interviews to ensure they are aware of the consequences of lying and to confirm they understand the reasoning behind the in-depth questioning; this should encourage applicants to offer truthful answers. Equally, decision-makers should be aware that those fleeing a situation in their home countries are unlikely to have documentation to prove their accounts. When safety is their main concern, ensuring they collect potentially relevant documents before they leave will never be a priority; this should not count against asylum seekers in their claims.

For statutory organisations that provide support services, training is required based on the fact that they interact with people facing any number of vulnerabilities. While the staff member's main role may not be to identify or act upon those vulnerabilities, it is fundamental that they are at least able to signpost individuals in need to organisations that may be able to support them. In failing to offer such potentially vital information, these statutory organisations risk allowing the perpetuation of exploitation, or leaving people in a situation where they are unaware of their options and, as a result, may believe that they have little choice but to accept exploitation. This training should also be expanded so that professionals are made aware of any implicit bias they may have regarding depictions of the 'ideal victim'. By highlighting the possession of agency held by victims leading up to their situations of exploitation, I push for understandings of victims to move beyond the notion of weak and passive individuals to recognise a degree of agency that has been enacted in response to a restriction of viable options. It is essential that practitioners recognise the impact of decisions based on depictions of the ideal victim and understand that victims all have unique experiences and will present in different ways; therefore, not being weak and passive does not diminish their experiences or entitlements to support.

A scoping study of the training trends of statutory organisations that work with service users would be incredibly valuable here. This research could identify whether there are certain sectors or geographical regions that are more proficient than others at training their staff to recognise and signpost vulnerable clients. While there may be some difficulty in drawing direct correlations, these findings could also be compared with NRM reporting data to identify whether higher rates of training correlate to larger numbers of referrals into the NRM in the corresponding geographical locations.

Similarly, information packs could be offered to all immigrants on arrival to the UK. While this may fail to reach those who enter clandestinely, it should be available regardless of whether the migrants have visas or intend to claim asylum. This information would include details of their rights, including the national minimum wage and the importance of not sharing a bank account or a national insurance number. It should also include information on support services that migrants could contact should they require assistance or advice, be that at the time they receive the information or in the future. Such information could be distributed with visa applications, travel tickets, upon arrival at the UK border, or as they begin an asylum application.

There is also an important need for better information on receipt of an asylum decision, be that decision positive or negative. The current lack of information means that even those who are granted asylum are left confused about their entitlements and therefore at risk of homelessness or of entering the labour market through illegitimate means, only to experience exploitation despite having the right to work. This could easily be rectified if, along with the paperwork outlining the decision of an asylum seeker's claim, they were provided with information (in the applicant's language) of what the decision means; the options that are available to them; their entitlements as a result of the decision; and organisations they can contact for more information, advice, or support.

This point leads to some of the larger-scale changes that could be implemented from the findings of this research. Initially, more robust support following an asylum decision would decrease the likelihood that both refugees and refused asylum seekers would find themselves victims of exploitation. This is reflected in the difference between the experiences of those who enter the UK on a resettlement programme and those who enter as asylum seekers. The former receive effective support for a year after arriving in the country, assistance in integrating into their new communities, and advice on entitlements; the latter are left to do all this for themselves and the differences in their experiences as a result are significant. While it could be anticipated that receiving a positive asylum decision would equate to receiving some form of support to reflect the need that has clearly been identified by receiving this decision, research shows that this is not the case. After receiving a positive asylum decision, refugees are provided with little, if any, information on how they could, or should, proceed. This lack of support only serves to push such people to turn to others for advice which holds an inherent risk of leading them into exploitation when they are unaware of their entitlements. Clearly for those who receive a negative decision and therefore have no entitlements, this risk of exploitation is heightened.

Another change that the UK government should make to reduce the likelihood of asylum seekers in the UK becoming vulnerable to modern slavery is to end their forced destitution upon the receipt of a negative asylum decision. While offering asylum seekers the right to work is currently claimed to be a pull factor for immigration, leaving those who are denied asylum without the right to work serves only to generate substantial vulnerabilities among this group, especially for those who are unable to leave the UK. Putting refused asylum seekers in this position leaves them with little choice but to accept exploitative labour, the conditions of which have the potential to become severe when employers become aware of their illegal status and manipulate this to their advantage. Ideally the right to work should be extended to all asylum seekers. It is evident that the current statutory support they receive is not enough to prevent the search for a supplementary income and there are employers ready to exploit asylum seekers' illegal working status to receive significant labour for little remittance. Such a change would also have a significantly positive economic impact as, if asylum seekers were permitted to work, this would benefit the UK economy by an estimated £97.8 million each year (Lift the Ban, no date).

Additional research could offer further useful insight into the experiences of asylum seekers in the UK. The asylum-seeking respondents I interviewed for this research all came from significantly different backgrounds. They were politicians, business owners, factory workers, and stallholders. They were male, female, religious, atheist, rich, and poor. And yet after arriving in the UK their identities and experiences were homogenised. Despite the disparity in their backgrounds, the countries they came from, the methods they used to reach the UK, and the reasons that they left their home countries, upon claiming asylum the vast intersectional aspects of their identities were all reduced to one: asylum seeker. Valuable research could be undertaken into how standardising all asylum seekers into one group has essentially created a new class of (non-) citizen. Understanding the methods and the reasons behind homogenising asylum seekers in this way could provide insight into how the UK government justifies treating this social class in a way that would be considered unacceptable if applied to UK citizens. Understanding these justifications could assist in making changes to the asylum system to increase social integration, to reduce the negative impact on mental health, and to reduce the likelihood that such individuals will need to turn to exploitative labour simply to be able to survive while they wait for a decision on their claim.

Linking to support after a decision, the new Recovery Needs Assessment part of the NRM requires a detailed evaluation to understand its effectiveness in curbing the previous, almost instantaneous, drop off in support after a victim left the NRM. The Recovery Needs Assessment was introduced at the beginning of 2021 to try and ensure long-term support for individuals as they left the dedicated NRM support. While this is surely a positive step in encouraging ongoing assistance to the point that individuals no longer need specialised help, there are early indications of disparity of care between British and non-British nationals (Heys et al., 2022). Further, there is still a significant gap in support for those who receive negative decisions through the NRM. If someone has been referred into the NRM, it means that a trained professional has recognised enough signs of exploitation to fear that they fit the definition of being a victim of modern slavery. However, not all these potential victims will meet the requirements stipulated by the two-tier decision-making process of the NRM and may receive negative decisions at the Reasonable or Conclusive Grounds stages. Should an individual receive a negative Conclusive Grounds decision when they are already receiving support, they have nine days to exit any housing or emergency support that has been provided to them through the NRM. It is expected that in these nine days any move-on support will be organised, meaning that referrals should be made for any requirements such as housing and healthcare. However, nine days is not a significant amount of time to secure ongoing support and the levels of success of this short turnaround time, if collected at all, have not been publicly shared. Overall, the introduction of the Recovery Needs Assessment is a positive step to encourage ongoing support post-NRM. However, further evaluation should be conducted into the effectiveness of the process when an individual receives a negative decision through the NRM to establish whether there is any risk of inadequate long-term provisions increasing vulnerabilities to exploitation.

Particularly reflective of the system prior to the Recovery Needs Assessment which saw a cliff-edge drop-off in care, further research could also expand upon the possibility that a person's experience of modern slavery could be considered preferable to their previous situation, or even to life after escaping their exploitation. With this research focusing on people who have experienced conflict, there is the possibility that the experience of modern slavery—especially where there has been the provision of food, accommodation, and employment (albeit exploitative)—may be deemed preferable to the conflict situation where perhaps there was no safe housing, no access to food, and no way of earning an income. Although this is a moral, philosophical dilemma that has no clear answer, gaining a thorough understanding of this ethical quandary could influence policy regarding the duty of care that a government has to an individual experiencing modern slavery that is preferable to their previous situation, and also in ensuring that their experience post-exploitation is preferable to their modern slavery experience. It could also lead to debate regarding judicial decisions on offences committed by perpetrators of slavery in such instances and whether their sentencing should take into consideration the fact that, although they held someone in a situation of modern slavery, it was preferable to the situation from which they helped them to escape.

The UK government should also reframe its focus of concentrating on vulnerabilities in source countries and how these could be addressed to reduce the likelihood of migration into slavery. Statistics indicate that the largest group of those identified as victims of modern slavery in the UK experienced their exploitation only in the UK. As such, the government must turn its attention to understanding and tackling the reasons why the UK poses such a threat. This insight should encourage a new approach to prevention efforts where the UK government recognises the role that it plays in limiting the agency of people arriving in the country and in pushing policies that encourage and perpetuate situations of modern slavery. In reality, an individual's experience after arriving in the UK is more indicative than the situation they are fleeing of whether they will go on to experience modern slavery.

Overall, this title has used first-hand accounts of those who have experienced conflict and modern slavery to identify the precise vulnerabilities that conflict causes. It uncovers that conflict reduces a person's options, often leaving them to choose between situations that all hold inherent risk, therefore leaving them with little option but to choose what appears to be the lesser evil. This all occurs in a context which simultaneously decreases an individual's support networks, leaving them with nowhere safe to turn when they need help. While being able to make these choices means that the individuals still have a level of agency, the decisions are limited by the context of the conflict. However, it is also evident that the development of these vulnerabilities is not unique to conflict. This title investigates some of the contexts in the UK that generate the same vulnerabilities to demonstrate how some UK policies are creating environments that actually serve to increase the risk of modern slavery.

While most victims do still have some level of agency in the time leading up to their exploitation, responses to modern slavery should not focus purely on the decisions or actions that victims take, as such an approach fails to engage with the complex interplay between structure and agency. Effective interventions will rest on approaching modern slavery as an interaction between those agentic decisions and the environments in which they are undertaken, recognising that many actions and decisions are significantly influenced by the context in which they exist.

References

Acharya, A. K. 2004. *Agrarian Conflict, Internal Displacement and Trafficking of Mexican Women: The Case of Chiapas State*. Boston, MA: Universidad Nacional Autónoma de México.

Ackerman, P., and J. DuVall. 2000. *A Force More Powerful: A Century of Non-Violent Conflict*. New York: Palgrave Macmillan.

Agnew, R., and J. M. Kaufman. 2010. *Anomie, Strain and Subcultural Theories of Crime*. Burlington: Ashgate.

Alachkar, M. 2016. 'Victims or Survivors?'. *Avicenna Journal of Medicine* 6 (3): p. 89.

Allain, J., K. Bales, A. Bunting, J. Cairns, W. M. Carter Jr, H. Cullen, S. Drescher, S. Engerman, P. Finkelman, B. Freamon, A. Gorsuch, R. Helmholz, R. Hickey, A. Honoré, A. McQuade, O. Patterson, J. Penner, J. Quirk, J. Sarich, and R. Scott. 2012. 'Bellagio-Harvard Guidelines on the Legal Parameters of Slavery'. In *The Legal Understanding of Slavery: From the Historic to the Contemporary*, edited by J. Allain, pp. 375–81. Oxford: Oxford University Press.

All Party Parliamentary Group on Refugees. 2017. *Refugees Welcome? The Experience of New Refugees in the UK*. All Party Parliamentary Group on Refugees.

Amnesty International. 2004. *'So Does That Mean I Have Rights?' Protecting the Human Rights of Women and Girls Trafficked for Forced Prostitution in Kosovo*. London: Amnesty International.

Anti-Slavery International. 2017. *Official: Forced Marriage is Slavery*. https://www.antislavery.org/official-forced-marriage-slavery [Accessed 26/10/2022].

Anti-Trafficking Monitoring Group. 2014. *The National Referral Mechanism: A Five Year Review*. https://www.ecpat.org.uk/the-national-referral-mechanism-a-five-year-review [Accessed 26/10/2022].

Aradau, C. 2004. 'The Perverse Politics of Four-Letter Words: Risk and Pity in the Securitisation of Human Trafficking'. *Journal of International Studies* 33 (2): pp. 251–77.

Archer, M. S. 1995. *Realist Social Theory: The Morphogenetic Approach*. Cambridge: Cambridge University Press.

Atkinson, R., and J. Flint. 2001. 'Accessing Hidden and Hard-to-Reach Populations: Snowball Research Strategies'. *Social Research Update* 33 (1): pp. 1–4.

Avis, W. 2020. *Key Drivers of Modern Slavery. Knowledge, Evidence and Learning for Development*. Brighton, UK: Institute of Development Studies. https://opendocs.ids.ac.uk/opendocs/bitstream/handle/20.500.12413/15581/855_Mode rn_Slavery.pdf?sequence=1&isAllowed=y [Accessed 26/10/2022].

Baker, C. N. 2013. 'Moving Beyond "Slaves, Sinners, and Saviors": An Intersectional Feminist Analysis of US Sex-Trafficking Discourses, Law and Policy'. *Journal of Feminist Scholarship* 10: pp. 1–23.

Bales, K. 2006. *Testing a Theory of Modern Slavery*. Washington, DC: Free the Slaves.

Bales, K. 2007. *Ending Slavery: How We Free Today's Slaves*. London: University of California Press.

Bales, K., and L. Mayblin. 2018. 'Unfree Labour in UK Detention Centres: Exploitation and Coercion of a Captive Immigrant Workforce'. *Economy and Society* 47 (2): pp. 191–213.

Bales, K., and P. T. Robbins. 2001. 'No One Shall be Held in Slavery or Servitude: A Critical Analysis of International Slavery Agreements and Concepts of Slavery'. *Human Rights Review* 2 (2): pp. 18–28.

Bales, K., and Z. Trodd. 2008. *To Plead Our Own Cause*. New York: Cornell University Press.

Barbour, B., and B. Gorlick. 2008. 'Embracing the "Responsibility to Protect": A Repertoire of Measures Including Asylum for Potential Victims'. *International Journal of Refugee Law* 20 (4): pp. 533–66.

Barlow, C. H. 2019. 'Child Criminal Exploitation: A New Systemic Model to Improve Professional Assessment, Investigation and Intervention'. (PhD dissertation, University of Hull, 2019).

Barner, J. R., D. Okech, and M. A. Camp. 2014. 'Socio-Economic Inequality, Human Trafficking and the Global Slave Trade'. *Societies* 4: pp. 148–60.

Basedow, J., and L. Doyle. 2016. *England's Forgotten Refugees: Out of the Fire and into the Frying Pan*. Refugee Council.

Bauman, Z. 2001. 'Foreword: Individually Together'. In *Individualization: Institutionalized Individualism and its Social and Political Consequences*, edited by U. Beck, and E. Beck-Gernsheim, pp. xiv–xix. London; Thousand Oaks; New Delhi: Sage.

BBC. 2017. Two-tier system leaving refugees in UK destitute, says report. *BBC*. 25 April. https://www.bbc.co.uk/news/uk-politics-39700596 [Accessed 26/10/2022].

BBC. 2018. Oxfam sex scandal: Haiti suspends charity's operations. *BBC*. 22 February. http://www.bbc.co.uk/news/uk-43163620 [Accessed 26/10/2022].

Beck, U., and E. Beck-Gernsheim. 2001. *Individualization: Institutionalized Individualism and its Social and Political Consequences*. London; Thousand Oaks; New Delhi: Sage.

Belandra, N. 2007. 'Defining Armed Conflict'. *Cardozo Law Review* 29: p. 2461.

Bellamy, A. 2017. Safe passage: an integral component of the responsibility to protect. *Beyond Slavery and Trafficking, openDemocracy*. 3 March. https://www.opendemocracy.net/en/beyond-trafficking-and-slavery/safe-passage-integral-component-of-responsibility-to-protect/ [Accessed 26/10/2022].

Berent, P. H. 1966. 'The Depth Interview'. *Journal of Advertising Research* 6 (2): pp. 32–39.

Bernard, H. R. 2002. *Research Methods in Anthropology: Qualitative and Quantitative Approaches*, 3rd ed. Walnut Creek, CA: Alta Mira Press.

Beutin, L. P. 2017. 'Black Suffering for/from Anti-Trafficking Advocacy'. *Anti-Trafficking Review* 9: pp. 14–30.

Binberg Peirce and Partners, Medical Justice, and the National Coalition of Anti Deportation Campaigns. 2008. *Outsourcing Abuse: The Use and Misuse of State-Sanctioned Force During the Detention and Removal of Asylum Seekers.*

London: Binberg Peirce and Partners, Medical Justice, and the National Coalition of Anti Deportation Campaigns.

Birks, M., and J. Mills. 2011. *Grounded Theory: A Practical Guide*. London: Sage.

Blazek, M., J. Esson, and D. P. Smith. 2018. 'Relational Geographies of Human Trafficking: Inequality, Manoeuvring and Im/mobility Across Space and Time'. *Transactions of the Institute of British Geographers* 44 (1): pp. 1–16.

Bloch, A. 1999. 'Carrying Out a Survey of Refugees: Some Methodological Considerations and Guidelines'. *Journal of Refugee Studies* 12 (4): pp. 367–83.

Bloch, A. 2013. 'The Labour Market Experiences and Strategies of Young Undocumented Migrants'. *Work, Employment and Society* 27 (2): pp. 272–87.

Bloch, A., and L. Schuster. 2002. 'Asylum and Welfare: Contemporary Debates'. *Critical Social Policy* 22 (3): pp. 393–413.

Blume, S. 2015. *Masculinity and the 'Ideal Victim' in the US trafficking Discourse. Working Paper WP-2015-124*. Oxford: Centre on Migration, Policy and Society, University of Oxford.

Bollas, C. 1993. *Being a Character*. London: Routledge.

Bonilla, T., and C. Mo. 2018. 'The Evolution of Human Trafficking Messaging in the United States and its Effect on Public Opinion'. *Journal of Public Policy* 39 (2): pp. 201–34.

Bosworth, M., C. Hoyle, and M. M. Dempsey. 2011. 'Researching Trafficked Women: on Institutional Resistance and the Limits to Feminist Reflexivity'. *Qualitative Inquiry* 17 (9): 769–79.

Brekke, J. P., and G. Brochmann. 2015. 'Stuck in Transit: Secondary Migration of Asylum Seekers in Europe, National Differences, and the Dublin Regulation'. *Journal of Refugee Studies* 28 (2): pp. 1–18.

Brickell, K., and D. Cuomo. 2019. 'Feminist Geolegality'. *Progress in Human Geography* 43 (1): pp. 104–22.

Broome, A., and J. Quirk. 2015. The politics of numbers: the global slavery index and the marketplace of activism. *Beyond Slavery and Trafficking, openDemocracy*. 10 March. https://www.opendemocracy.net/en/beyond-trafficking-and- slavery/politics-of-numbers-global-slavery-index-and-marketplace-of-ac/ [Accessed 26/10/2022].

Brown, C. 2012. 'Rape as a Weapon of War in the Democratic Republic of the Congo'. *Torture* 22: pp. 24–37.

Bruch, E. 2004. 'Models Wanted: The Search for an Effective Response to Human Trafficking'. *Journal of International Law* 40 (1): pp. 1–46.

Brysk, A., and A. Choi-Fitzpatrick. 2012. 'Introduction: Rethinking Trafficking'. In *From Human Trafficking to Human Rights: Reframing Contemporary Slavery*, edited by A. Brysk, and A. Choi-Fitzpatrick, pp. 1–10. Philadelphia: University of Pennsylvania Press.

Bulman, M. 2018a. The human impact of Theresa May's hostile environment policies. *Independent*. 21 April. https://www.independent.co.uk/news/uk/home-news/hostile-environment-policy-theresa-may-migrants-windrush-a8315806.html [Accessed 26/10/2022].

Bulman, M. 2018b. Government thwarted in bid to deport modern slavery victim who feared he would be killed if returned. *Independent*. 13 June. https://www.

independent.co.uk/news/uk/home-news/government-thwarted-in-bid-to-deport-modern-slavery-victim-a8397561.html [Accessed 26/10/2022].

Burland, P. 2017. Smoke but no fire: how not to read UK government trafficking statistics. *Beyond Slavery and Trafficking, openDemocracy.* 28 April. https://www.opendemocracy.net/en/beyond-trafficking-and-slavery/smoke-but-no-fire-how-not-to-read-uk-government-trafficking-statistics/ [Accessed 26/10/2022].

Butler-Sloss, E. 2011. Human trafficking is modern slavery. *The Guardian.* 2 July. https://www.theguardian.com/law/2011/jul/02/elizabeth-butler-sloss-human-trafficking [Accessed 26/10/2022].

Byrne, B., R. Marcus, and T. Powers-Stevens. 1995. 'Gender, Conflict and Development Volume II: Case Studies: Cambodia; Rwanda; Kosovo; Algeria; Somalia; Guatemala and Eritrea'. *Research Report* 1 (34). Brighton: Institute for Development Studies, pp. 1–148.

Cameron, S., and E. Newman. 2008. 'Trafficking in Humans: Structural Factors'. In *Trafficking in Humans: Social, Cultural and Political Dimensions*, edited by S. Cameron, and E. Newman, pp. 21–57. Tokyo and New York: United Nations University Press.

Chacon, J. 2017. 'Human Trafficking, Immigration Regulation, and Subfederal Criminalization'. *New Criminal Law Review* 20 (1): pp. 96–129.

Charmaz, K. 2006. *Constructing Grounded Theory: A Practical Guide Through Qualitative Analysis Introducing Qualitative Methods.* London: Sage.

Chase, R. T. 2015. 'We Are Not Slaves: Rethinking the Rise of Carceral States through the Lens of the Prisoners' Rights Movement'. *Journal of American History* 1 (1): pp. 73–86.

Chase, S. 1951. *Roads to Agreement.* New York: Harper.

China Daily. 2005. UN soldiers arrested for alleged sexual abuse. 16 February. http://www.china.org.cn/english/international/120416.htm. [Accessed 26/10/2022].

Choi-Fitzpatrick, A. 2012. 'Rethinking Trafficking: Contemporary Slavery'. In *From Human Trafficking to Human Rights: Reframing Contemporary Slavery*, edited by A. Brysk, and A. Choi-Fitzpatrick, pp. 13–24. Philadelphia: University of Pennsylvania Press.

Christie, N. 1986. 'The Ideal Victim'. In *From Crime Policy to Victim Policy: Reorienting the Justice System*, edited by E. Fattah, pp. 17–30. Basingstoke: Palgrave Macmillan.

Clugston, H. 2021. Crown Prosecution Service 'failing' on modern slavery as four in five suspects walk free from court. *Hartlepool Mail.* 15 February. https://www.hartlepoolmail.co.uk/read-this/crown-prosecution-service-failing-on-modern-slavery-as-four-in-five-suspects-walk-free-from-court-3135185 [Accessed 26/10/2022].

Cohen, S. 2002. 'Dining with the Devil: the 1999 Immigration and Asylum Act and the Voluntary Sector'. In *From Immigration Controls to Welfare Controls*, edited by S. Cohen, B. Humphries, and E. Mynott, pp. 141–56. London: Routledge.

Conaghan, J. 2009. 'Intersectionality and the Feminist Project in Law'. In *Intersectionality and Beyond: Law, Power and the Politics of Location*, edited by E. Grabham, D. Cooper, J. Krishnadas, and D. Herman, pp. 21–48. Oxon and New York: GlassHouse.

Conlon, D., and N. Hiemstra. (editors) 2016. *Intimate Economies of Immigration Detention: Critical Perspectives*. London: Routledge.

Cooper, C., O. Hesketh, N. Ellis, and A. Fair. 2017. *A Typology of Modern Slavery Offences in the UK: Research Report 93*. London: Home Office.

Council of Europe. 2010. *European Convention on Human Rights*. Strasbourg: Council of Europe.

Craig, G., A. Gaus, M. Wilkinson, K. Skrivankova, and A. McQuade. 2007. *Contemporary Slavery in the UK: Overview and Key Issues*. York: Joseph Rowntree Foundation.

Crates, E. 2020. *Operation Fort: What Businesses Should Learn from the UK's Largest Anti-Slavery Prosecution*. Independent Anti-Slavery Commissioner.

Crawley, H. 2006. 'Forced Migration and the Politics of Asylum: The Missing Pieces of the International Migration Puzzle?' *International Migration* 44 (1): pp. 21–26.

Crawley, H., F. Duvell, K. Jones, S. McMahon, and N. Sigona. 2016. *Destination Europe? Understanding the Dynamics and Drivers of Mediterranean Migration in 2015*. MEDMIG Final Report.

Crenshaw, K. 1989. 'Demarginalizing the Intersection Between Race and Sex: A Black Feminist Critique of Anti-Discrimination Doctrine, Feminist Theory and Anti-Racist Politics'. *University of Chicago Legal Forum* 1989 (1): pp. 139–67.

Cresswell, J. W., and V. L. Plano Clark. 2011. *Designing and Conducting Mixed Method Research*, 2nd ed. Thousand Oaks, CA: Sage.

Crown Prosecution Service. 2020. *Modern slavery: news, international and organised crime*. 9 October. https://www.cps.gov.uk/cps/news/modern-slavery [Accessed 26/10/2022].

Cucumanova, V. 2010. *South Africa at the Crossroads of Human Trafficking: War-Pushed and Hope-Driven*. Southern African Catholic Bishop's Conference: Catholic Parliamentary Liaison Office.

d'Albis, H., E. Boubtane, and D. Coulibaly. 2018. 'Macroeconomic Evidence Suggests that Asylum Seekers are not a "Burden" for Western European Countries'. *Science Advances* 4 (6): pp. 1–5.

Dahrendorf, R. 1958. 'Toward a Theory of Social Conflict'. *The Journal of Conflict Resolution* 2 (2): pp. 170–83.

Darling, J. 2014. 'Another Letter from the Home Office: Reading the Material Politics of Asylum'. *Environment and Planning D: Society and Space* 32: 484–500.

Darling, J. 2016. 'Privatising Asylum: Neoliberalisation, Depoliticisation and the Governance of Forced Migration'. *Transactions of the Institute of British Geographers* 41 (3): pp. 230–43.

David, K. 1998. *The Disarmament, Demobilisation and Reintegration of Child Soldiers in Liberia. 1994–1997. The Process and Lessons Learned*. New York; Monrovia: UNICEF.

Davies, P. 2007. 'Lessons from the Gender Agenda'. In *Handbook of Victims and Victimology*, edited by S. Walklate, pp. 175–201. Cullompton: Willan.

De Angelis, M. 2016. *Women's Stories of Agency*. Cambridge: Cambridge Scholars Publishing.

De Genova, N. 2002. 'Migrant "Illegality" and "Deportability" in Everyday Life'. *Annual Review of Anthropology* 31: pp. 419–47.

Demetriou, D. 2015. '"Tied visas" and Inadequate Labour Protections: A Formula for Abuse and Exploitation of Migrant Domestic Workers in the United Kingdom'. *Anti-Trafficking Review* 5: pp. 69–88.

Dempsey, M. M. 2010. 'Sex Trafficking and Criminalization: in Defense of Feminist Abolitionism'. *University of Pennsylvania Law Review* 158 (6): pp. 1729–78.

Deutsch, M. 1949. 'A Theory of Cooperation and Competition'. *Human Relations* 2: pp. 129–51.

de Watteville, N. 2002. 'Addressing Gender Issues in Demobilisation and Reintegration Programs'. *World Bank Africa Region Working Paper Series* 33: pp. 1–35.

Dodds, P. 2017. AP exclusive: UN child sex ring left victims but no arrests. *AP News Online*. 12 April. https://apnews.com/article/africa-arrests-united-nations-only-on-ap-e6ebc331460345c5abd4f57d77f535c1 [Accessed 26/10/2022].

Doezema, J. 1998. 'Forced to Choose: Beyond the Voluntary v Forced Prostitution Dichotomy'. In *Global Sex Workers. Rights, Resistance and Redefinition*, edited by K. Kempadoo, and J. Doezema, pp. 34–50. London and New York: Routledge.

Doezema, J. 2001. 'Ouch! Western Feminists' "Wounded Attachment" to the "Third World Prostitute"'. *Feminist Review* 67: pp. 16–38.

Dottridge, M. 2017. Eight reasons why we shouldn't use the term 'modern slavery'. *Beyond Slavery and Trafficking, openDemocracy*. 17 October. https://www.opendemocracy.net/en/beyond-trafficking-and-slavery/eight-reasons-why-we-shouldn-t-use-term-modern-slavery/ [Accessed 26/10/2022].

Dowler, L., and J. Sharp. 2001. 'A Feminist Geopolitics? '*Space and Polity* 5 (3): pp. 165–76.

Dugan, E. 2022. Home Office reclassifies modern slavery as illegal immigration issue. *The Guardian*. 13 October. https://www.theguardian.com/world/2022/oct/13/home-office-reclassifies-modern-slavery-as-immigration-issue [Accessed 26/10/2022].

Dunhill, A., and A. Kidd. 2020. 'How Definitions of "Child Soldiers" Exclude Girls from Demobilisation Efforts'. In *Human Trafficking in Conflict: Context, Causes and the Military*, edited by J. Muraszkiewicz, T. Fenton, and H. Watson, pp. 183–97. Cham, Switzerland: Palgrave Macmillan.

Dunn, J. L. 2005. '"Victims" and "Survivors": Emerging Vocabularies of Motive for "Battered Women who Stay"'. *Sociological Inquiry* 75 (1): pp. 1–30.

Durkheim, E. 1897. *Suicide: A Study in Sociology*, translated by J. A. Spaulding and G. Simpson. Glencoe, IL: Free Press.

Duxbury, A. 2007. 'Drawing Lines in the Sand: Characterizing Conflicts for the Purposes of Teaching International Humanitarian Law'. *Melbourne Journal of International Law* 8 (2): pp. 259–72.

Dwyer, P. J. 2005. 'Governance, Forced Migration and Welfare'. *Social Policy Administration* 39 (6): pp. 622–39.

Dwyer, P., and D. Brown. 2004. 'Meeting Basic Needs? The Survival Strategies of Forced Migrants'. *Paper to the Social Policy Association Annual Conference, University of Nottingham*, July 2004, pp. 1–22.

Dwyer, P., S. Hodkinson, H. Lewis, and L. Waite. 2016. 'Socio-Legal Status and Experiences of Forced Labour Among Asylum Seekers and Refugees in the UK'. *Journal of International and Comparative Social Policy* 32 (3): 182–98.

Ehrenreich, N. 2002. 'Subordination and Symbiosis: Mechanisms of Mutual Support between Subordinating Systems'. *UMKC Law Review* 71: pp. 251–324.

Farr, V. A. 2012. *Gender-Aware Disarmament, Demobilisation and Reintegration (DDR): A Checklist*. New York: United Nations Development Fund for Women .

Faugier, J., and M. Sargeant. 1997. 'Sampling Hard to Reach Populations'. *Journal of Advanced Nursing* 26 (4): pp. 790–97.

FLEX. 2021. Bad Decisions: the creation of an Immigration Enforcement Competent Authority will undermine identifying and protecting victims of crime. https://www.labourexploitation.org/publications/bad-decisions-creation-immigration-enforcement-competent-authority-will-undermine [Accessed 17/02/2023].

Fink, C. 1968. 'Some Conceptual Difficulties in the Theory of Social Conflict'. *Journal of Conflict Resolution* 12 (4): pp. 412–60.

Foucault, M. 1977. *Discipline and Punish: The Birth of the Prison*. London: Allen Lane.

Gadd, D., and R. Broad. 2018. 'Troubling Recognitions in British Responses to Modern Slavery'. *British Journal of Criminology* 58: pp. 1440–61.

Gallagher, A. 2014. The Global Slavery Index: seduction and obfuscation. *Beyond Slavery and Trafficking, openDemocracy*. 4 December. https://www.opendemocracy.net/en/5050/global-slavery-index-seduction-and- obfuscation/ [Accessed 26/10/2022].

Giddens, A. 1986. *The Constitution of Society*. Cambridge: Polity Press.

Glaser, B. G., and A. L. Strauss. 1999. *The Discovery of Grounded Theory: Strategies for Qualitative Research*. New Brunswick, N.J.: Aldine.

Glorius, B., J. Doomernik, and J. Darling. 2016. 'Asylum in Austere Times: Instability, Privatization and Experimentation within the UK Asylum Dispersal System'. *Journal of Refugee Studies* 29 (4): pp. 483–505.

Gong-Gershowitz, J. 2009. 'Forced Marriage: a "New" Crime Against Humanity?' *Northwestern Journal of International Human Rights* 8 (1): pp. 52–76.

Gower, M. 2021. *Refugee Resettlement in the UK: Recent Developments*. Briefing Paper Number 9017. House of Commons Library.

Green, S. 2015. 'Transcending the Carceral Archipelago: Existential, Figurational and Structurational Perspectives on Power and Control'. *Oñati Socio-Legal Series* 5 (3): pp. 919–44.

Greenfield, P. 2018. Red Cross finds 21 cases of sexual misconduct in last three years. *The Guardian*. 24 February. https://www.theguardian.com/world/2018/feb/24/red-cross-21-staff-members-left-due-to-sexual-misconduct-in-past-three-years [Accessed 26/10/2022].

Haer, R., C. M. Faulkner, and B. E. Whitaker. 2019. 'Rebel Funding and Child Soldiers: Exploring the Relationship Between Natural Resources and Forcible Recruitment'. *European Journal of International Relations* 26 (1): pp. 236–62.

Hayden, S. 2018. Exclusive: refugees in Sudan allege chronic corruption in UN resettlement process. *IRIN*. 15 May. https://www.irinnews.org/investigations/2018/05/15/exclusive-refugees-sudan-allege-chronic-corruption-un-resettlement-process [Accessed 26/10/2022].

Haynes D. F. 2014. 'The Celebritization of Human Trafficking'. *The ANNALS of the American Academy of Political and Social Science* 653 (1): pp. 25–45. doi:10.1177/0002716213515837

Hebblethwaite, A., A. Hames, M. Donkin, M. Colman, and A. Forsyth. 2007. 'Investigating the Experiences of People who Have Been Homeless and are in Contact with Learning Disability Services'. *Tizard Learning Disability Review* 12 (3): pp. 25–34.

Helvey, R. L. 2004. *On Strategic Nonviolent Conflict: Thinking about the Fundamentals*. Boston: The Albert Einstein Institution.

Herlihy, J., and S. Turner. 2006. 'Should Discrepant Accounts Given by Asylum Seekers be Taken as Proof of Deceit?'. *Torture* 16 (2): pp. 81–92.

Hesketh, O., and A. Balch. 2021. *Modern Slavery and International Development*. London: Modern Slavery and Human Rights Policy and Evidence Centre.

Heys, A., C. Barlow, C. Murphy, and A. McKee. 2022. 'A Review of Modern Slavery in Britain: Understanding the Unique Experience of British Victims and Why it Matters'. *Journal of Victimology and Victim Justice* 5 (1): pp. 54–70.

Hilhorst, D., L. Weijers, and M. van Wessel. 2012. 'Aid Relations and Aid Legitimacy: Mutual Imaging of Aid Workers and Recipients in Nepal'. *Third World Quarterly* 33 (8): pp. 1439–57.

Hogeland, C., and K. Rosen. 1990. *Dreams Lost, Dreams Found: Undocumented Women in the Land of Opportunity. A Survey Research Project of Chinese, Filipina and Latina Undocumented Women*. San Francisco: Immigrant Women's Task Force, Coalition for Immigrant and Refugee Rights and Services.

Holloway, I. 2008. *A–Z of Qualitative Research in Healthcare*, 2nd ed. Oxford: Blackwell.

Home Office. 2014. *Modern Slavery Strategy*. https://www.gov.uk/government/uploads/system/uploads/attachment_data/file/383764/Modern_Slavery_Strategy_FINAL_DEC2015.pdf [Accessed 26/10/2022].

Home Office. 2020. *Modern Slavery: National Referral Mechanism Statistics UK, End of Year Summary, 2019*. https://assets.publishing.service.gov.uk/government/uploads/system/uploads/attachment_data/file/876646/national-referral-mechanism-statistics-uk-end-of-year-summary-2019.pdf [Accessed 26/10/2022].

Home Office. 2021. *Modern Slavery: National Referral Mechanism and Duty to Notify Statistics UK, End of Year Summary, 2020*. https://assets.publishing.service.gov.uk/government/uploads/system/uploads/attachment_data/file/970995/modern-slavery-national-referral-mechanism-statistics-end-year-summary-2020-hosb0821.pdf [Accessed 26/10/2022].

Home Office. 2022a. *Modern Slavery: National Referral Mechanism and Duty to Notify Statistics UK, End of Year Summary, 2021*. https://www.gov.uk/government/statistics/modern-slavery-national-referral-mechanism-and-duty-to-notify-statistics-uk-end-of-year-summary-2021/modern-slavery-national-referral-mechanism-and-duty-to-notify-statistics-uk-end-of-year-summary-2021#:~:text=In%202021%2C%20the%20NRM%20received,referrals%20since%20the%20NRM%20began. [Accessed 26/10/2022]. Note that some information is taken from the data tables accessible through this report rather than from the report directly.

Home Office. 2022b. *Modern Slavery: National Referral Mechanism and Duty to Notify statistics UK, Quarter 3 2022 – July to September*. https://www.gov.uk/gov

ernment/statistics/national-referral-mechanism-and-duty-to-notify-statistics-uk-july-to-september-2022/modern-slavery-national-referral-mechanism-and-duty-to-notify-statistics-uk-quarter-3-2022-july-to-september [Accessed 17/02/2023].

Home Office. 2022c. *Modern Slavery: Statutory Guidance for England and Wales (under s49 of the Modern Slavery Act 2015) and Non-Statutory Guidance for Scotland and Northern Ireland.* https://assets.publishing.service.gov.uk/government/uploads/system/uploads/attachment_data/file/1133140/Modern_Slavery_Statutory_Guidance__EW__Non-Statutory_Guidance__SNI__v3.0.pdf [Accessed 21/02/2023].

Home Office. 2023. *Modern Slavery: Statutory Guidance for Engalnd and Wales (under s49 of the Modern Slavery Act 2015) and Non-Statutory Guidance for Scotland and Nothern Ireland. Version 3.0.* https://assets.publishing.service.gov.uk/government/uploads/system/uploads/attachment_data/file/1133140/Modern_Slavery_Statutory_Guidance__EW__Non-Statutory_Guidance__SNI__v3.0.pdf [Accessed 17/02/2023].

Hopper, E., and J. Hidalgo. 2006. 'Invisible Chains: Psychological Coercion of Human Trafficking Victims'. *Intercultural Human Rights Law Review* 1: pp. 185–210.

Horowitz, D. 1985. *Ethnic Groups in Conflict*. Berkeley: University of California Press.

Housing Act UK. 1996. Chapter 52. https://www.legislation.gov.uk/ukpga/1996/52/contents [Accessed 26/10/2022].

Human Rights Watch. 2002. 'Hopes Betrayed: Trafficking of Women and Girls to Post-Conflict Bosnia and Herzegovina for Forced Prostitution'. *Human Rights Watch 14* (9): pp. 1–75.

Human Rights Watch. 2003. 'Stolen Children: Abduction and Recruitment in Northern Uganda'. *Human Rights Watch* 15 (7A): pp. 1–25.

Human Rights Watch, and S. Brett. 2003. *You'll Learn Not to Cry: Child Combatants in Colombia*. New York: Human Rights Watch.

Human Trafficking Foundation. 2015. *Life Beyond the Safehouse: for Survivors of Modern Slavery in London, Gaps and Options Review.* https://static1.squarespace.com/static/599abfb4e6f2e19ff048494f/t/599eeb28914e6b9ddcceace2/1503587117886/Web_Life+Beyond+the+Safe+House.pdf [Accessed 26/10/2022].

Human Trafficking Foundation. 2016. *Day 46: Is There Life after the Safe House for Survivors of Modern Slavery?* https://static1.squarespace.com/static/599abfb4e6f2e19ff048494f/t/599eec35a803bb09254f7d0d/1503587392258/Human+Trafficking+Foundation+Report+2016+Day+46.PDF [Accessed 26/10/2022].

Hunter, R., and T. de Simone. 2009. 'Identifying Disadvantage: Beyond Intersectionality'. In *Intersectionality and Beyond: Law, Power and the Politics of Location*, edited by E. Grabham, D. Cooper, J. Krishnadas, and D. Herman, pp. 159–82. Oxon and New York: GlassHouse.

Hunter, S. V. 2010. 'Evolving Narratives about Childhood Sexual Abuse: Challenging the Dominance of the Victim and Survivor Paradigm'. *Australian & New Zealand Journal of Family Therapy* 31: pp. 176–90.

Hyndman, J. 2004. 'Mind the Gap: Bridging Feminist and Political Geography through Geopolitics'. *Political Geography* 23: pp. 307–22.

Hynes, P., and R. Sales. 2010. 'New Communities: Asylum Seekers and Dispersal'. In *Race and Ethnicity in the 21st Century*, edited by A. Bloch, and J. Solomos, pp. 39–61. London: Routledge.

Independent Anti-Slavery Commissioner. 2018. *Priority 5: International Collaboration.* https://www.antislaverycommissioner.co.uk/priorities/priority-5-international-collaboration/ [Accessed 15/7/2018. No longer a live webpage].

International Committee of the Red Cross. 1949. *Geneva Convention for the Amelioration of the Condition of the Wounded and Sick in Armed Forces in the Field* (First Geneva Convention), 12 August 1949, 75 UNTS 31.

International Committee of the Red Cross. 2008. *How is The Term 'Armed Conflict' Defined in International Humanitarian Law?* https://www.icrc.org/eng/resources/documents/article/other/armed-conflict-article-170308.htm [Accessed 26/10/2022].

International Criminal Tribunal for the Former Yugoslavia. 2005. *The Prosecutor v Fatmir Limaj.* Judgment IT-03-66-T, 30 November. http://www.icty.org/x/cases/limaj/tjug/en/lim-tj051130-e.pdf [Accessed 26/10/2022].

International Labour Organization. 2005. *A Global Alliance Against Forced Labour.* Geneva: International Labour Office.

International Organization for Migration. 2001. *Victims of Trafficking in the Balkans.* Geneva: International Organization for Migration.

International Organization for Migration. 2011. *World Migration Report.* Geneva: International Organization for Migration.

Jagpal, P., K. Saunders, G. Plahe, S. Russell, N. Barnes, R. Lowrie, and V. Paudyal. 2020. 'Research Priorities in Healthcare of Persons Experiencing Homelessness: Outcomes of a National Multi-Disciplinary Stakeholder Discussion in the United Kingdom'. *International Journal for Equity in Health* 19 (86): pp. 1–7.

Jain, N. 2009. 'Forced Marriage as a Crime Against Humanity: Problems of Definition and Prosecution'. *Journal of International Criminal Justice* 6 (5): pp. 1013–32.

Jean-Charles, R. 2014. 'Toward a Victim-Survivor Narrative: Rape and Form in Yvonne Vera's *Under the Tongue* and Calixthe Beyala's *Tu T'appelleras Tanga*'. *Research in African Literatures* 45 (1): 39–62.

Jessop, B. 1999. 'The Changing Governance of Welfare: Recent Trends in its Primary Functions, Scale and Modes of Coordination'. *Social Policy and Administration* 33 (4): pp. 348–59.

Kalyaan. 2021. *Stolen Rights: It's Time to Give Migrant Domestic Workers their Rights Back.* http://www.kalayaan.org.uk/campaign-posts/stolen-rights-its-time-to-give-migrant-domestic-workers-their-rights-back/. [Accessed 26/10/2022].

Kaplan, C. D., D. Korf, and C. Sterk. 1987. 'Temporal and Social Contexts of Heroin-Using Populations: An Illustration of the Snowball Sampling Technique'. *Journal of Mental and Nervous Disorders* 175 (9): p. 566.

Kara, S. 2009. *Sex Trafficking: Inside the Business of Modern Slavery.* New York: Columbia University Press.

KarmaNirvana. 2022. *What is Forced Marriage?* https://karmanirvana.org.uk/get-help/what-is-forced-marriage/ [Accessed 26/10/2022].

Kassaw, E. S. 2019. 'Major Problems in Street Life of People at "Risk", the Case of Selected Areas of Harari Region Ethiopia'. *International Journal of Education and Literacy Studies* 7 (1): pp. 66–76.

Kaye, M., and A. McQuade. 2007. *Poverty, Development and the Elimination of Slavery*. Anti-Slavery International.

Kaytaz, E. 2016. 'Afghan Journeys to Turkey: Narratives of Immobility, Travel and Transformation'. *Geopolitics* 21 (2): pp. 284–302.

Kelly, A. 2017. Latest figures reveal more than 40 million people are living in slavery. *The Guardian*. 19 September. https://www.theguardian.com/global-development/2017/sep/19/latest-figures-reveal-more-than-40-million-people-are-living-in-slavery?CMP=Share_iOSApp_Other [Accessed 26/10/2022].

Kempadoo, K. 2015. The white man's burden revisited. *Beyond Slavery and Trafficking, openDemocracy*. 11 January. https://www.opendemocracy.net/en/beyond-trafficking-and-slavery/white-mans-burden-revisited/ [Accessed 26/10/2022].

Kidd, A., E. Faulkner, and L. Arocha. 2019. How UK asylum system creates perfect conditions for modern slavery and exploitation to thrive. *The Conversation*. 8 April. https://theconversation.com/how-uk-asylum-system-creates-perfect-conditions-for- modern-slavery-and-exploitation-to-thrive-113778 [Accessed 26/10/2022].

Kirby, P. 2012. 'How is Rape a Weapon of War? Feminist International Relations, Modes of Critical Explanation and the Study of Wartime Sexual Violence'. *European Journal of International Relations* 19 (4): pp. 797–821.

Kjaerum, M. 2002. 'Refugee Protection between State Interests and Human Rights: Where is Europe Heading?' *Human Rights Quarterly* 24: pp. 513–36.

Klopcic, A. 2004. 'Trafficking in Human Beings in Transition and Post-Conflict Countries'. *Human Security Perspectives* 1 (1): pp. 7–12.

Koser, K. 2000. 'Asylum Policies, Trafficking and Vulnerability'. *Journal of International Migration* 38 (3): pp. 91–111.

Kotecha, A. 2020. 'Human Trafficking, Conflict and Money Flows'. In *Human Trafficking in Conflict: Context, Causes and the Military*, edited by J. Muraszkiewicz, T. Fenton, and H. Watson, pp. 61–80. Cham, Switzerland: Palgrave Macmillan.

Kotiswaran, P., and S. Okyere. 2015. The role of the state and law in trafficking and modern slavery. *Beyond Slavery and Trafficking, openDemocracy*. 24 March. https://www.nottingham.ac.uk/icemic/documents/the-role-of-the-state-and-law-in-trafficking-and-modern-slavery.pdf [Accessed 26/10/2022].

Kuhl, M. 2011. 'Modern day slavery and human trafficking: an overlooked issue'. (BA thesis. Salve Regina University, 2011).

Kuschminder, K. 2017. 'Afghan Refugee Journeys: Onwards Migration Decision-Making in Greece and Turkey'. *Journal of Refugee Studies* 31 *(4): pp. 566–87*.

Labott, S. M., T. P. Johnson, M. Fendrich, and N. C. Feeny. 2013. 'Emotional Risks to Respondents in Survey Research: Some Empirical Evidence'. *Journal of Empirical Research on Human Research Ethics* 8 (4): pp. 53–66.

Landman, T. 2018. 'Out of the Shadows: Trans-Disciplinary Research on Modern Slavery'. *Peace Human Rights Governance* 2 (2): pp. 143–62.

Lave, J., and S. Kvale. 1995. 'What is Anthropological Research? An Interview with Jean Lave by Steiner Kvale'. *International Journal of Qualitative Studies in Education* 8 (3): 219–28.

LeBaron, G. 2015. Slaves of the state: American prison labour past and present. *Beyond Slavery and Trafficking, openDemocracy.* 23 April. https://www.opendemocracy.net/en/beyond-trafficking-and-slavery/slaves-of-state-american-prison-labour-past-and-present/ [Accessed 26/10/2022].

LeBaron, G., N. Howard, C. Thibos, and P. Kyritsis. 2019. Confronting root causes: forced labour in supply chains. *Beyond Slavery and Trafficking, openDemocracy.* 19 March. https://www.opendemocracy.net/en/beyond-trafficking-and-slavery/confronting-root-causes/ [Accessed 26/10/2022].

LeVine, R. 1961. 'Anthropology and the Study of Conflict: Introduction'. *Journal of Conflict Resolution* 5 (1): pp. 3–15.

Lewis, H., P. Dwyer, S. Hodkinson, and L. Waite. 2013. *Precarious Lives: Experiences of Forced Labour Among Refugees and Asylum Seekers in England.* Leeds: University of Leeds.

Lewis, H., P. Dwyer, S. Hodkinson, and L. Waite. 2014. 'Hyper-Precarious Lives: Migrants, Work and Forced Labour in the Global North'. *Progress in Human Geography* 39 (5): pp. 580–600.

Lewis, H., and L. Waite. 2015. 'Asylum, Immigration Restrictions and Exploitation: Hyper-Precarity as a Lens for Understanding and Tackling Forced Labour'. *Anti-Trafficking Review* 5: pp. 50–68.

Lift the Ban. No Date. *Lift the Ban: Why Giving People Seeking Asylum the Right to Work is Common Sense.* https://www.refugee-action.org.uk/wp-content/uploads/2020/07/Lift-The-Ban-Common-Sense.pdf. [Accessed 26/10/2022].

Limanowska, B. 2005. *Trafficking in Human Beings in South Eastern Europe.* Sarajevo: United Nations Development Programme .

Lister, R. 2004. *Poverty*. Cambrid ge: Polity Press.

Little, D. 2006. 'Religion, Conflict and Peace'. *Case Western Reserve Journal of International War* 31 (1): 95–103.

Lobasz, J. 2009. 'Beyond Border Security: Feminist Approaches to Human Trafficking'. *Security Studies* 18 (2): pp. 3193–44.

McCall, L. 2009. 'The Complexity of Intersectionality'. In *Intersectionality and Beyond: Law, Power and the Politics of Location*, edited by E. Grabham, D. Cooper, J. Krishnadas, and D. Herman, pp. 49–76. Oxon and New York: GlassHouse.

McCosker, H., A. Barnard, and R. Gerber. 2001. 'Undertaking Sensitive Research: Issues and Strategies for Meeting the Safety Needs of all Participants'. *Forum: Qualitative Social Research* 2 (1).

McFayden, J., and J. Rankin. 2016. 'The Role of Gatekeepers in Research: Learning from Reflexivity and Reflection'. *Global Science and Technology Forum Journal of Nursing and Healthcare* 4 (1): pp. 82–88.

McGough, M. 2013. 'Ending Modern-Day Slavery: Using Research to Inform U.S. Anti- Human Trafficking Efforts'. *National Institute of Justice Journal* 271: pp. 26–32.

McGrath, S. 2014. The US' troubling turn as global anti-trafficking sheriff. *Beyond Slavery and Trafficking, openDemocracy.* 26 August. https://www.opendemocr

acy.net/en/opensecurity/us-troubling-turn-as-global-antitrafficking-sheriff/ [Accessed 26/10/2022].

McIntyre, N. 2018. Private contractors paid millions to run UK detention centres. *The Guardian.* 10 October. https://www.theguardian.com/uk-news/2018/oct/10/private-contractors-paid-millions-uk-detention-centres-some-firms-making-30-percent-profit [Accessed 26/10/2022].

McKay, S., and D. Mazurana. 2004. *Where Are The Girls? Girls in Fighting Forces in Northern Uganda, Sierra Leone and Mozambique: Their Lives During and After War.* Montreal: International Centre for Human Rights and Democratic Development.

Mack, R. W. 1965. 'The Components of Social Conflict'. *Social Problems* 22 (4): pp. 388–97.

Martens, J., M. Pieczkowski, and B. van Vuuren-Smyth. 2003. *Seduction, Sale & Slavery: Trafficking in Women & Children for Sexual Exploitation in Southern Africa*, 3rd ed. Pretoria: International Organization for Migration.

Martin, L. 2015. 'Noncitizen Detention: Spatial Strategies of Migrant Precarity in US Immigration and Border Control'. *Annales de Géographie* 124 (702–703): pp. 231–47.

Martins, A. 2016. 'Interview with Julia O'Connell Davidson on Modern Slavery'. *Theory, Culture and Society* 33 (7–8): pp. 381–90.

Massaro, V. A., and J. Williams. 2013. 'Feminist Geopolitics'. *Geography Compass* 7 (8): pp. 567–77.

May, T. 2016. My government will lead the way in defeating modern slavery. *The Telegraph.* 4 July. https://www.telegraph.co.uk/news/2016/07/30/we-will-lead-the-way-in-defeating-modern-slavery [Accessed 26/10/2022].

May, T., and B. Cazeneuve. 2015. Migrants think our streets are paved with gold. *The Telegraph.* 1 August. https://www.telegraph.co.uk/news/uknews/immigration/11778396/Migrants-think-our-streets-are-paved-with-gold.html [Accessed 26/10/2022].

Mayblin, L., and P. James. 2019. 'Asylum and Refugee Support in the UK: Civil Society Filling the Gaps?'. *Journal of Ethnic and Migration Studies* 45 (3): pp. 375–94.

Mazurana, D., S. A. McKay, K. Carlson, and J. C. Kasper. 2002. 'Girls in Fighting Forces and Groups: Their Recruitment, Participation, Demobilization, and Reintegration'. *Peace and Conflict: Journal of Peace Psychology* 8 (2): pp. 97–123.

Meillassoux, C. 1991. *The Anthropology of Slavery: The Womb of Iron and Gold.* Chicago: University of Chicago Press.

Mendelson, S. E. 2005. *Barracks and Brothels: Peacekeepers and Human Trafficking in the Balkans.* Washington: The Centre for Strategic and International Studies .

Miers, S., and I. Kopytoff. 1977. *Slavery in Africa: Historical and Anthropological Perspectives.* Wisconsin: The University of Wisconsin Press.

Milano, V. 2020. 'The Due Diligence Duty and the Role of the Military in the Identification and Protection of Human Trafficking Victims'. In *Human Trafficking in Conflict: Context, Causes and the Military*, edited by J. Muraszkiewicz, T. Fenton, and H. Watson, 2020, pp. 173–96. Cham, Switzerland: Palgrave Macmillan.

Mnookin, R., and A. Verbeke. 2009. 'Persistent Nonviolent Conflict with No Reconciliation: The Flemish and Walloons in Belgium'. *Law and Contemporary Problems* 72 (2): pp. 151–86.

Modern Slavery Act UK. 2015. Chapter 30. https://www.legislation.gov.uk/ukpga/2015/30/contents/enacted [Accessed 26/10/2022].

Morris, D. 1997. 'About Suffering: Voice, Genre and Moral Community'. In *Social Suffering*, edited by A. Kleinman, and J. Kleinman, pp. 25–45. Berkeley, Los Angeles and London: University of California Press.

Moss, J. 2011. 'Trafficking: A Human Rights Abuse, Not an Immigration Offence'. *50.50, openDemocracy*, 17 August. https://www.opendemocracy.net/en/5050/trafficking-human-rights-abuse-not-immigration-offence/ [Accessed 26/10/2022].

Mountz, A., and J. Hyndman. 2006. 'Feminist Approaches to the Global Intimate'. *Women's Studies Quarterly* 34 (1–2): pp. 446–63.

Muraszkiewicz, J., T. Fenton, and H. Watson. 2020a. 'Introduction'. In *Human Trafficking in Conflict: Context, Causes and the Military*, edited by J. Muraszkiewicz, T. Fenton, and H. Watson, pp. 1–18. Cham, Switzerland: Palgrave Macmillan.

Muraszkiewicz, J., O. Ianelli, and P. Wieltschnig. 2020b. 'Typology'. In *Human Trafficking in Conflict: Context, Causes and the Military*, edited by J. Muraszkiewicz, T. Fenton, and H. Watson, pp. 21–42. Cham, Switzerland: Palgrave Macmillan.

Muraszkiewicz, J., T. Fenton, and H. Watson. 2020c. (editors) *Human Trafficking in Conflict: Context, Causes and the Military*. Cham, Switzerland: Palgrave Macmillan.

Murphy, C. 2020. *A Game of Chance? Long-term Support for Survivors of Modern Slavery*. The Centre for the Study of Modern Slavery, St Mary's University Twickenham.

Murphy, L. T. 2014. *Survivors of Slavery: Modern-Day Slave Narratives*. New York: Columbia University Press.

National Crime Agency. 2014. *National Referral Mechanism Statistics 2013*. https://nationalcrimeagency.gov.uk/who-we-are/publications/374-national-referral-mechanism-statistics-2013/file [Accessed 26/10/2022].

National Crime Agency. 2015. *National Referral Mechanism Statistics—End of Year Summary 2014*. https://nationalcrimeagency.gov.uk/who-we-are/publications/373-national-referral-mechanism-statistics-end-of-year-summary-2014/file [Accessed 26/10/2022].

National Crime Agency. 2016. *National Referral Mechanism Statistics—End of Year Summary 2015*. https://nationalcrimeagency.gov.uk/who-we-are/publications/364-national-referral-mechanism-statistics-end-of-year-summary-2015/file [Accessed 26/10/2022].

National Crime Agency. 2017. *National Referral Mechanism Statistics—End of Year Summary 2016*. https://nationalcrimeagency.gov.uk/who-we-are/publications/60-modern-slavery-and-human-trafficking-national-referral-mechanism-statistics-end-of-year-summary-2016/file [Accessed 26/10/2022].

National Crime Agency. 2018. *National Referral Mechanism Statistics—End of Year Summary 2017*. https://nationalcrimeagency.gov.uk/who-we-are/publications/

159-modern-slavery-and-human-trafficking-national-referral-mechanism-statistics-annual-report-2017/file [Accessed 26/10/2022].

National Crime Agency. 2019. *National Referral Mechanism Statistics—End of Year Summary 2018*. https://nationalcrimeagency.gov.uk/who-we-are/publications/282-national-referral-mechanism-statistics-end-of-year-summary-2018/file [Accessed 26/10/2022].

Nationality and Borders Act. 2022. Chapter 36. https://www.legislation.gov.uk/ukpga/2022/36/contents/enacted [Accessed 17/02.2023].

Nejati, V., M. A. Salehinejad, and A. Sabayee. 2018. 'Impaired Working Memory Updating Affects Memory for Emotional and Non-Emotional Materials the Same Way: Evidence from Post-Traumatic Stress Disorder (PTSD)'. *Cognitive Processing* 19: pp. 53–62.

Nelson, S., J. Guthrie, and P. S. Coffey. 2004. *Literature Review and Analysis Related to Human Trafficking in Post-Conflict Situations*. Washington DC: United States Agency for International Development.

Newman, C. 2014. 'No One to Stand by Us: Reintegrating Formerly Abducted Child-Mothers in Uganda'. *Journal of Intervention and Statebuilding* 8 (4): pp. 357–80.

Nunkoosing, K. 2005. 'The Problems with Interviews'. *Qualitative Health Research* 15: pp. 698–706.

O'Connell Davidson, J. 2006. 'Will the Real Sex Slave Please Stand Up?' *Feminist Review* 83: pp. 4–22.

O'Connell Davidson, J. 2010. 'New Slavery, Old Binaries: Human Trafficking and the Borders of "Freedom"'. *Global Networks* 10 (2): pp. 244–61.

O'Connell Davidson, J. 2013a. Viewpoint: what's wrong with modern slavery? Why Theresa May in Wilberforce's clothing won't appeal to all. *Discover Society*. 24 October. https://archive.discoversociety.org/2013/11/05/586/ [Accessed 26/10/2022].

O'Connell Davidson, J. 2013b. 'Troubling Freedom: Migration, Debt and Modern Slavery'. *Migration Studies* 1 (2): pp. 176–95.

O'Connell Davidson, J. 2015. *Modern Slavery: The Margins of Freedom*. London: Palgrave Macmillan.

O'Connell Davidson, J. 2016. 'De-canting "Trafficking in Human Beings", Re-centring the State'. *The International Spectator: Italian Journal of International Affairs* 51 (6): pp. 58–73.

O'Connell Davidson, J. 2017. The presence of the past: lessons of history for anti-trafficking work. *Beyond Slavery and Trafficking, openDemocracy*. 19 October. https://www.opendemocracy.net/en/beyond-trafficking-and-slavery/presence-of-past-lessons-of-history-for-anti-trafficking-work/ [Accessed 26/10/2022].

O'Connell Davidson, J., and N. Howard. 2015. On freedom and (im)mobility: how states create vulnerability by controlling human movement. *Beyond Slavery and Trafficking, openDemocracy*. 18 May. https://www.opendemocracy.net/en/beyond-trafficking-and-slavery/on-freedom-and-immobility-how-states-create-vulne/ [Accessed 26/10/2022].

Office of the Special Adviser on Gender Issues and Advancement of Women. 2000. *Resolution 1325*. http://www.un.org/womenwatch/osagi/wps/ [Accessed 26/10/2022].

Olsson, L., I. Skjelsbaek, E. Fredrikk Barth, and K. Hostens. 2004. 'Gender Aspects of Conflict Interventions: Intended and Unintended Consequences'. *Final Report to the Norwegian Ministry of Foreign Affairs*. Oslo: International Peace Research Institute.

Oppong, S. H. 2012. 'Human Trafficking through Organized Crime'. *International Journal of Humanities and Social Science* 20 (2): pp. 37–43.

Oxford English Dictionary. No Date. *Conflict*. Available via oed.com [Accessed 26/10/2022].

Pain, R., and L. Staeheli. 2014. 'Introduction: Intimacy-Geopolitics and Violence'. *Area* 46 (4): pp. 344–60.

Papendick, M., G. and Bohner. 2017. *'Passive Victim—Strong Survivor'? Perceived Meaning and Labels Applied to Women who were Raped*. Bielefeld: Bielefeld University.

Parker, S. 2015. '"Unwanted Invaders": The Representation of Refugees and Asylum Seekers in the UK and Australian Print Media'. *Myth and Nation*, eSharp (23): pp. 1–21.

Patterson, O. 1982. *Slavery and Social Death: A Comparative Study*. Massachusetts: Harvard University Press.

Patton, M. 2002. *Qualitative Research and Evaluation Methods*, 3rd ed. Thousand Oaks, CA: Sage.

Pearson, E. 2003. *Trafficking in Women in East Africa*. Eschborn Germany: Deutsche Gesellschaft für Technische Zusammenarbeit (GTZ).

Peck, J., and A. Tickell. 2002. 'Neoliberalizing Space'. *Antipode* 34 (3): pp. 380–404.

Pehlic, A. 2020. 'Occurrence of Human Trafficking in a Conflict/Peacebuilding Context: Bosnian Experience'. In *Human Trafficking in Conflict: Context, Causes and the Military*, edited by J. Muraszkiewicz, T. Fenton, and H. Watson, pp. 123–42. Cham, Switzerland: Palgrave Macmillan.

Peternelj-Taylor, C. 2015. 'Patient, Victim or Survivor: Does Language Matter? A Conversation with Claudia Bayliff'. *Journal of Forensic Nursing* 11 (2): pp. 63–65.

Phillips, N. 2015. What has forced labour to do with poverty? *Beyond Slavery and Trafficking, openDemocracy*. 17 February. https://www.opendemocracy.net/en/beyond-trafficking-and-slavery/what-has-forced-labour-to-do-with-poverty/ [Accessed 26/10/2022].

Picarelli, J. T. 2002. 'Trafficking, Slavery and Peacekeeping: the Need for a Comprehensive Training Program'. *A Conference Report Hosted by the Transnational Crime and Corruption Centre, American University and the UN Interregional Crime and Justice Research Institute*. Turin, 9–10 May 2002.

Platts-Folwer, D., and D. Robinson. 2011. *An Evaluation of the Gateway Protection Programme*. Turin: Home Office.

Pratt, G., and V. Rosner. 2006. 'The Global and the Intimate'. *Women's Studies Quarterly* 34 (1–2): pp. 13–24.

Quirk, J. 2011. *The Anti-Slavery Project*. Philadelphia: University of Pennsylvania Press.

Quirk, J. 2015a. The rhetoric and reality of 'ending slavery in our lifetime'. *Beyond Slavery and Trafficking, openDemocracy*. 30 January. https://www.opendemocr

acy.net/en/beyond-trafficking-and-slavery/rhetoric-and-reality-of-ending-slavery-in-our-lifetime/ [Accessed 26/10/2022].

Quirk, J. 2015b. Reparations are too confronting: let's talk about 'modern slavery' instead. *Beyond Slavery and Trafficking, openDemocracy*. 7 May. https://www.opendemocracy.net/en/beyond-trafficking-and-slavery/reparations-are-too-confronting-lets-talk-about-modernday-slavery-instea/ [Accessed 26/10/2022].

Quirk, J., and G. LeBaron. 2015. The use and abuse of history: slavery and its contemporary legacies. *Beyond Slavery and Trafficking, openDemocracy*. 21 April. https://www.opendemocracy.net/en/beyond-trafficking-and-slavery/use-and-abuse-of-history-slavery-and-its-contemporary-leg/ [Accessed 26/10/2022].

Quirk, J., and J. O'Connell Davidson. 2015. Introduction: moving beyond popular representations of trafficking and slavery. *Beyond Slavery and Trafficking, openDemocracy*. 11 January. https://www.opendemocracy.net/en/beyond-trafficking-and-slavery/introduction-moving-beyond-popular-representations/ [Accessed 26/10/2022].

Quirk, J., and M. Richter. 2015. Human trafficking and Africa's 'pornography of pain': the pitfalls of CSR. *Beyond Slavery and Trafficking, openDemocracy*. 2 September. https://www.opendemocracy.net/en/beyond-trafficking-and-slavery/human-trafficking-and-africas-pornography-of-pain-pitfal/ [Accessed 26/10/2022].

Quirk, J., E. Kenway, and C. Thibos. 2021. It's time to get off the fence on sex workers' rights. *Beyond Slavery and Trafficking, openDemocracy*. 16 August. https://www.opendemocracy.net/en/beyond-trafficking-and-slavery/its-time-to-get- off-the-fence-on-sex-workers-rights/ [Accessed 26/10/2022].

Ramsbotham, O., T. Woodhouse, and H. Miall. 2011. *Contemporary Conflict Resolution*, 3rd ed. Cambridge: Polity Press.

Rape, Abuse and Incest National Network. 2009. *Key Terms and Phrases*. https://rainn.org/news-room/key-terms-sexual-violence. [Accessed 26/10/2022].

Raymond, J. G., J. D'Cunha, S. R. Dzuhayatin, H. P. Hynes, Z. R. Rodriguez, and A. Santos. 2002. *A Comparative Study of Women Trafficked in the Migration Process: Patterns, Profiles and Health Consequences of Sexual Exploitation in Five Countries (Indonesia, the Philippines, Thailand, Venezuela and the United States)*. New York: Coalition Against Trafficking Women International.

Refugee Council. 2018. *Refugee Resettlement: The Facts*. https://www.refugeecouncil.org.uk/what_we_do/refugee_services/resettlement_programme/refugee_resettlement_the_facts [Accessed 26/10/2022].

Refugee Legal Aid Information. 2021. *Resettlement to the UK*. https://www.refugeelegalaidinformation.org/resettlement-uk [Accessed 26/10/2022].

Rhys Jones, D. 2013. Is she a victim or an illegal immigrant? The UK Border Agency decides. *Shine a Light, openDemocracy*. 18 March. https://www.opendemocracy.net/en/shine-a-light/is-she-victim-or-illegal-immigrant-uk-border-agency-decides/ [Accessed 26/10/2022].

Robinson, A. 2017. Damning stats show police failing UK's modern slaves. *Sky News*. 24 October. https://news.sky.com/story/modern-slavery-conviction-rate-is-less-than-2-11095938 [Accessed 26/10/2022].

Rosenblatt, K. 2014. 'Determining the Vulnerability Factors, Lures and Recruitment Methods Used to Entrap American Children into Sex Trafficking'. (PhD dissertation, Nova Southeastern University, 2014).

Russell, A. M. 2014. '"Victims of trafficking": The Feminisation of Poverty and Migration in the Gendered Narratives of Human Trafficking'. *Societies* 4: pp. 532–48.

R v Brecani [2021] EWCA Crim 731. In the Court of Appeal (Criminal Division) on Appeal from the Crown Court at Woolwich.

R v DS [2020]. EWCA Crim 285. In the Court of Appeal (Criminal Division) on Appeal from the Maidstone Crown Court.

Sales, R. 2002. 'The Deserving and the Undeserving? Refugees, Asylum Seekers and Welfare in Britain'. *Critical Social Policy* 22 (3): pp. 456–78.

Salt, J., and J. Stein. 1997. 'Migration as a Business: The Case of Trafficking'. *Journal of International Migration* 35 (4): pp. 467–94.

Sammut-Scerri, C., A. Abela, and A. Vetere. 2012. 'Ethical Dilemmas of a Clinician/Researcher Interviewing Women Who Have Grown Up in a Family Where There Was Domestic Violence'. *International Journal of Qualitative Methods* 11 (2): pp. 102–31.

Sandelowski, M. 2002. 'Reembodying Qualitative Inquiry'. *Qualitative Health Research* 12: pp. 104–15.

Schmidt, S. M., and T. A. Kochan. 1972. 'Conflict: Toward Conceptual Clarity'. *Administrative Science Quarterly* 17 (3): pp. 359–70.

Schneider, E. M. 1993. 'Feminism and the False Dichotomy of Victimization and Agency'. *New York Law School Review* 38: pp. 387–99.

Schwark, S., and G. Bohner. 2019. 'Sexual Violence—"Victim" or "Survivor": News Images Affect Explicit and Implicit Judgments of Blame'. *Violence Against Women* 25 (12): pp. 1491–509.

Sen, A. 1985. 'Well-being, Agency and Freedom: the Dewey Lectures 1984'. *Journal of Philosophy* 82: pp. 169–221.

Sen, A. 1999. *Development as Freedom*. New York: Alfred A Knopf.

Sentencing Council. 2021. *Modern Slavery Offences: Data Tables*. https://www.sentencingcouncil.org.uk/publications/item/modern-slavery-offences-data-tables/ [Accessed 26/10/2022].

Sigona, N. 2012. '"I Have Too Much Baggage": The Impacts of Legal Status on the Social Worlds of Irregular Migrants'. *Social Anthropology* 20 (1): pp. 50–65.

Silverman, S., M. Griffiths, and P. W. Walsh. 2021. Immigration detention in the UK. *The Migration Observatory at The University of Oxford*. 16 September. https://migrationobservatory.ox.ac.uk/resources/briefings/immigration-detention-in-the-uk/ [Accessed 26/10/2022].

Singer, K. 1949. 'The Resolution of Conflict'. *Social Research: An International Quarterly*, 16 (2): 230–45.

Skrivankova, K. 2010. *Between Decent Work and Forced Labour: Examining the Continuum of Exploitation*. York: Joseph Rowntree Foundation.

Skrivankova, K. 2011. Modern slavery—the reality. *The Guardian*. 12 September. https://www.theguardian.com/commentisfree/2011/sep/12/modern-slavery-reality [Accessed 26/10/2022].

Sloan, A. 2015. UK tied visa system 'turning domestic workers into modern-day slaves'. *The Guardian.* 17 March. https://www.theguardian.com/world/2015/mar/17/uk-tied-visa-system-turning-domestic-workers-into-modern-day-slaves [Accessed 26/10/2022].

Smith, C. A., and B. Miller-de la Cuesta. 2010. 'Human Trafficking in Conflict Zones: The Role of Peacekeepers in the Formation of Networks'. *Human Rights Review* 12: pp. 287–99.

Smith, C. A., and H. M. Smith. 2010. 'Human Trafficking: The Unintended Effects of United Nations Intervention'. *International Political Science Review* 32 (2): pp. 123–45.

Smucker, G. R., and G. F. Murray. 2004. *The Uses of Children: A Study of Trafficking in Haitian Children.* Port-au-Prince: United States Agency for International Development.

Solomon, M. K., and C. Thibos. 2017. Interview: is rights-based 'good migration governance' possible? *Beyond Slavery and Trafficking, openDemocracy.* 22 February. https://www.opendemocracy.net/en/beyond-trafficking-and-slavery/interview-is-rights-based-good-migration-governan/ [Accessed 26/10/2022].

Sommers, M. 2002. *Children, Education and War: Reaching Education for All (EFA). Objectives in Countries Affected by Conflict.* Washington DC: The World Bank.

Srikantiah, J. 2007. 'Perfect Victims and Real Survivors: The Iconic Victim in Human Trafficking Law'. *Boston University Law Review* 87 (1): pp. 157–211.

Steiner, J. 1969. 'Nonviolent Conflict Resolution in Democratic Systems: Switzerland'. *Journal of Conflict Resolution* 13 (3): pp. 295–304.

Steinfeld, R. J. 2001. *Coercion, Contract and Free Labor in the Nineteenth Century.* Cambridge: Cambridge University Press.

Stephan, M. J., and E. Chenoweth. 2008. 'Why Civil Resistance Works: The Strategic Logic of Nonviolent Conflict'. *International Security* 33 (1): pp. 7–44.

Stepnitz, A. 2012. 'A Lie More Disastrous Than the Truth: Asylum and The Identification of Trafficked Women in the UK'. *Anti-Trafficking Review* 1: pp. 104–19.

Stevens, D. 2017. 'Asylum, Refugee Protection and the European Response to Syrian Migration'. *Journal of Human Rights Practice* 9 (2): pp. 184–89.

Strauss, A., and J. Corbin. 1997. 'Introduction'. In *Grounded Theory in Practice,* edited by A. Strauss, and J. Corbin, pp. vii–viii. Thousand Oaks: Sage.

Strauss, K. 2016. 'Sorting Victims from Workers: Forced Labour, Trafficking and the Process of Jurisdiction'. *Progress in Human Geography* 41 (2): pp. 140–58.

Symonds, T. 2021. Brooke House detention centre whistleblower 'abuse' inquiry begins. *BBC.* 24 November. https://www.bbc.co.uk/news/uk-england-sussex-59388291 [Accessed 26/10/2022].

Testart, A. 2002. 'The Extent and Significance of Debt Slavery'. *Revue Française de Sociologie* 43 (1): pp. 173–204.

The Dublin Regulation. 2003. No. 604/2013 EU: UNHCR.

The Freedom Fund. 2016. *Modern Slavery and Trafficking in Conflict: The UN's Response.* https://freedomfund.org/our-reports/modern-slavery-and-trafficking-in-conflict-the-uns-response/ [Accessed 26/10/2022].

The Passage 2017. *Understanding and Responding to Modern Slavery within the Homelessness Sector.* Independent Anti-Slavery Commissioner.

The Salvation Army. 2021. *New 2021 Victim Care Contract.* https://www.salvationarmy.org.uk/modern-slavery/new-victim-care-contract [Accessed 26/10/2022].

Thibos, C., and S. Topouzova. 2017. Global compacts, detention centres, and safe passage: can the world change course on migration? *Beyond Slavery and Trafficking, openDemocracy.* 20 February. https://www.opendemocracy.net/en/beyond-trafficking-and-slavery/global-compacts-detention-centres-and-safe-passage-can-/ [Accessed 26/10/2022].

Tjosvold, D. 2006. 'Defining Conflict and Making Choices About Its Management. Lighting the Dark Side of Organisational Life'. *International Journal of Conflict Management* 17 (2): pp. 87–95.

Tyldum, G. 2013. 'Dependence and Human Trafficking in the Context of Transnational Marriage'. *International Migration* 53 (4): pp. 103–15.

UK Visas and Immigration. 2021. *Vulnerable Persons and Vulnerable Children's Resettlement Schemes Factsheet, March 2021.* https://www.gov.uk/government/publications/uk-resettlement-schemes-factsheet-march-2021/vulnerable-persons-and-vulnerable-childrens-resettlement-schemes-factsheet-march-2021 [Accessed 26/10/2022].

UNHCR (United Nations High Commissioner for Refugees). 2003. *Sexual and Gender-Based Violence Against Refugees, Returnees and Internally Displaced Persons.* Geneva: United Nations High Commissioner for Refugees.

UNHCR (United Nations High Commissioner for Refugees). No Date a. *UNHCR Solutions.* https://www.unhcr.org/uk/solutions.html [Accessed 26/10/2022].

UNHCR (United Nations High Commissioner for Refugees). No Date b. *UNHCR Resettlement.* http://www.unhcr.org/uk/resettlement.html [Accessed 26/10/2022].

UNHCR (United Nations High Commissioner for Refugees). No Date c. *Resettlement Submission Categories.* https://www.unhcr.org/558bff849.pdf [Accessed 26/10/2022].

UNHCR (United Nations High Commissioner for Refugees). No Date. *Information on UNHCR Resettlement.* https://www.unhcr.org/uk/information-on-unhcr-resettlement.html#:~:text=In%202018%2C%2027%20countries%20around,%2C%20and%20Sweden%20(4%2C900). [Accessed 26/10/2022].

UNHCR (United Nations High Commissioner for Refugees). No Date e. *Resettlement Data.* https://www.unhcr.org/resettlement-data.html [Accessed 26/10/2022].

UNHCR (United Nations High Commissioner for Refugees). 2008. *Policy and Procedural Guidelines: Addressing Resettlement Fraud Perpetrated by Refugees.* Geneva: United Nations High Commissioner for Refugees.

UNHCR (United Nations High Commissioner for Refugees). 2013. *Strategic Framework for the Prevention of Fraud and Corruption.* United Nations High Commissioner for Refugees.

UNHCR (United Nations High Commissioner for Refugees). 2018. *2017 in Review.* http://www.unhcr.org/uk/5a9d507f7 [Accessed 26/10/2022].

UNICEF (United Nations Children's Fund). 2002. *Adult Wars, Child Soldiers. Voices of Children Involved in Armed Conflict in the East Asia and Pacific Region.* Bangkok: UNICEF East Asia and Pacific Regional Office.

UNICEF (United Nations Children's Fund). 2021. *Children Recruited by Armed Forces*. https://www.unicef.org/protection/children-recruited-by-armed-forces [Accessed 26/10/2022].

United Nations. No Date. *Responsibility to Protect*. https://www.un.org/en/genocideprevention/about-responsibility-to-protect.shtml [Accessed 26/10/2022].

United Nations Department of Economic and Social Affairs. 2005. *World Youth Report: Young People Today and in 2015* (30 July 2005, ST/ESA/301). New York: United Nations.

United Nations General Assembly. 1926. *Slavery Convention* (25 September 1926). http://www.ohchr.org/EN/ProfessionalInterest/Pages/SlaveryConvention.aspx [Accessed 26/10/2022].

United Nations General Assembly. 1948. *Universal Declaration of Human Rights* (10 December 1948, 217 A). http://www.ohchr.org/EN/UDHR/Documents/UDHR_Translations/eng.pdf [Accessed 26/10/2022].

United Nations General Assembly. 1998. *Rome Statute of International Criminal Court, Final Act of the United Nations Diplomatic Conference of Plenipotentiaries on the Establishment of an International Criminal Court* (17 July 1998, U.N. Doc. A/CONF.183/10). http://legal.un.org/icc/statute/finalfra.htm [Accessed 26/10/2022].

United Nations General Assembly. 2000a. *Protocol to Prevent, Suppress and Punish Trafficking in Persons, Especially Women and Children, Supplementing the United Nations Convention Against Transnational Organized Crime* (15 November 2000, Res 55/25). http://www.ohchr.org/EN/ProfessionalInterest/Pages/ProtocolTraffickingInPersons.Aspx [Accessed 26/10/2022].

United Nations General Assembly. 2000b. *Protocol Against the Smuggling of Migrants by Land, Sea and Air*. https://www.ohchr.org/EN/ProfessionalInterest/Pages/TransnationalOrganizedCrime.aspx [Accessed 26/10/2022].

Van Dijk, J. 2009. 'Free the Victim: A Critique of the Western Conception of Victimhood'. *International Review of Victimology* 16: pp. 1–33.

Varshney, A. 2002. *Ethnic Conflict and Civic Life: Hindus and Muslims in India*. New Haven and London: Yale University Press.

Veale, A., and G. Dona. 2003. 'Street Children and Political Violence: a Socio-Demographic Analysis of Street Children in Rwanda'. *Child Abuse & Neglect* 27 (3): pp. 253–69.

Verhey, B. 2001. 'Child Soldiers: Preventing, Demobilizing and Reintegrating'. *Africa Region Working Paper Series* 23: pp. 1–31.

Vickers T. 2015. 'The Contribution of UK Asylum Policy 1999–2010 to Conditions for the Exploitation of Migrant Labour'. In *Vulnerability, Exploitation and Migrants*, edited by L. Waite, G. Craig, H. Lewis, and K. Skrivankova, pp. 101–14. London: Palgrave Macmillan.

Vité, S. 2009. 'Typology of Armed Conflicts in International Humanitarian Law: Legal Concepts and Actual Situations'. *International Review of the Red Cross* 91 (873): pp. 69–94.

Waite, L. 2017. 'Asylum Seekers and the Labour Market: Spaces of Discomfort and Hostility'. *Social Policy & Society* 16 (4): pp. 669–79.

Ward, C. L., and J. R. Seager. 2010. 'South African Street Children: A Survey and Recommendations for Services'. *Development Southern Africa* 27 (1): pp. 85–100.

Watchlist. 2003. *The Impact of Armed Conflict on Children in the Democratic Republic of Congo (DRC)*. New York: Watchlist.

Weber, M. 1964. *The Theory of Social and Economic Organization*. New York: Free Press.

Weitzer, R. 2007. 'The Social Construction of Sex Trafficking: Ideology and Institutionalization of a Moral Crusade'. *Politics & Society* 35: pp. 447–75.

Weitzer, R. 2014. 'New Directions in Research of Human Trafficking'. *The Annals of the American Academy of Political and Social Science* 653: pp 6–24.

Wieviorka, M. 2009. *Violence, a New Approach*. London: Sage.

Williams, K. 2004. *Textbook of Criminology*, 5th ed. Oxford: Oxford University Press.

Williamson, J., and K. Serna. 2017. 'Reconsidering Forced Labels: Outcomes of Sexual Assault Survivors Versus Victims (and Those Who Choose Neither)'. *Violence Against Women* 24 (6): pp. 668–83.

Wilson, M., and E. O'Brien. 2016. 'Constructing the Ideal Victim in the United States of America's Annual Trafficking in Persons Report'. *Crime, Law and Social Change* 65 (1): pp. 29–45.

Wölte, S. 1997. *Human Rights Violations Against Women During War and Conflict*. Geneva: Women's International League for Peace and Freedom.

Women's International League for Peace and Freedom. 2012. *Human Trafficking and Related Crimes in the Context of Peacekeeping: State Organisation and Individual Responsibilities and Accountabilities*. Women's International League for Peace and Freedom. Report of Conference held November 15–16.

Wuilbercq, E. 2021. Factbox: ten facts about child soldiers around the world. *Reuters*. 12 February. https://www.reuters.com/article/us-global-childsoldiers-factbox-trfn-idUSKBN2AC0CB [Accessed 26/10/2022].

Yea, S. 2015. 'Trafficked Enough? Missing Bodies, Migrant Labour Exploitation, and the Classification of Trafficking Victims'. *Singapore Antipode* 47 (4): pp. 1080–100.

Index

For the benefit of digital users, indexed terms that span two pages (e.g., 52–53) may, on occasion, appear on only one of those pages.

Tables are indicated by *t* following the page number